Communications in Computer and Information Science 634

Commenced Publication in 2007
Founding and Former Series Editors:
Alfredo Cuzzocrea, Dominik Ślęzak, and Xiaokang Yang

More information about this series at http://www.springer.com/series/7899

Tieniu Tan · Guoping Wang
Shengjin Wang · Yue Liu
Xiaoru Yuan · Ran He
Sheng Li (Eds.)

Advances in Image and Graphics Technologies

11th Chinese Conference, IGTA 2016
Beijing, China, July 8–9, 2016
Proceedings

Editors
Tieniu Tan
Institute of Automation
Chinese Academy of Sciences
Beijing
China

Guoping Wang
Peking University
Beijing
China

Shengjin Wang
Tsinghua University
Beijing
China

Yue Liu
Beijing Institute of Technology
Beijing
China

Xiaoru Yuan
Peking University
Beijing
China

Ran He
Institute of Automation
Chinese Academy of Sciences
Beijing
China

Sheng Li
Peking University
Beijing
China

ISSN 1865-0929   ISSN 1865-0937 (electronic)
Communications in Computer and Information Science
ISBN 978-981-10-2259-3   ISBN 978-981-10-2260-9 (eBook)
DOI 10.1007/978-981-10-2260-9

Library of Congress Control Number: 2016947926

This Springer imprint is published by Springer Nature
The registered company is Springer Science+Business Media Singapore Pte Ltd.

Preface

It was a pleasure and an honor to have organized the 11th Conference on Image and Graphics Technologies and Applications. The conference was held during July 8–9, 2016, in Beijing, China. The conference series is the premier forum for presenting research in image processing and graphics and their related topics. The conference provides a rich forum for sharing the progress in the areas of image processing technology, image analysis and understanding, computer vision and pattern recognition, big data mining, computer graphics and VR, image technology application, with the generation of new ideas, new approaches, new techniques, new applications, and new evaluations. The conference is organized under the auspices of the Beijing Society of Image and Graphics, in Peking University, Beijing, China.

The conference program includes keynotes, oral papers, posters, demos, and exhibitions. For this year's conference, we received 138 papers for review. Each of these was assessed by at least two reviewers, with some of the papers being assessed by three reviewers; finally, 27 submissions were selected for oral and poster presentation.

We are grateful for the effort of everyone who helped to make this conference a reality. We thank all the reviewers for completing the reviewing process on time. The local host, Peking University, facilitated many of the local arrangements for the conference and provided a warm welcome to all of the delegates.

The conference continues to be a leading forum for cutting-edge research and case study in image and graphics. We hope you enjoy reading these proceedings.

July 2016   Guoping Wang

Organization

General Conference Chairs

Tan, Tie-niu   Chinese Academy of Sciences, China
Wang, Guo-ping   Peking University, China

Executive and Coordination Committee

Ruan, Qiu-qi   Beijing Jiaotong University, China
Wang, Run-sheng   China Aero Geophysical Survey & Remote Sensing Center for Land and Resources, China
Chen, Chao-wu   The First Research Institute of the Ministry of Public Security of P.R.C., China
Zhou, Ming-quan   Beijing Normal University, China
Jiang, Zhi-guo   Beihang University, China

Program Committee Chairs

Wang, Sheng-jin   Tsinghua University, China
Yuan, Xiao-ru   Peking University, China
He, Ran   Chinese Academy of Sciences, China

Organizing Chairs

Li, Sheng   Peking University, China
Liu, Yue   Beijing Institute of Technology, China

Organizing Committee

Ma, Hui-min   Tsinghua University, China
Yang, Lei   Communication University of China, China
Di, Kai-chang   Chinese Academy of Sciences, China
Lei, Jing-wen   Peking University, China

Program Committee

Ran He   National Laboratory of Pattern Recognition, China
Fengjun Zhang   Chinese Academy of Sciences, China
Xin Geng   Southeast University, China
Muhammad Rauf   Chinese Academy of Science (CASIA), China

Huijie Zhao	Beihang University, China
Xuelong Hu	Yangzhou University, China
Guangyou Xu	Tsinghua University, China
Xiaochun Cao	Chinese Academy of Sciences, China
Hua Lin	Beijing University of Technology, China
Guangda Su	Tsinghua University, China
Xueqiang Lv	Beijing Information Science and Technology University, China

Contents

A New Approach for Measuring Leaf Projected Area for Potted Plant Based on Computer Vision

Kaiyan Lin, Huiping Si[✉], Jie Chen, and Junhui Wu

Modern Agricultural Science and Engineering Institute of Tongji University,
No. 1239 Siping Road, Shanghai 200092, China
sihuiping@tongjii.edu.cn

Abstract. Leaves are the main organs for plant photosynthesis and transpiration, and thus accurate and rapid measurements of their surface area are of great significance in plant growth studies. A novel method was developed to utilize computer vision to determine the leaf projected area for potted plants using a reference object. During leaf extraction, the excess green vegetation index and the Otsu algorithm were used for image binarization. Blob analysis was then performed to eliminate noise and extract leaf images. After grey level transform and obtaining the binary image, the Sobel operator and Hough transform were utilized to detect pot's external boundary. The image including the extracted leaves and the detected reference borders were then processed using a Geometric correction to improve the measurement accuracy, and based on this, the leaf projected area was calculated. Results of the experimental image showed that this newly proposed method proved is effective and can continuously measure the plant's leaf area for non-destructive monitoring.

Keywords: Image segmentation · Edge detection · Hough transform · Projected area · Image correction

1 Introduction

Leaf area is frequently expressed as the leaf area index (LAI), which is defined as the total one-sided area of leaf tissue per unit ground area [1]. LAI is an important crop parameter that determines the radiation intercepted by the crop canopy, and has a strong impact on the calculation of crop canopy photosynthesis and transpiration [2]. In crops like tea, tobacco, and green leafy vegetables, where leaves are the major commercial product, leaf area is a good direct indicator of product yields. Since leaf area plays an important role in photosynthesis, light interception, water and nutrient use, crop growth, and yield potential, measurement of leaf area is valuable in plant growth studies [3, 4]. The importance of leaf area determination in plant sciences has stimulated the use of many leaf area measurement methods.

Researchers have studied the use of machine vision technology in the measurement of the leaf area. Trooien and Heermann [5] developed a simulation model of potato canopy architecture to evaluate an image-processing leaf-area measurement method. Kacira et al. [6] used features derived from top-projected canopy area (TPCA) to detect

© Springer Science+Business Media Singapore 2016
T. Tan et al. (Eds.): IGTA 2016, CCIS 634, pp. 1–7, 2016.
DOI: 10.1007/978-981-10-2260-9_1

plant water stress. Igathinathane et al. [3] measured detached leaf area that required human intervention using semi-automatic interactive software. Story et al. [7] combined TPCA and color information to develop a vision system to detect lettuce calcium deficiency. Xia et al. [8] proposed a quick on-line measuring method of tobacco leaf area for analyzing tobacco strip size distribution. Tong et al. [9] studied machine vision techniques to calculate the leaf area of seedlings for quality evaluation. However, the problems associated with most existing methods are that the measurements were performed in controlled environments, requiring that the camera maintains a perpendicular orientation to the projection plane, and the leaf area was expressed in pixels of the projected object instead of the actual area. These shortcomings limit their application to actual crop production.

Thus, the objective of this study is to develop a new approach for accurate and rapid measurement of leaf area using a reference object that can be used in actual production. The potted plant is a common cropping pattern in greenhouses, where the pot is regular and can be used as a reference object. Using our approach, Hough transform (HT) was carried out after edge detection to determine the reference object's boundaries. The HT is robust for determining a regular object's boundaries. In this paper, to improve measurement accuracy, the images were processed using a geometric correction, based on which leaf area and the size of the reference were calculated. Once the reference's size is known, the actual projected area of the leaf is easy to calculate.

2   Materials and Methods

2.1   Plants and Image Acquisition

Experiments on plants were performed in the agricultural park of Tongji University in the Jiading district. For potted plants, white rectangular pots were selected for the tests.

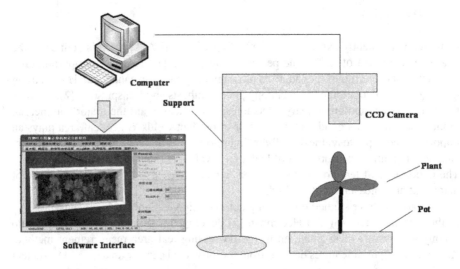

Fig. 1. Image acquisition system

Figure 1 shows the image acquisition system for plants, which comprised a support to fix the CCD camera. The image processing system worked on an Intel Core 2 computer equipped with 4 GB memory. Top-view plant images were captured in natural light every day at a given time and were then digitized into 24-bit red-green-blue (RGB) images with a resolution of 4000 × 2248 pixels. As shown in Fig. 2, each basin contains 3 plants and the pot was selected as the reference object.

Fig. 2. Image of lettuce in a white rectangular pot

2.2 LAI Calculation with Image Processing

Figure 3 shows the system block diagram, which illustrates the algorithms used and the order during image processing. The diagram shows that leaf extraction and calculation of the pot's outer boundary are two important steps in measuring a plant's projected area. During leaf extraction, the excess green (ExG) index and Otsu approach are combined to obtain a binary image. To segment vegetation from soil, researchers have employed different kinds of indices [10–13]. We selected the ExG index for calculation, which yielded results similar to binary images. The ExG index is defined as:

$$ExG = 2G - R - B \tag{1}$$

The area of interest is green vegetation, and the color component differences between leaves and background are obvious. The difference in the background area is slight and the leaf area can be extracted easily with a suitable threshold, which was determined using Otsu's approach [14] in this paper. Then, blob analysis was used to eliminate noise and extract the leaf image.

Our main aim was to use HT to determine the pot boundary. The first step in pot boundary determination was pot segmentation, which was achieved using the gray level transform and image binarization with a suitable threshold value. The gray level transform formula is given by:

$$L = 0.299R + 0.587G + 0.114B \tag{2}$$

A binary image could be obtained by manually selecting the appropriate threshold based on histogram analysis and application to the gray image resulting from Eq. (2).

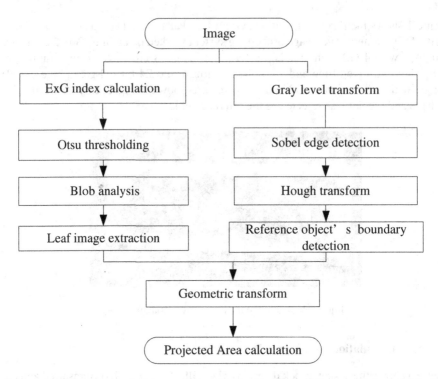

Fig. 3. LAI calculation block diagram, illustrating the algorithms followed and the order during image processing

This value was thus selected as a fixed threshold that could affect binary image segmentation. After gray level transform, the Sobel operator and HT were utilized to calculate the reference object's outer boundary position. Geometric transform is performed to overcome image distortion due to the camera view not being perpendicular to the ground, thereby improving measurement accuracy. The leaf area and the reference area in the image are then calculated. Because the size of the pot is known, the actual projected area of the leaves is easy to compute.

3   Results and Discussion

The proposed approach was verified using the experimental images and C# programming with the Aforge Imaging library from the Aforge.net Framework. Formula (1) was utilized to calculate the ExG index to obtain the gray image in Fig. 1. A grey level image resulted from the ExG, and to convert this grey level image to a binary image, an Otsu approach was performed to achieve the optimized threshold. After segmenting the image, there were noise residues (Fig. 4 (a)). Blob analysis was implemented to eliminate the noise that was less than 100 pixels and to fill the holes in the object (Fig. 4(b)), and the leaf images were then extracted. Results are illustrated in Fig. 4(c).

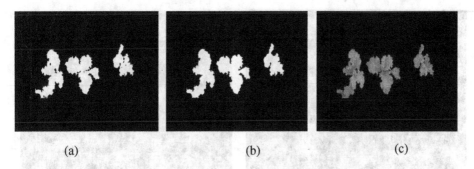

Fig. 4. Plant image extraction. (a) Image segmentation using the ExG index and the Otsu approach; (b) Filtering and filling with blob analysis; (c) Extracting the leaf image

Pot segmentation was the first step in detecting the pot's boundaries. With formula (2), grey level transform was carried out and an appropriate threshold (T = 220) was selected using histogram analysis to obtain the binary image (Fig. 5(a)). The Sobel operator was then used to detect boundary edges, as illustrated in Fig. 5(b). Similar to leaf extraction, noise was removed using blob analysis as displayed in Fig. 5(c), and there were several lines present. The position of these lines could be detected using HT. In our approach, the four most outer lines were needed to define the pot's boundary.

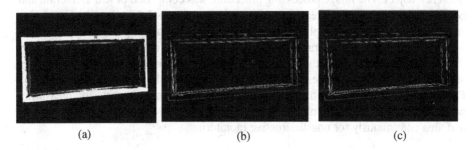

Fig. 5. Pot edge detection. (a) Image segmentation with grey level transform; (b) Sobel edge detection; (c) Blob filtering to eliminate noise

According to the result of HT, the four boundary lines were selected and labeled in red in Fig. 6. The boundary line and the leaf image were then corrected using GT (Fig. 7), based on which the leaf area and pot area (in pixels) were calculated. Because the pot real area Apt is known, it is easy to compute the leaf-projected area Apj, which is defined as follows:

$$A_{pj} = \frac{A_l}{w \times h} A_{pt} \tag{3}$$

where w and h are the width and height of pot after GT, and Al is the area of leaf in pixels. In Fig. 2, the Apj is 352.3 cm^2, the real projected area calculated with a leaf area meter (AM-300, ADC, UK) is 352.1 cm^2. The error is small and our approach is effective.

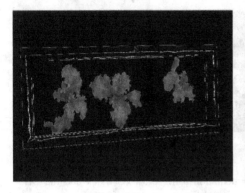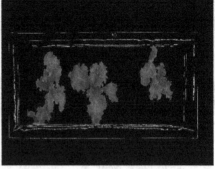

Fig. 6. Leaf image extracted using Blob analysis and boundary detected using Hough transform

Fig. 7. Image after geometric correction

4   Conclusion

An image processing method was developed for non-destructive measurement of the leaf area using a reference object. For potted plants, the pot was naturally selected as a reference object. The image processing procedure was comprised of leaf extraction and boundary detection. During leaf extraction, the Otsu approach based on the ExG index and the blob analysis were applied to obtain leaf images. An image processing procedure, which comprised grey level transform, noise removal, edge detection and HT, was used to detect the reference object's boundaries. Moreover, the image containing the leaves and the boundary was processed using GT to improve the measurement accuracy. Experiments demonstrated that the proposed approach was effective for measuring projected leaf area for potted plants. This newly proposed method can measure a plant's leaf area continuously for non-destructive monitoring.

Acknowledgment. This work was supported by Grant No. 2014BAD05B05 from the Ministry of Science and technology of China and the fundamental research funds for the central universities of China.

References

1. Breda, N.J.: Ground-based measurements of leaf area index, a review of methods: instruments and current controversies. J. Exp. Bot. **54**(11), 2403–2417 (2003)
2. Xu, R., Dai, J., Luo, W., et al.: A photothermal model of leaf area index for greenhouse crops. Agric. For. Meteorol. **150**, 541–552 (2010)
3. Igathinathane, C., Prakash, V.S.S., Padma, U.: Interactive computer software development for leaf area measurement. Comput. Electron. Agric. **51**, 1–16 (2006)
4. Cho, Y.Y., Oh, S.B., Oh, M.M., Jung, E.S.: Estimation of individual leaf area, fresh weight, and dry weight of hydroponically grown cucumbers (Cucumis sativus L.) using leaf length, width, and SPAD value. Sci. Hortic. **111**, 330–334 (2007)

5. Trooien, T.P., Heermann, D.R.: Measurement and simulation of potato leaf area using image processing III. Measur. Trans. ASAE **35**(5), 1719–1721 (1992)
6. Kacira, M., Ling, P.P., Short, T.H.: Machine vision extracted plant movement for early detection of plant water stress. Trans. ASAE **45**(4), 1147–1153 (2002)
7. Story, D., Kacira, M., Kubota, C., Akoglu, A., An, L.L.: Lettuce calcium deficiency detection with machine vision computed plant features in controlled environments. Comput. Electron. Agric. **74**, 238–243 (2010)
8. Xia, Y.W., Xu, D.Y., Du, J.S.: On-line measurement of tobacco leaf area based on machine vision. Trans. Chin. Soc. Agric. Mach. **43**(10), 167–173 (2012)
9. Tong, J.H., Li, J.B., Jiang, H.Y.: Machine vision techniques for the evaluation of seedling quality based on leaf area. Biosyst. Eng. **115**, 369–379 (2013)
10. Kataoka, T., Kaneko, T., Okamoto, H., Hata, S.I.: Crop growth estimation system using machine vision. In: Proceedings of the IEEE/ASME International Conference on Advanced Intelligent Mechatronics, pp. 1079–1083 (2003)
11. Meyer, G.E., Neto, J.C.: Verification of color vegetation indices for automated crop imaging applications. Comput. Electron. Agric. **63**, 282–293 (2008)
12. Perez, A.J., Lopez, F., Benlloch, J.V., Christensen, S.: Color and shape analysis techniques for weed detection in cereal fields. Comput. Electron. Agric. **25**, 197–212 (2000)
13. Woebbecke, D.M., Meyer, G.E., Bargen, K.V., Mortensen, D.A.: Color indices for weed identification under various soil residue and lighting conditions. Trans. ASAE **38**, 259–269 (1995)
14. Otsu, N.: A threshold selection method from gray-level histograms. IEEE Trans. Syst. Man Cybern. **9**(1), 62–66 (1979)

Research of Meso-pore Structures of Eco-material

Gaoliang Tao[✉], Liang Bai, Xinshan Zhuang, and Qizhi Hu

School of Civil Engineering and Architectural, Hubei University of Technology,
Wuhan 430068, China
tgl1979@126.com

Abstract. A proposed method was introduced to study the meso-pore structures of eco-material in this paper. Firstly, the samples were solidified by using the mixtures of epoxy resin, triethanolamine and blue organic dyestuff. Then, the sections were obtained by cutting the solidified samples and the digital images were gathered by using high resolution camera. At last, the IPP technique was used to analyze the digital images for studying the meso-pore structures. Experimental results show that pore number of eco-material increases with the decrease of pore-size, and the number of pores of pore-size smaller than 0.24 mm is about 30 % of total. Further more, smoother pore number distribution curve indicates more stable structure. With the increase of wet-dry cycles, the total porosity of eco-material of 3 ~ 9 cm depth tends to decrease, while that of 12 ~ 18 cm depth shows a tendency to increase.

Keywords: Eco-material · Meso-pore structures · Sampling depth · Wet-dry cycles

1 Introduction

Pore structures and macro physical mechanics properties of rock and soil are closely linked, and the pore structure is the foundation to carry out the study on relation between macro physical mechanical characteristics and pore structure. With the continuous development of experimental techniques, mercury injection technique and SEM technology were used to study the micro-pore structure of the rock and soil materials and the experiment had become easy (Zhang et al., 2008; Tao et al., 2010). For the study of meso-pore structure, the corresponding experiment is relatively difficult (Skopp et al., 1981; Singh et al., 1991; Tang et al., 1963). Although CT technology has been applied in the study of pore distribution of rock and soil medium in 3D space, the resolution of CT image is low and the precision is not high. In addition, application equipment and expensive testing also limits the CT technology. In soil science, in general, after the sample being solidified using the cured resin, the pore structure is analyzed by the polarizing microscope. A method was put forward to study the meso-pore structure by color photography scanner or high resolution digital camera and the pore distribution data was gained by computer image analysis software (Li et al., 2002; He et al., 2002). Based on the above method, a new method will be presented and applied to the research of the eco-material pore structure.

© Springer Science+Business Media Singapore 2016
T. Tan et al. (Eds.): IGTA 2016, CCIS 634, pp. 8–16, 2016.
DOI: 10.1007/978-981-10-2260-9_2

2   Materials and Methods

Sample preparation: Referring to the proposed experimental methods (Li et al., 2002; He et al., 2002), a new method to study the meso-pore structure is introduced. The steps of sample preparation and sections cutting are as follows:

(a) Sampling. The light rain weather is very fit for sampling (eco-material humidity is moderate, convenient for sampling). In the field test site of ecological material, a plastic barrel, whose diameter is 11 cm, height is 20 cm and wall thickness is about 2 mm, is slowly put into the eco-materials. Then, the small range of materials near cylinder is hollowed out. In the representative area, 4 samples were made.

(b) Wet-dry cycles. In 4 samples, 3 samples are chosen as the samples of drying and watering cycle.

(c) Specimen impregnation. Before immersion, the specimens were sealed. Then, the samples were put in drying cylinder to dry out, with control temperature at 70°C. In the same time, E44 epoxy resin of a certain volume was heated in the oven until the liquidity achieved to the ideal state. Then, triethanolamine was added into the epoxy resin according to volume ratio of 15 %. Afterward, blue dye of 5 g: 1 L was added. This process took time, so the fluidity of epoxy resin might become worse. Therefore, it need take impregnating agent in the oven for heating, until mobility was in the ideal state. Afterward, impregnating agent was injected slowly into the barrel along the inside. The whole process should be controlled within 30 min.

(d) Specimen solidifying. After completing previous steps, it need continue to heat the samples in the oven, at a temperature about 70°C. In general, samples can be solidified after about 7 h.

(e) Sample cutting. Along the vertical height, each sample was cut at intervals of about 3 cm. Then, 6 representative sections were acquired for each sample and the sections were marked.

Table 1. Sample number of eco-material and corresponding sampling depth and wet-dry cycles

Sample number	Sampling depth (cm)	Wet-dry cycles	Sample number	Sampling depth (cm)	Wet-dry cycles
S1-1	3	0	S3-1	3	3
S1-2	6	0	S3-2	6	3
S1-3	9	0	S3-3	9	3
S1-4	12	0	S3-4	12	3
S1-5	15	0	S3-5	15	3
S1-6	18	0	S3-6	18	3
S2-1	3	1	S4-1	3	7
S2-2	6	1	S4-2	6	7
S2-3	9	1	S4-3	9	7
S2-4	12	1	S4-4	12	7
S2-5	15	1	S4-5	15	7
S2-6	18	1	S4-6	18	7

According to the above experimental methods, 4 samples respectively corresponding to 0, 1, 3, 7 wet-dry cycles were solidified, and each sample was cut into 6 representative sections. The relationship between sample number, sampling depth and wet-dry cycles is shown in Table 1.

Image acquisition and processing: A scale mark of 2 cm was put near by the sample section and the high resolution image was acquired for each representative section. Then, by using the IPP software, the color photographs were converted to binary image of black and white. In the processing, threshold adjustment function was chosen to complete pore and particle segmentation in IPP. The binary image of black and white must be compared with the original color image, guaranteeing the black and white image can reflect the actual situation. The same work should be completed by one or more peoples. If the error is within 10 %, it may be a black and white image which can reflect the actual situation.

Figure 1 shows the binary image of eco-material standard sample with 2 cm scale signs nearby. By impregnating liquidity constraints, it will inevitably lead to not fully filled pores, so that pores of color photographs are divided into two kinds, one is dipping agent filled pores with the color of blue; another is not filled with color of black. In binary image of the black and white, black represents pore, and the white represents the particle.

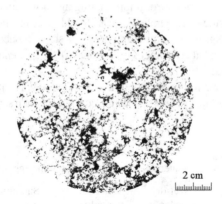

2 cm

Fig. 1. Binary images of standard samples of eco-material

3　Results and Discussion

Using IPP software, the statistics and analysis work of pore-size distributions of eco-material was completed. Although the sampling barrel diameter is 11 cm, the samples generally have the volume shrinkage, which lead to smaller diameter. To avoid the pore caused by volume shrinkage, 10 cm was chosen as the circular diameter of analysis region.

Pore-size distribution and the porosity: In accordance with the pore-size range, the pore distribution data of IPP software was divided into 13 to 16 pore-size level, the number and pore area corresponding to pore-size level were counted. In particular, according to the resolution of digital cameras, the minimum pore-size is 0.16 mm.

Figure 2 gives pore-size distributions using the porosity for pore-size grade, in which all the abscissa is used in logarithmic form. As you can see from Fig. 2, each pore-size interval porosity distribution is relatively uniform on the whole, the porosity of pore-size smaller than 1 mm is relatively small, and porosity of pore-size larger than 1 mm is relatively big. For part samples, the porosity of pore-size larger than 10 mm presents obvious increasing intend, such as sample 1-1, and there exists a large pore, the corresponding porosity approaches 50 % of total porosity. The reason may be that corresponding sample has loose structure, and that many connected large pores form large pores. These pores should be the main pore water preferential flow, which easily leads to nutrient loss of eco-materials.

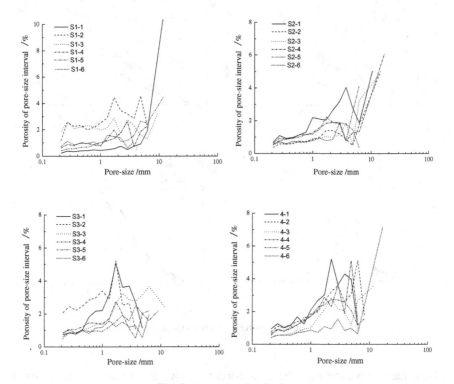

Fig. 2. Pore-size distribution

For the sampling depth, porosity of the same pore-size interval decreases with the increase of sampling depth on the whole. The reason is that, larger action of gravity of deeper eco-material leads to smaller porosity. Due to the pore distribution's variability of eco-materials with space, porosity of pore-size interval of some samples shows the opposite trend, i.e. the porosity increases with the increase of depth. For example, the porosity of small pore-size interval of surface sample 1-1 is smaller than the deeper samples.

Figure 3 shows the changes of cumulative porosity with the pore-size. On the whole, the growth trend of porosity is relatively stable. The reason is that porosity distribution of each pore-size interval is uniform on the whole. However, for individual samples, the growth rate of porosity of pore-size interval shows mutations. For example, the sample 1-1, porosity growth rate of pore-size interval presents significant accelerating trend when pore-size is larger than 8 mm. The reason is that, for the sample 1-1, a bigger proportion of total porosity is occupied by the larger pores, whose porosity shows sudden changes with pore-size.

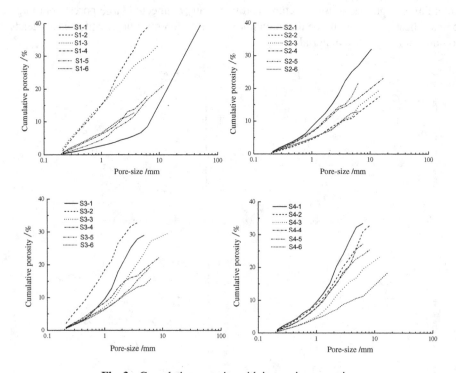

Fig. 3. Cumulative porosity with increasing pore-size

With the depth increases, the total porosity shows an overall decreasing trend. Smaller the total porosity is, more slowly the cumulative porosity increases.

Pore number distribution: Fig. 4 shows the distribution curves of pore number. As you can see from Fig. 4, pore number increases with the decrease of pore-size, and the number of pores of pore-size smaller than 0.24 mm is about 30 % of total. A few specimens, such as sample 1-2, appear obvious inflection point at about 0.24 mm, and shows decreasing trend for smaller pores.

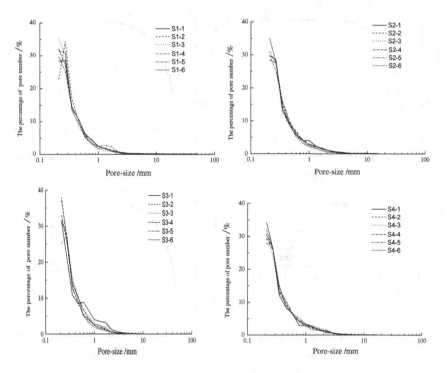

Fig. 4. Distribution of pore number

Pore number distribution curve of surface eco-materials shows large fluctuation. However, the number distribution curves of deeper layers are relatively smooth. The reason may be that the effects of vegetation and soil erosion lead to the discontinuous pore distributions. It can be considered that, smoother pore distribution curves are, more stable the pore structures are.

Figure 5 gives the accumulated number distributions of pores smaller than a certain pore-size. All curves of 24 samples are shown on the corresponding convex, because smaller pore number increases more quickly than larger pores. On the whole, all distribution curves are relatively concentrated. With the increase of depth, the curve tends to be plumper.

For sample 3-1, the curve is not plump, which indicates the structure is most unstable.

The change rule of total porosity: Fig. 6 compares the total porosity of different sampling depths of eco-material. Figure 6 shows that, with the increase of sampling depth, total porosity of eco-material decreases on the whole. This shows that, with increasing sampling depth, eco-material structure becomes tighter. The reason is that, on the one hand, many pores in surface eco-material were produced due to vegetation growth, on the other hand, the deeper eco-material become more compact because of gravity.

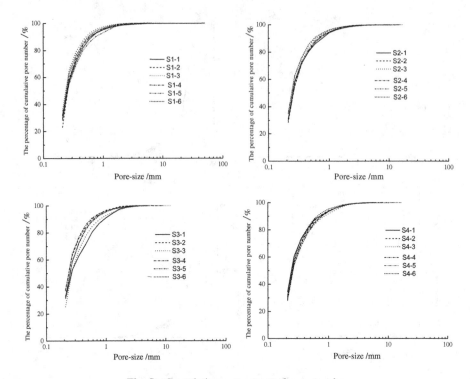

Fig. 5. Cumulative percentage of pore number

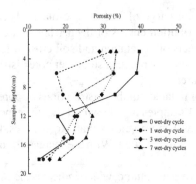

Fig. 6. Variation law of porosity with sampling depth

The total porosity of eco-material of different wet-dry cycles is compared in Fig. 7. It is shown that, with the increase of wet-dry cycles, the total porosity of eco-material of 3 ~ 9 cm depth tends to decrease, and that of 12 ~ 18 cm depth shows a tendency to increase. The reason is that, on the one hand, due to the existing of some large pores, structure collapse phenomenon happens in superficial layer in cyclic wet-dry conditions, so that the total porosity decreases; on the other hand, the wet volume expansion is larger than dry volume shrinkage for deeper eco-material, so that the total porosity increases with increase of wet-dry cycles.

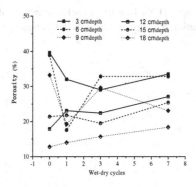

Fig. 7. Variation law of porosity with wet-dry cycles

4 Conclusion

Experimental results show that the proposed approach is perfect for the research of meso-pore structures of soils. Pore number of eco-material increases with the decrease of pore-size, and the number of pores of pore-size smaller than 0.24 mm is about 30 % of total. Further more, Smoother pore number distribution curve indicates more stable structure. With the increase of sampling depth, total porosity of eco-material decreases on the whole. With the increase of wet-dry cycles, the total porosity of eco-material of 3 ~ 9 cm depth tends to decrease, and that of 12 ~ 18 cm depth shows a tendency to increase.

Acknowledgment. The authors wish to thank National Natural Science Foundation of China (51209084, 51409097) and Project of Natural Science Foundation of Hubei Province (2015CFB297, 2014CFB591) for their financial supports.

References

1. Zhang, J.R., Huang, L., Zhu, J., Huang, W.J.: SEM analysis of soil pore and its fractal dimension on micro scale. Acta Pedol. Sin. **45**(2), 22–30 (2008)
2. Tao, G.L., Zhang, J.R., Huang, L., Yuan, L.: Description of pore property of porous materials using fractal theory. J. Build. Mater. **13**(5), 678–681 (2010)
3. Skopp, J.: Comment on "micro, meso, and macroposity of soil". Soil Sci. Soc. Am. J. **45**, 1246 (1981)
4. Singh, P., Rameshwa, K.S., Thompson, M.L.: Measurement and characterization of macropores by using AUTOCAD and automatic image analysis. J. Environ. Qual. **20**, 289–294 (1991)
5. Tang, H.C., Zhu, H.Z.: New method of loose rock and soil sample sheet. Chin. Sci. Bull. **8**, 65–66 (1963)

6. Li, D.C., Velde, B., Delerue, J.F., Zhang, T.L.: Characteristics of pore structure at various places of a low-hill using the techniques of soil sections and digital images. Chin. J. Soil Sci. **33**(1), 6–8 (2002)
7. He, S.R., Huang, C.M., Zhou, H.Y.: Features of microstructure of diagnostic horizons and lower categorical classification of stagnic anthrosols in Chengdu plain. J. Mt. Sci. **20**(2), 157–163 (2002)

Application of Typical Set on Automatic Counting of Round Brilliant Cut Gems

Minghua Pan[1], Hengbing Wei[1,2(✉)], and Shaohua Sun[1,3]

[1] Guangxi Colleges and Universities Key Laboratory of Image Processing and Intelligent Information System, Wuzhou University, Wuzhou, China
{panmhwz, weihengbing}@qq.com, sshhgx@sohu.com
[2] College of Mechanical and Material Engineering,
Wuzhou University, Wuzhou, China
[3] School of Information and Communication,
Guilin University of Electronic Technology, Guilin, China

Abstract. Counting is an important part of gems trade, especially in large quantities. To develop a fast and automatic method for gems counting is necessary. According to the structure of round brilliant cut gem and the typical set property, typical gems were defined by high circularity and probability. Using the characters of typical gems and the relationship between number and area, gems were counted adaptively. The experiments were shown that the processing speed was fast and the accuracy of counting was high enough for large number of gems trading.

Keywords: Typical set · Gems · Round brilliant cut · Image processing · Counting

1   Introduction

Artificial gems [1, 2], hereinafter referred to as gems, as substitutes for diamonds, with variety, style, beauty and, in particular, huge price advantage, are being well received by buyers. Wuzhou, a city in south of China that has close links with the Pearl River Delta, is widely held to be a gems trading center that serves China and the rest of the world and known as 'the world capital for artificial gems'. Every year, the volume of processing, distributing and exchanging of gems in Wuzhou has reached more than 13 billion. Counting is important during the gems trading, especially in large quantities. Thus, to develop a fast and automatic method for gems counting is necessary. In order to make gems become more beautiful and personalized, consequently, improve their exchange values, one of the most important ways to aggregate value of the gems is lapidary, including the cutting and polishing processes. Due to physical properties similar to diamond, cubic zirconia is widely processed for artificial gems. Here, we focus on the gems processed into round brilliant cut which is the most popular cutting in gems, for this brilliant cut model maximizing the return of incident light, and consequently, making gems more sparkly and fascinating [2, 3].

As the development of image processing technology, image processing is used to counting in many applications, such as cells counting in medicine [4, 5], counting for

© Springer Science+Business Media Singapore 2016
T. Tan et al. (Eds.): IGTA 2016, CCIS 634, pp. 17–26, 2016.
DOI: 10.1007/978-981-10-2260-9_3

vegetable or fruits in agriculture [6–8]. However, there is still no universal method to counting especially for adhesive objects. Different methods would be useful just in special applications. During gems trading, the number of gems is so huge that the gems counting must be automatic and rapid. The methods are presented in referents [4–8] maybe more exactly but not so effective in gems counting for their complex calculations and processing.

In this article, we present a method based on typical set of gems, and then use the relationship between number and area of gems to count gems rapidly. In the following Sect. 2, we present the definition and the property of typical set. In Sect. 3, we present the structure of round brilliant cut gems, analysis the shape features of gems, and moreover we address how to select typical gems. In Sect. 4, the method to calculate the number of gems is present by using the typical gems feature and the relationship between area and number of gem. The complete procession of gems counting and some experimental results are presented in Sect. 5. At last, we give the conclusion that all the gems can be counted exactly by this method, at the same time the whole processing can be automatic done by the computer.

2 Typical Set

Typical set and its applications are very important in information theory. The elements in typical set are proved with high probability and will determine the average behavior of a large sample, thus most of our attention will be on the typical elements.

Definition 1 [9]. The typical set with respect to p(x) is the set of sequences $(X_1, X_2, \ldots, X_n) \in X^n$ with the property

$$2^{-n(H(X)+\varepsilon)} \leq p(X_1, X_2, \ldots, X_n) \leq 2^{-n(H(X)-\varepsilon)} \tag{1}$$

where n is the number of elements, H(x) is the Shannon entropy $H(p_x) = - p_x \log_2(p_x)$, and p_x is the probability of element x.

From the definition of $A_\varepsilon^{(n)}$, it is clear that $A_\varepsilon^{(n)}$ is a fairly set that contains most of the probability. The typical set has probability nearly 1, all elements of the typical set are nearly equiprobable. This enables us to divide the set of all elements into two sets, the typical set, where the sample entropy is close to the true entropy, and the nontypical set, which contains the other sequences. Any property that is proved for the typical elements will then be true with high probability and will determine the average behavior of a large sample. Thus, for gems counting, if we can find out the typical gems with high probability satisfying these properties, we can just focus on typical gems, and then use the features of typical gems to count gems.

3 Geometric Structure and Features of Gems

3.1 Structure of Round Brilliant Cut Gems

Lapidary techniques are still being developed in terms of producing even more sophisticated models, seeking to control color saturation, to maximize the return of incident light from the observer perspective, to obtain interesting distortion effects of light rays inside the gem, to reduce wastage in the raw material cutting, or simply to allow the setting of the gemstone on the jewel assembly [2, 3]. The round brilliant cut for gems can satisfy this demand and make gems more shiny and sparkly.

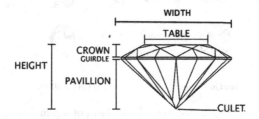

Fig. 1. Nomenclature of a round brilliant cut gemstone

The structure and nomenclature of a round brilliant cut gem [2] are shown in Fig. 1. For the sake of simplicity, we ignore its internal structure without affect the accuracy of counting. A round brilliant cut gem can be divided into three parts, Crown (C), Girdle (G) and Pavillion (P). Support W is the width of the Girdle which usually also is defined as the width or diameter of a gem. In different references and applications [2, 10], the ratios of each part to width are different. Here, we adopt as the follows.

The ratio of Pavilion to Width is

$$R_P = P/W = 0.43 \pm 0.03 \tag{2}$$

The ratio of Crown to Width is

$$R_C = C/W = 0.14 \pm 0.03 \tag{3}$$

The ratio of Girdle to Width is

$$R_G = G/W = 0.03 \pm 0.02 \tag{4}$$

The ratio of Table to Width is

$$R_T = T/W = 0.58 \pm 0.05 \tag{5}$$

3.2 Shape Features of Round Brilliant Cut Gems

In gems trading, the gems are classified by size and category for different size or category gems have different prices. So the gems in one time counting are in same shapes and sizes. But the same gems may present different shapes as circle or elliptic or other shapes in image under the light and camera.

If placed one gem randomly on platform, the gem should be bearing on table or pavilion surface [11]. Different visual planes of a gem on table and on pavillion bearing

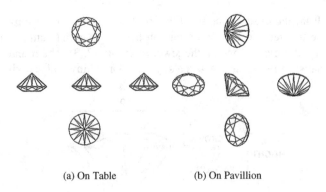

(a) On Table   (b) On Pavillion

Fig. 2. Different visual planes of a gem

surface are showed in Fig. 2. When a gem is placed exactly under the light and camera at the same time, if on table bearing surface, the gem is a circle with the diameter as the diameter of the gem, else if on pavillion bearing surface, the gem is an ellipse with the length also as the diameter of the gem. There may be other shapes for not all the gems will present exactly under the light and camera. Luckily, the probability of this case will be small.

When a gem on table bearing surface, the gem is a circle as under vertical view of the gem with the diameter as the diameter of the gem, its area is

$$S_C = \pi\left(\frac{w}{2}\right)^2 \tag{6}$$

When a gem is on pavilion bearing surface, then the gem is elliptic under vertical view, its area is

$$S_E = \pi a W \tag{7}$$

where a is the width of the ellipse. From the structure of the gem

$$a \approx \frac{W^2}{2\sqrt{\frac{W^2}{4} + P^2}} \tag{8}$$

where P is the height of Pavilion. Hence, we get

$$S_E = \frac{W^3}{2\sqrt{\frac{W^2}{4} + P^2}} \approx 0.63\, S_C \tag{9}$$

4   Method to Count Gems

According to 3.1, if we can find out the typical gems with high probability satisfying typical set properties and will determine the average behavior of a large sample, then we can just focus on the features of typical gems and use the features to count gems rapidly.

4.1 Typical Set of Gems

The probability of gems on table bearing surface is much higher than on pavilion [11], in other words, the probability of circle is much higher than elliptic and other shapes. When the gems are on table bearing surface, they are nearly equiprobable. According to the definition of typical set, we can definition the gems on table bearing surface with high probability as the typical gems. Hence we can use the circle gems to character the feature of gems. For fast counting, we use the circularity and area to describe gems.

4.2 Gems Circularity

In image processing, circularity is used to measure the degree of a circle. Hence, the circularity and the area are the features of a gem to judge a region is a single gem or noise or adhesive gems. The circularity of a gem is computed as follows.

> Step 1: Label all the connected regions, then get the total number of all the labeled regions as N_C, the area as S and the boundary coordinates (x, y) of each region;
> Step 2: Differentiate the boundary coordinates and square sum to get the perimeter as L.
> Step 3: Calculate the area S_L of the circle which the perimeter is L.

$$S_L = (\frac{L^2}{4\pi}) \tag{10}$$

> Step 4: Compute the circularity

$$deg = \frac{S}{S_L} = 4\pi \frac{S}{L^2} \tag{11}$$

The circularity ranges from 0 to 1, the closer to 1 the circular degree is higher, and more accurately to determine whether a region is a typical gem or not.

4.3 Gems Counting

According the above presented, we can get the method to count gems based on feature of gems. We firstly select out the typical gems with high circularity and probability, and then calculate the average area of all the typical gems as the area of the single standard gem noting S_{sd}. After select out the typical gems, the rest thing is to count the other single nontypical gems and adhesive gems and get rid of noise.

The area of a single gem is between 0.63 to 1 times of the area S_{sd} of a typical standard gem according to the shape features of round brilliant cut gems in Sect. 3B. And from large sampling tests, we found that the area of a single gem generally between 0.6 to 1.2 times of S_{sd}. In order to obtain a universal formula to count gems automatic and fast, according to the prior knowledge that the relationship of the number and the area of gems is approximate linear, without loss of general, we appropriately use the area S of a connected region is 0.5 to 1.5 times of the area S_{sd} of a single standard gem as a single gem. If the area S out of this scope, the region will be considered as noise or adhesive gems. Move elaborate describe as follows.

Case1: The area S belongs to 0.5 and 1.5 times the area S_{sd} of a single typical gem as a single gem. Then we need to do nothing for we have counted gems in the number N_C of the original labeled regions.

Case2: When the area S of a region is smaller than the lower bound of a single gem, that is $S < 0.5S_{sd}$, we consider the region as noise and do not count it. Hence, support the number of the noises is n and we should minus n from the number N_C of the original labeled regions. Namely, the number of gems is

$$N = N_C - n \tag{12}$$

Case3: When the connected area is larger than the upper bound of a single gem, that is $S > 1.5S_{sd}$, we consider the region as adhesive gems.

Support the number of adhesive region is m, the number of gems is N_i in the i-th adhesive region. In order to obtain a universal formula to count gems automatic and fast, without loss of general, the round of the connected region area (S) divided by a single gem standard area as the actual number of gems, i.e.

$$N_i = round(S/S_{sd}) \tag{13}$$

Thus, the number of gems is

$$N = N_C + \sum_{i=1}^{m} [N_i - 1] \tag{14}$$

To sum up the above discussions, the number of all gems is

$$N = N_C - n + \sum_{i=1}^{m} [N_i - 1] \tag{15}$$

5 Experiments and Results

5.1 Experimental Process

In order to count gems more accurate and save time, we disperse gems by mechanics device. But there are still some adhesive gems or pseudo adhesive gems due to high reflection and refraction of gems in the image under the light which are the critical of the gems counting. The procession to count gems by computer image processing is as in Fig. 3. More elaborate description and the experiment with MATLAB are as follows.

Step 1: Place gems on plane under the camera, and disperse gems by mechanical device. In the case of the number of gems is huge, the mechanical device divides gems into suitable volume which makes gems can be counted in batches.

Step 2: Take the image of gems by image acquisition, as shown Fig. 4.

Step 3: Do image preprocessing of the image of gems. First, change the image into a gray image to improve data processing speed of the system; Then, binary image and remove background; In the end, morphology of binary image processing, using circular structure elements to open and close combination operations, to smooth boundary and remove noise and impurities, as shown Fig. 5.

Step 4: Statistics the information of gems image. According to the image edge information, adopt the eight neighborhood connected area method, record the basic information of the labeled image, such as, the total number (N_C) of connected regions, the area (S) and the centroid coordinates, the boundary coordinates of each connected region.

Step 5: According to the characteristics of the gems as present in Sect. 3, compute the circularity of regions, select out the gems with high probability and circularity as the typical gems, as shown in Figs. 6 and 7. Then compute the numbers and areas of all the typical regions.

Step 6: Compute the average area of all the typical gems as the area of a single standard gem and note it as S_{sd}.

Step 7: Judge the stats of gems and decide they are single gems or noise or adhere gems by 3.4. To clear the result of gems counting, we label the number of gems in each region as shown in Fig. 8. From Fig. 8, we can see that all the gems are counted exactly.

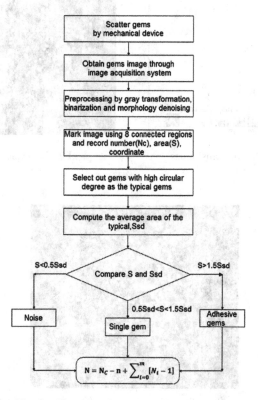

Fig. 3. Algorithm flow chart of counting gems

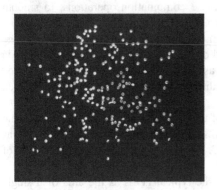

Fig. 4. Original gems image

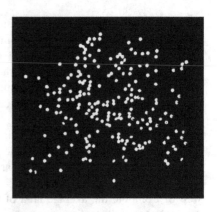

Fig. 5. Gems image after preprocessing

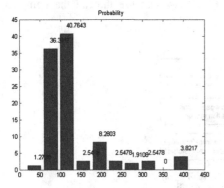

Fig. 6. Probability of gems' areas

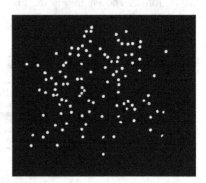

Fig. 7. Typical gems

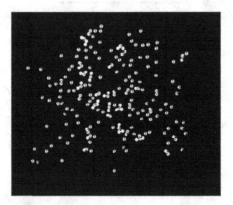

Fig. 8. Result of gems counting

5.2 Experiments and Discussion

To demonstrate the efficient performance of the proposed counting method, the experiments were done to compare with other methods under different conditions and gems sizes, as summarized in Table 1. The datum were tested by MATLAB (R2013a) under Windows XP with the size of figure about 720*600 pixels. The Table 1 shows that when the width of gems is larger than 2.0 mm, the accuracy of the algorithm based on the character of typical gems almost 100 %, even gems are heavy adhesive which satisfy that the probability of single typical gems is large enough. In Table 1, the picture (c) of gems is taken under the poor light and the width of these gems is 1.0 mm which is the smallest size in the market. In that case, the accuracy is dropped but also is large than 95 % by the proposed method. If the poor light and the image pixels are improved, the accuracy will be improved. Compare to other methods, the performance of the proposed methods is best as its high accuracy and stabilization. The time consumption is little more than other simple image processing algorithms taken but is 100 times faster than the handwork taken when the number of gems is large then 200.

Table 1. Experiments with different methods under different conditions and gems sizes

Gems images	(a)W=2.0mm,NO.=210			(b)W=3.0mm,NO.=210			(c)W=1.0mm,NO.=193			(d)W=3.5mm,NO.=134		
Algorithms	No.	Precise	Time	No.	Precise	Time	No.	Precise	Time	No.	Precise	Time
Regions	161	76.7%	0.57 ± .02	67	31.9%	0.66 ± 0.03	186	96.4%	0.66 ± 0.02	118	88.1%	0.54 ± 0.01
Mean Area	189	90.0%	0.65 ± 0.03	80	38.1%	0.72 ± 0.03	192	99.4%	0.72 ± 0.01	133	99.3%	0.63 ± 0.03
Morphology	185	88.1%	0.78 ± 0.02	100	47.6%	0.87 ± 0.02	175	90.6%	0.79 ± 0.02	130	97.0%	0.77 ± 0.03
Typical set	210	100%	0.97 ± 0.03	210	100%	0.95 ± 0.05	188	97.4%	1.08 ± 0.04	134	100%	0.94 ± 0.04
Handwork	208 ± 2	99.1± 0.9%	105 ± 12	209 ± 5	99.5± 2.4%	102 ± 5	196 ± 5	98.4± 2.6%	114 ± 11	123 ± 3	99.3± 2.2%	53 ± 2

Note. The algorithms in Table 1 are as follows. *Regions:* Use the number of the connected regions; *Mean Area:* Use the mean area of connected regions as the area of a signal gem instead of the mean area of typical gems; *Morphology:* Do morphological corrosion with circle element whose radius is 50% of the radius of mean area of connected regions to separate adhesive gems. *Typical set:* The proposed algorithm in this paper. *Handwork:* Count by mankind.

6 Conclusion

According to the probability of circle is much higher than other shapes of gems, we definite the typical gems. Furthermore we select out the gems with high circularity as single typical gems. Here we complete the gems counting just use the characters of typical gems and the relationship between the number and the area, hence the counting is adaptive. With the help of mechanical device, the whole counting process can be automatic done by the computer, and as shown in the experiments that the processing speed is fast and the accuracy of counting is high enough for large number of gems trading.

Acknowledgments. The authors extend thanks to Zhenming Yu for helpful discussions and to the reviewers of IGTA2016 for providing comments to improve the manuscript. This work was supported by the Key Project of Wuzhou University Scientific Research under Grant No. 2015B008, and the Project of Wuzhou Scientific Research and Technology Development under Grant No. 2014A05003.

References

1. Kun, W., Shuli, Z., Lin, Z., et al.: Enduring gem processing industry in Wuzhou. Superhard Mater. Eng. **23**(6), 54–58 (2011)
2. Mol, A.A., Martins-Filho, L.S., da Silva, J.D.S., et al.: Efficiency parameters estimation in gemstones cut design using artificial neural networks. Comput. Mater. Sci. **38**, 727–736 (2007)
3. Shi, B., Yuan, X.: Study on emulation model and principle of optical effect of round brilliant cut diamond. J. Gems Gemmol. **9**(2), 8–12 (2007)
4. Chaudhury, B., Kramer, K., Elozory, D., et al.: A novel algorithm for automated counting of stained cells. In: Proceedings of the 25th IEEE International Symposium on Computer-Based Medical Systems (2012). doi:10.1109/CBMS.2012.6266296
5. Kothari, S., Chaudry, Q., Wang, M.D., et al.: Automated cell counting and cluster segmentation using concavity detection and ellipse fitting techniques. In: Biomedical Imaging: From Nano to Macro, pp. 795–799. IEEE (2009)
6. Song, Y., Glasbey, C.A., Horgan, G.W., Polder, G., et al.: Automatic fruit recognition and counting from multiple images. Biosyst. Eng. **118**, 203–215 (2014)
7. Font, D., Pallejà, T., Tresanchez, M., et al.: Counting red grapes in vineyards by detecting specular spherical reflection peaks in RGB images obtained at night with artificial illumination. Comput. Electron. Agric. **108**, 105–111 (2014)
8. Linker, R., Cohen, O., Naor, A.: Determination of the number of green apples in RGB images recorded in orchards. Comput. Electron. Agric. **81**, 45–57 (2012)
9. Thomas, M.C., Thomas, J.A.: Elements of Information Theory, 2nd edn. Wiley, New York (2006)
10. Liu, P., Yuan, X., Shi, B., et al.: Study on measuring brilliance of round brilliant cut cubic zirconia under ring light. J. Gems Gemmol. **16**(1), 62–69 (2014)
11. Pan, M.: Research on features of round brilliant cut gemstones of stochastic equilibrium. Sci. Technol. Eng. **28**(15), 170–173, 178 (2015)

An Algorithm for Automatic Recognition
of Manhole Covers Based on MMS Images

Zhang Chong[1]([✉]) and Liu Yang[1,2]

[1] School of Geomatics and Urban Information,
Beijing University of Civil Engineering and Architecture,
No. 1, Exhibition Hall Road, Xicheng District, Beijing 100044, China
13521173436@163.com
[2] The Key Laboratory for Urban Geomatics of National Administration
of Surveying, Mapping and Geoinformation,
Beijing University of Civil Engineering and Architecture,
No. 1, Exhibition Hall Road, Xicheng District, Beijing 100044, China

Abstract. Considering difficulties in performing automatic recognition for manhole covers under complex background, this paper proposed a Hough transform algorithm to locating the possible positions of the manhole covers based on features of ellipse geometry extracting from images by Mobile Mapping Systems (MMS). Firstly, the original images need to be preprocessed by image enhancement, edge detection, and morphological closing operation. Then the processed image was filled, the image noises with very small areas were removed, and the remaining blocks were identified. A ratio of the ellipse area to its outer rectangle area was calculated as the threshold value to eliminate large amount of image noises so as to obtain the maximum likely positions of manhole covers. Finally, the Hough transform was used to identify the accurate locations of the manhole covers. Experiments with fifty images have showed that the proposed algorithm can achieve a 88 % accuracy of identifying the manhole covers correctly, automatically and quickly.

Keywords: Manhole cover · Automatic recognition · Geometric properties · Coarse positioning · Hough transform

1 Introduction

Along with the accelerated process of urbanization in China, the city infrastructure construction change rapidly. The number of manhole covers in water supply and drainage, electricity, gas, fire, heat, communication is also increasing [1]. A comprehensive understanding of the distribution and number of manhole covers, to ensure the correctness, real-time and reliability of data so that provide effective help for the management department of municipal manhole cover. However, the traditional census method was relying on humans mainly, resulting in heavy workload and low efficiency. Now we proposes the implementation of the digital management of urban road manhole cover is the main direction to solve the problem, relying on the information and network technology, using digital means to process, analyze and manage [2] manhole covers.

© Springer Science+Business Media Singapore 2016
T. Tan et al. (Eds.): IGTA 2016, CCIS 634, pp. 27–34, 2016.
DOI: 10.1007/978-981-10-2260-9_4

In this paper proposes images captured by Mobile Mapping Systems (MMS). According to the characteristics of elliptic geometry covers using image processing technology to identify the manhole covers under complex background, and laying a foundation for the digital management. There were many ways to identify the ellipse in the existing literature. The reference [3] puts forward a method which was based on invariant moments, this method is sensitive to noise, large computation and complex algorithm, it was not applicable to practical applications. Reference [4–6] proposes least square and its improvement method. The least square method was that when the random error is normal distribution, it is an optimal estimation technique introduced by the maximum likelihood method, it makes the square of measurement error minimum, so it was also regarded as one of the most reliable methods to find out a set of unknown quantity in a set of measured values [1]. Some scholars put forward the algebraic distance least squares fitting ellipse [5]. It can solve the problem when there was an error in the sample and avoiding to the larger fitting error. Reference [7–11] put forward based on Hough transform and its improved method. The basic idea of Hough transform is to transform the image space domain into the parameter domain, and if the parameter of the ellipse was known, then the traditional Hough transform detection can be used, however, there were some problems in large scale of computing, large memory, and restricted by the quantization precision of parameter domain. In order to overcome the above defects, some scholars put forward random Hough transform technology (RHT). Multiple to one mapping were used to avoid the huge computational, and dynamic linked list structure were used to reduce the memory footprint. However, with the increase of the amount of data, invalid cumulative increased, it will affect the performance of RHT. Therefore, this paper proposes an improved Hough transform algorithm based on the rough localization of the ellipse geometry, it reduces the Hough transform computation and memory to realize the automatic recognition of manhole covers faster and more accurate.

2 Image Preprocessing

The images collected by MMS was influenced by time, scene, illumination and so on. The background information was very complex and there were a large number of random noise images seriously affect the accurate identification of manhole covers. Therefore, image preprocessing to make the output image has a better effect at first, and to lay the foundation for the subsequent image detection and recognition.

In this paper, the original image was processed by gray-scale transformation and filtering technology. Then using the double threshold method in Canny operator edge detection technology [14] to detect the edge information. The flexibility of edge detection was improved by setting two thresholds, and the feature of image edge was guaranteed. Finally, in order to eliminate the redundant edge information in the image, and connect disconnected edge effectively, it adopts mathematical morphology method such as closing operation which is using the structure elements of circular ring shape repeatedly, to eliminate interference information of small area, and to reduce the amount of computation in image recognition. As a result, the image preprocessing operation was completed (Fig. 1).

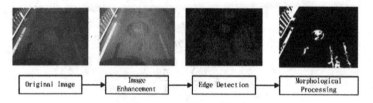

Fig. 1. Image preprocessing steps

3 A Hough Transform Algorithm Based on Rough Localization of Ellipse Geometry

The preprocessed image were filled, and combined with the removal of a small area of the image noise, leaving only a few blocks of different shapes in different area of fill area. Then the image information block identified (shown in Fig. 2) in order to prepare for the rough location of manhole covers.

Fig. 2. Block marks image information

Manhole covers are round in our country. Because the different camera angles by MMS, the different degree of deformation caused when the oblique projection covers, lead to the manhole cover in the shape of ellipse. Therefore, this paper analyzes the characteristics of ellipse (Fig. 3):

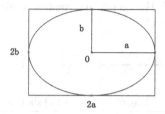

Fig. 3. Ellipse and its external rectangle sketch map

$$S = \pi \times a \times b \tag{1}$$

$$W = 4 \times a \times b \tag{2}$$

$$K = \frac{S}{W} = \frac{\pi}{4} \tag{3}$$

'S' represents an ellipse area, 'W' represents an enclosing rectangle area, 'a' is the minor semi-axis of ellipse, 'b' is the major semi-axis of ellipse. The ratio of ellipse area and rectangle area is 'K', and the fixed value of 'K' is $\frac{\pi}{4}$, approximately equal to 0.7854. In this paper, traverse each area and calculate the area of the area and the ratio of the rectangular area to the outside. According to the value of K setting threshold range is [0.75 0.79], If the calculation results were in the threshold range, then the region was selected as ellipse, otherwise the image information was deleted. The results of rough localization based on the ellipse geometry were shown in Fig. 4.

Fig. 4. Results of rough localization by elliptic geometry

After the initial rough positioning of the image information, the complexity was significantly reduced. At this time, the traditional Hough transform algorithm is used to detect the ellipse can be improved the detection speed significantly. Correction of the large amount of computation and memory occupation in the traditional Hough transform.

Standard elliptic equation is shown in the formula (4), the (x_0, y_0) is the ellipse center, 'a' is the minor semi-axis, 'b' is the major semi-axis. In the actual situation, the long and short axis of the ellipse may not be parallel to the axis, so the coordinate axis can be translated and rotated. Hypothesis the rotation angle is θ, the elliptic equation can be written as the formula (5).

$$\frac{(x - x_0)^2}{a^2} + \frac{(y - y_0)^2}{b^2} = 1 \tag{4}$$

$$\frac{[(x - x_0)\cos\theta + (y_0 - b)\sin\theta]^2}{a^2} + \frac{[(x - x_0)\sin\theta + (y_0 - b)\cos\theta]^2}{b^2} = 1 \tag{5}$$

Finding all the contours on the edge of the binary image (including the closed and non closed contours), Hough transformation was carried out in the sub image with the center of each contour based on the contour list [9]. The first step in the processing cycle contour of each pixel, the establishment of the accumulator, the initial value was zero. The second step is to assume a point of the ellipse center O, to calculate the Euclidean distance between each point and the O point in the current profile, to find the distance between the maximum value was set to the length of the half axis A and save the contour point P. Third step if you find the contour point P points P, O connection and the angle between the X axis, or repeat the second step. The fourth step according to the loop current contour of every pixel, calculating elliptical short half axis b, at the same time will add 1 corresponding accumulator. Finally, if the value of the short half axis was in the set threshold, the corresponding a, b, O and θ were the necessary parameters for the elliptic equation. Therefore, the ellipse object can be accurately identified from the image of the coarse positioning.

4 Experimental Results and Analysis

In this paper, on the Windows7 platform, based on the Matlab 2010 development tools to achieve the above algorithm. The experimental data were collected from the 1392 × 1040 color image (shown in Fig. 6(a)) by MMS. The experimental steps were as follows (Fig 5):

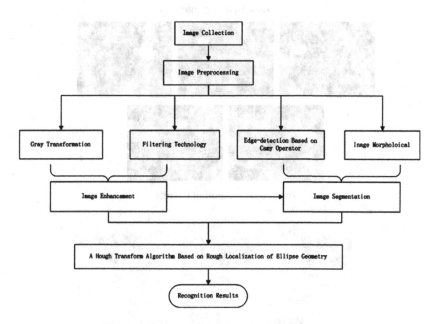

Fig. 5. The recognition of road covers flowchart

This paper collected 50 pieces of different environment images, which can be correctly identified road manhole covers image 44 pieces, correct rate of 88 %, shown in Table 1. Undetected refers to the presence of cover image recognition but without success. Error refers to the meaning of the original image does not exist, but because of the influence of the light shadow, the error is detected as an ellipse.

Table 1. Statistics of experimental results

	Total number	Correct	Undetected	Error
Quantity	50	44	4	2
Percentage	100 %	88 %	8 %	4 %

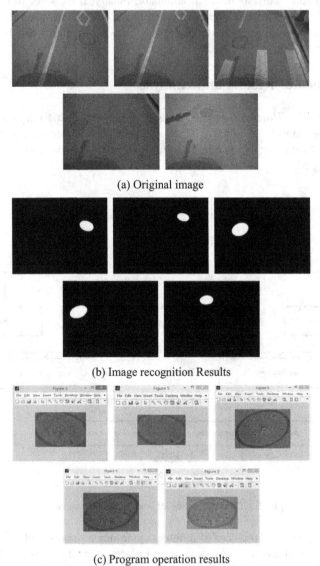

(a) Original image

(b) Image recognition Results

(c) Program operation results

Fig. 6. Results of image recognition

The evaluation of real-time identification method of manhole covers. Comparative analysis the method 1 based on the invariant moment of recognition of ellipse, method 2 based on the Hough transform recognition of ellipse and this paper recognition method, the results were shown in Fig. 7. With the increase of the experimental samples, the recognition speed of the three algorithms is gradually decreased. The number of the samples is 'm', total recognition time is 't', recognition velocity is 'v' as the time required to process the image of the unit $\frac{m}{t}$. This situation was due to the huge image data lead to a gradual increase in the amount of computation, and the recognition rate was reduced.

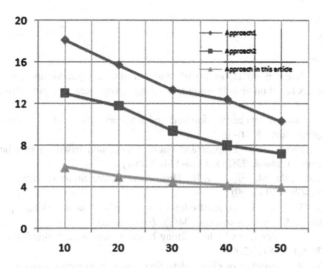

Fig. 7. Relationship between image recognition speed and experimental sample

Experimental results show that compared to the methods 1 and 2, the algorithm speed was faster in this paper, so real time effect is better, and it can meet the requirement of real-time processing of road manhole covers recognition system.

5   Conclusion

In this paper, a Hough transform algorithm based on the rough localization of ellipse geometry was proposed, in order to fast and effective identify the target of manhole cover. The innovation of this paper was to use the geometric properties of the ellipse, introducing the concept of the ratio of the ellipse area to the enclosing rectangle area to set the threshold. Then if the ratio was consistent with the range of threshold, it may be the manhole cover. The coarse location of image after preprocessing was realized and removing most of the interference information in front of the traditional Hough transform. Improved the speed of recognition effectively, reduced memory usage, and satisfied the needs of real-time processing. Experimental results show that this algorithm has high efficiency and performance under complex background. However, for some special circumstances, such as the road surface has a large area of shadow and other strong interference factors. Further practice and research were needed to identify the accuracy of the algorithm in this paper.

Fund Project. Supported by Beijing Nova Program (No. Z121106002512025) and its matching supporting program by Beijing University of Civil Engineering and Architecture (No. 21221214116), Importation and Development of High-Caliber Talents Project of Beijing Municipal Institutions (No. CIT&TCD201504032), Beijing Municipal Organization Department Talents Project (No. 2012D005017000001), Scientific Research Project of Beijing Educational Committee (No. KM201410016008).

References

1. Jianhua, L.: Research on algorithm of automatically recognizing and positioning road manhole covers based on vehicle—mounted sensors. Appl. Res. Comput. **28**(8), 3139–3140 (2011)
2. Qi, Z.: Discussion on data acquisition and updating methods of urban components. Urban Geotech. Invest. Surv. **3**, 16–18 (2011)
3. Xiuming, L., Zhaoyao, S.: Ellipses and circles recognition based on invariant moments. J. Beijing Univ. Technol. **33**(11), 1136–1140 (2007)
4. Fitzgibbon, A., Pilu, M., Fisher, R.B.: Direct least square fitting of elipses. IEEE Trans. PAMI **21**(5), 476–480 (1999)
5. Pei, Y., Bin, W., Yuan, L.: Optimal ellipse fitting method based on least-square principle. J. Beijing Univ. Aeronaut. Astronaut. **34**(3), 296–298 (2008)
6. Yimin, Z., Bo, W.: Fragmental ellipse fitting based on least-square algorithm. Chin. J. Sci. Instrum. **27**(7), 808–812 (2006)
7. Jingdong, Z.: An algorithm of ellipse detection based on Hough transform. Optoelectron. Technol. **28**(3), 379–384 (2010)
8. Lei, X., Erkki, O.: Randomized Hough transform (RHT): basic mechanisms, algorithms and computational complexities. CVGIP: Image Underst. **57**(2), 131–154 (1993)
9. Ying, C., Zhang, X., Yunhong, W.: Improved classical Hough transform applied to the manhole cover's detection and location. Opt. Tech. **37**, 504–508 (2006)
10. Pao, D.C.W., Li, H.F., Jayakumar, R.: Shapes recognition using the straight line Hough transform: theory and generalization. IEEE Trans. Pattern Anal. Mach. Intell. **14**(11), 1076–1089 (1992)
11. Farsi, H., Joly, J.L., Miscevic, M., et al.: An experimental and theoretical investigation of the transient behavior of a two-phase closed thermosyphon. Appl. Therm. Eng. **23**(15), 1895–1912 (2003)
12. Taiwen, Q.: Chord midpoint Hough transform based ellipse detection method. J. Zhejiang Univ.: Eng. Sci. **39**(8), 1132–1135 (2005)
13. Guiming, S., Qingtao, W., Fansheng, M.: Image edge detection algorithm based on canny operator. Mod. Electron. Tech. **38**(12), 92–94 (2015)
14. Xiaochuan, Z., Hao, H., Yuancheng, M., et al.: MATLAB digital image processing. China Mach. Press 94–97 (2013)
15. Magda, E.F., Cosmin, S., Loan, L.A.: Image search algorithms. In: International Conference on Electronics, Computers and Artificial Intelligence, pp, 36–40 (2015)

An Adaptive Error Concealment Algorithm Based on Partition Model

Chengxing Li[1], Li Xu[1(✉)], Feng Ye[1,2], and Jiazhen Chen[1]

[1] School of Mathematics and Computer Science, Fujian Normal University, Fuzhou, China
fjlcx2016@sina.com, {xuli,yefeng,jiazhen_chen}@fjnu.edu.cn
[2] Multimedia Telecommunication Centre, Beijing University of Posts & Telecoms,
Beijing, China

Abstract. In this paper, a novel error concealment method based on partition model is developed for video transmission over noisy channels. This method contains spatio-temporal restoration and spatial error concealment (SEC) strategy. In the spatial domain, the SEC strategy is used to select the appropriate spatial method by location information and Intra Mode of surrounding received macroblocks (MBs). In temporal domain, the Inter partition model (PM) of corrupted MB is estimated by the surrounding MBs, then the appropriate temporal method is used according to the Inter PM of corrupted MB. Experimental results show that the proposed algorithm has good subjective video quality in comparison with the traditional error concealment method in the H.264/AVC, and the average PSNR is improved by 0.3 dB.

Keywords: Error concealment · Spatio-temporal · H.264/AVC · Partition model

1 Introduction

In order to transmit video streams on the Internet, video compression technologies like H.264 are needed to reduce bit stream size and retain the video quality. Unfortunately, wireless channels or the Internet are not reliable enough, packet lost happens due to various reasons. To solve this problem, the missing data is needed to restore by error concealment (EC) techniques [1–3, 12]. The EC techniques can be classified into spatial error concealment (SEC) and temporal error concealment (TEC). The SEC is usually takes advantage of spatial correlations among the MBs in a frame and use correctly decoded MB to construct the missing MBs of a video frame. The TEC is used to estimate motion vector and replace the corrupted MB by using the motion compensation.

In general, the TEC is more efficient than the SEC method, since temporal correlation is much higher than spatial correlation in video sequences. In [11], the MB at the same spatial location in the previous frame is copied to conceal the missing one. In [7], the boundary matching algorithm (BMA) is proposed to select the motion vectors (MVs) that minimizes the total variation between the internal boundary and the external boundary of the reconstructed MB as the optimal one to recover the corrupted MBs. The [9]

T. Tan et al. (Eds.): IGTA 2016, CCIS 634, pp. 35–43, 2016.
DOI: 10.1007/978-981-10-2260-9_5

method considers the interframe partition mode of the correctly received MBs, and estimates the partition model of the corrupted MB, then recover the MVs. In [14], the TEC method based on motion object to reconstruct the missing blocks.

The spatial methods usually used in the pixel domain and frequency domain [1, 2]. The corrupted MBs can be estimated by means of the surrounding MB DC value [1]. In [4], the nearest neighbor MB boundary pixels are used to replace the corrupted pixels by weighted average calculation. The EC method proposed by [1, 4] has some disadvantages, such as the boundary effect. In [5, 6], the linear mask operation is performed by using the surrounding MB of missing MB, and the most probable edge direction is estimated, then the linear interpolation is performed along the boundary. In [8], the SEC strategy based on boundary strength to select used the nearest pixel linear interpolation (NPLI), directional interpolation (DI) and NMEC. Qaratlu et al. proposed the SEC algorithm for reconstruction of the lost MBs in the I frames of a video sequence [12].

By studying existing EC methods, we propose an improved adaptive EC method. The improvement is mainly in two aspects: in spatial domain, the adaptive SEC strategy uses location information of received MB and Intra mode in order to switch between improved DI and NPLI algorithm, the improved DI algorithm based on eight direction sobel 5×5 template for restoring corrupted MBs; In temporal domain, we analyze the PM of neighbor MBs to determine the PM of corrupted MB, then the suitable method is employed according to PM of corrupted MB.

This paper is organized as follows: in Sect. 2, we present the design of SEC method. In Sect. 3, the improved TEC method is presented. In Sect. 4, the experimental results are shown and discussed. Finally, conclusions are drawn in Sect. 5.

2   Proposed SEC Algorithm and Strategy

2.1   SEC Strategy Based on MB Location

The adaptive SEC strategy which switch between improved DI and NPLI method (simplify DN), the DN method is used to conceal the corrupted I frame. In Fig. 1(a), the methods [6, 8, 12] cannot recover the consecutive block errors very well, serious blurring artifact appears on the significant image edge after interpolation.

(a)   (b)

Fig. 1. (a) The frame of crew video, (b) The S is corrupted MB

The error detection and localization of the corrupted MBs is shown in the H. 264/AVC decoder [13]. For example, the S in Fig. 1(b) represents the corrupted MB that is currently restored. In most cases, the 1, 0 or 3 region give priority to conceal or correctly received (except the boundary of frame) due to error detection. In our work, if the S at the boundary of the frame, then use NPLI method. It is assumed that the S is not at the boundary of frame, and 0 region always are available or concealed. If sampling position of the pixels at 1 and 2 region when 1 and 2 are not available, the computation error will occur. This problem can be resolved in our SEC strategy in Fig. 2.

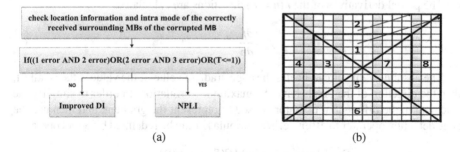

(a)   (b)

Fig. 2. (a) The proposed SEC strategy, (b) The region partition of MB

In the Intra mode of the H.264/AVC standard, the luminance MBs have two modes: 4×4 and 16×16. When the Intra mode of the correctly received surrounding MBs of the corrupted MBs are 4×4, which can be judged that usually have a lot of texture, we can use improved DI method. The T denotes the number of 4×4 Intra mode. According to the above description, we proposed the SEC strategy in Fig. 2(a), AND and OR representation logic operation, we use suitable algorithms according to analyze status of surrounding MB (Received, Error and Concealed) and Intra mode.

2.2   Improved Directional Interpolation

The DI method [8, 12], only the largest correlation direction interpolation solves the phenomenon of edge discontinuity, but interpolation error will be occur if edge direction calculation error is large or frame resolution is relatively large. To solve this problem, the eight direction interpolation is used to improve the accuracy of interpolation to restore edge: {$0°, 22.5°, 45°, 67.5°, 90°, 112.5°, 135°, 157.5°, 180°$}. In order to reduce computation complexity, the current corrupted MB is divided into eight regions, As illustrated in Fig. 2(b), the 16×16 MBs are partitioned into eight regions. For example, 22.5 degree direction of the 2 region is sampled at the top edge.

Edges, which play an important role in human perception of images. The edge region of video frame to form a gray change area, we use gray change rate and gray change direction to measure the whole change status of gray. Therefore, the gradient vector represents the change rate of the gray level, and the direction of the gradient vector represents the direction change of the gray level. If $f(x, y)$ represent the frame, the coordinates (x, y) in the gradient is a vector:

$$f(x, y) = \frac{\partial f}{\partial x}i + \frac{\partial f}{\partial y}j \qquad (1)$$

Where i and j are expressed as unit vectors (x, y), the edge gradient magnitude:

$$G = \sqrt{\left(\frac{\partial f}{\partial x}\right)^2 + \left(\frac{\partial f}{\partial y}\right)^2} \qquad (2)$$

The partial derivatives of the $n(n = 8)$ directions are calculated:

$$g_n = \frac{\partial f}{\partial n} \qquad (3)$$

The absolute value of g indicates the edge gradient value, if the value is the smallest, then the direction of the pixels have the maximum correlation. In order to simplify the calculation, the differential operator is used to represent the gradient, and then use the edge detection operator to estimate. The formula (3) can be redefined by Sobel operator:

$$D_{\min}(g_n(x, y)) = \min(C(S_n, f(x, y))) \qquad (4)$$

The S_n denotes Sobel template in [10] and C represents convolution function, $D_{\min}$ denotes the maximum correlation of direction. Therefore, interpolation of pixels along the minimum differential $D_{\min}$ direction.

Figure 3(a) shows the sample of surrounding pixels, the correlation that exists between a damaged MB and its adjacent MBs is relatively high. Therefore, the first and second line of the boundary pixels are used to recover lost pixels. In (b), P-number is obtained from the surrounding correctly received pixel in Fig. 3(a), which need to be calculated by convolution with the Sobel operator, the Y is need to restore. In order to reduce the computational complexity, luminance component uses in the improved DI algorithm. In Fig. 3(c), P_n is pixel, D_n is the distance in [8].

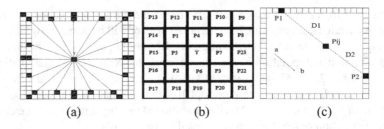

(a)   (b)   (c)

Fig. 3. (a) Eight direction sampling, (b) template, (c) directional interpolation

3   TEC Algorithm

In Fig. 4, the modes of the correctly received surrounding MBs of the missing MBs are checked first. If the surrounding MBs are all encoded as Skip Mode, it means that the corrupted MB has no motion at all, then zero MV is applied to recover the corrupted MB. The Inter PM of MB is mainly classified into three types, the first type is $4 \times 4, 4 \times 8, 8 \times 4$ mode, the second type is $8 \times 8, 8 \times 16, 8 \times 16$ mode, and the third type is 16×16 mode. If the PM of surrounding MBs is first type, then the surrounding area has complex motion information. Therefore, the corrupted MB is divided into sixteen 4×4 MBs, and we use 4×4 MB motion inpainting to conceal the corrupted MB, which can gain more accurate MVs for each 4×4 MB, after motion compensation, the status of the MB is set to "concealed". If the PM of surrounding MBs is second type, it means that have no complex motion, but possibly also contains relatively large motion, the corrupted MB is divided into four 8×8 MBs to use the simple 8×8 MB temporal interpolation method to recover the corrupted MB. If the PM of surrounding MBs is 16×16, it means that these regions with slow motion. Therefore, BMA method [7] is used to conceal the corrupted MB. If the PM of all surrounding MBs are Intra Mode, then DN method is used.

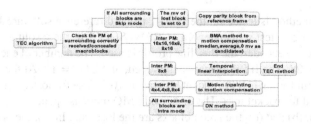

Fig. 4. Flow chart of the proposed TEC algorithm

In Fig. 5, if all the four surrounding MBs are correctly received, the MVs of outer edge blocks are recovered, then advance into inner ones in (a). If surrounding three MBs are correctly received, the repair order is shown in Fig. 5(b). If two surrounding MBs are both correctly received, we need to classify the situation into symmetrically and asymmetrically in Fig. 5(c), (d).

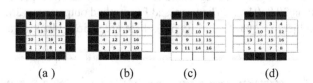

(a)   (b)   (c)   (d)

Fig. 5. The MVs inpainting order of 4×4 MB

In Fig. 5, the MV inpainting formula based on 4×4 blocks:

$$MV_{nt}(p_{nt}) = \frac{\sum_{q_{nt} \in H(p_{nt})} \omega(p_{nt}, q_{nt}) MV(q_{nt})}{\sum_{q_{nt} \in H(p_{nt})} \omega(p_{nt}, q_{nt})}$$

(5)

Where $n = 4$. p_{nt} is the error 4×4 block. $H(p_{nt})$ represents the correctly received MB next to p_{nt}, which is limited to four. q_{nt} is neighboring 4×4 block, $MV(q_{nt})$ is the motion vector of q_{nt}. $\omega(p_{nt}, q_{nt})$ expressed the weight coefficient in [9].

The temporal interpolation is employed when the Inter PM of surrounding MBs is 8×8, 8×16 or 16×8, which is used linearly interpolated to conceal a pixel by four pixel values in the reference frame. For each pixel C in a missing MB, four reference pixels are obtained using the motion vectors of the upper, lower, left and right MBs. They are denoted by C_{upper}, C_{lower}, C_{left} and C_{right}.

$$C = \frac{C_{upper}(N + 1 - y) + C_{lower} \cdot y + C_{left}(N + 1 - x) + C_{right} \cdot x}{2(N + 1)} \qquad (6)$$

Where (x, y) is the coordinates of pixel C, the N is set as 8. $x >= 1$ and $y <= 8$.

4 Experiment and Analysis

The proposed method is tested on the H.264 standard reference software JM14.2, The resolution 704×576 test sequence: ICE, CREW, SOCCER, the resolution 352×288: FOREMAN. At the encoder, the Baseline profile is used. The number of encoded frames is 60 and QP = 28. The IPPP format is employed, and GOP = 10. At the decoder, the file stream output format is RTP, packet loss rate is 10 %. The Rtploss.exe in the JM14.2 software is used for packet loss. The dispersed FMO mode is open.

In Fig. 6(a), (b) and (c), the green blocks are the lost data. In (a), the position of the corrupted MB is discrete, which can refer to the surrounding pixel to recover. In (b), The missing data are gathered together, which are difficult to recover. Under this circumstance, the proposed adaptive SEC strategy is used to recover lost data. In (e), The PSNR of JM14.2 is 32.4675 dB. The (h) represents the PSNR of improved algorithm is 32.8697 dB, which gets a 0.4 dB PSNR improvement gain comparing to JM 14.2. The (d) represents the PSNR of JM algorithm is 33.4872 dB. The (g) shows the PSNR of our algorithm is 33.9324 dB, better than the JM14.2, the gain is up to 0.4452 dB. The (i) represents the PSNR of proposed algorithm is 30.5834 dB. The (f) represents the PSNR of JM algorithm is 29.8691 dB. The proposed EC method outperforms JM 14.2 in both objective and subjective quality. In Fig. 6(e), there are serious blocking artifacts at the

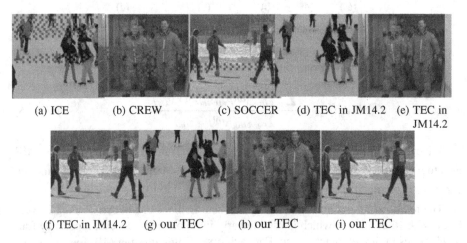

(a) ICE   (b) CREW   (c) SOCCER   (d) TEC in JM14.2   (e) TEC in JM14.2

(f) TEC in JM14.2   (g) our TEC   (h) our TEC   (i) our TEC

Fig. 6. Visual comparison of the video sequence. (Color figure online)

exit edge of the door, and blocking artifacts can be seen in the bright and dark junction of the door. In (d), there are significant blocking artifacts between the legs and the snow.

In Fig. 7(a–c) is the 46th frame of the test sequence which is P frame. The (d–f) are the IDR frames. (h), (b) and (e) are the decoded frames of the JM14.2, the PSNR is 32.2258 dB, 27.7341 dB and 31.489 dB, respectively. In (i), (c) and (f), the PSNR is 32.9614 dB, 28.9497 dB and 31.7963 dB, respectively. In (b), the blocking artifacts and edge discontinuity are very obvious. In (c) and (i), the blocking artifacts have been significantly reduced and also more smooth at the boundary, our method preserve edge continuity and sharpness. In (c), the forehead hair is recovered very well than (b), there are less blocking artifacts existing in the boundary of the loss blocks. That is because proposed method obtain a more accurate motion vector used for motion compensation. In (g) and (j), the PSNR is 32.5328 dB and 32.7148 dB, respectively. (i) is better than (g) and (j). In Fig. 8, our SEC technique is slightly better than [12]. By comparing the concealed frames, the results demonstrate that our method not only smooth boundary components also retain the low frequency information.

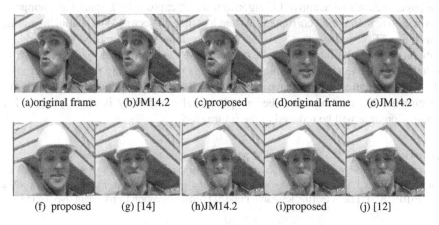

(a)original frame   (b)JM14.2   (c)proposed   (d)original frame   (e)JM14.2

(f) proposed   (g) [14]   (h)JM14.2   (i)proposed   (j) [12]

Fig. 7. FOREMAN sequence

(a) [12] technique   (b) Our SEC technique

Fig. 8. CREW sequence, (a) PSNR is 36.23 dB, (b) PSNR is 36.73 dB

In Table 1, the objective quality of the proposed EC algorithm is better than official EC method in JM14.2. the proposed method gets a 0.3 dB average PSNR improvement gain comparing to JM 14.2, which shows that the proposed algorithm is more accurate than the JM14.2 algorithm. Meanwhile, our method is slightly better than [14]. The intra mode is open when SEC technique is used. The average PSNR of proposed SEC is

33.80 dB, which has higher PSNR value compared with [12]. The objective quality of our proposed SEC method is better than the SEC method in [12].

Table 1. PSNR Comparison (unit: dB)

Video	SEC PSNR(dB)		TEC PSNR(dB)		
	[12]	Proposed	[14]	Proposed	JM14.2
ICE	33.67	34.13	32.36	32.37	32.13
CREW	34.72	35.41	33.31	33.26	33.19
FOREMAN	32.52	32.93	28.10	28.85	28.29
SOCCER	32.22	32.74	30.16	30.45	30.16
Average PSNR	33.28	33.80	30.98	31.23	30.94

5   Conclusion

This paper presents an adaptive EC algorithm which exploits both spatial and temporal information to reconstruct corrupted MB and lost motion vectors. The spatial inpainting mainly use SEC strategy that switches between improved DI and NPLI method. In temporal domain, the Inter PM of the corrupted MB is determined by the Inter PM of the neighboring MBs, then the suitable method is used according to PM of corrupted MB. The simulation results have shown that the proposed algorithm outperforms conventional EC methods, but the computational complexity is slightly high. The computation time will be reduced in the future work.

Acknowledgments. The work on this paper was supported by National Natural Science Foundation of China (Nos. 61072080, U1405255). Fujian Normal University Innovative Research Team (No. IRTL1207). Major science and technology project in Fujian province (No. 2014H61010105). The Scientific Research Fund of Fujian Education Department (No. JA15136).

References

1. Alkachouh, Z., Bellanger, M.G.: Fast DCT based spatial domain interpolation of blocks in images. IEEE Trans. Image Process. **9**, 729–732 (2000)
2. Meisinger, K., Kaup, A.: Spatial error concealment of corrupted image data using frequency selective extrapolation. In: Proceedings of the International Conference on Acoustics, Speech, and Signal Processing (ICASSP) (2004)
3. Wang, Y., Zhu, Q.-F.: Corrupted control and concealment for video communication: a review. IEEE Proc. **86**, 974–997 (1998)
4. Salama, P., Shroff, N.B., Delp, E.J.: Error concealment in encoded video streams. In: Katsaggelos, A.K., Galatsanos, N.P. (eds.) Signal Recovery Techniques for Image and Video Compression, pp. 199–233. Kluwer, Alphen aan den Rijn (1998). Chap. 7
5. Park, J., Park, D.-C., Marks, R.J., El-Sharkawi, M.A.: Macroblock loss recovery in DCT image encoding using POCS. In: Proceedings of the International Symposium on Circuits and Systems (ISCAS), pp. 245–248 (2002)
6. Kwok, W., Sun, H.: Multi-directional interpolation for spatial error concealment. IEEE Trans. Consum. Electron. **39**, 455–460 (1993)

7. Wang, Y.K., Hannuksela, M.M., Varsa, V., Hourunranta, A., Gabbouj, M.: The error concealment feature in the H. 26L test model. In: 2002 Proceedings of the International Conference on Image Processing, vol. 2, pp. II–729 (2002)
8. Rongfu, Z., Yuanhua, Z., Xiaodong, H.: Content-adaptive spatial error concealment for video communication. IEEE Trans. Consum. Electron. **50**, 335–341 (2004)
9. Wang, Y., Guo, X., Ye, F.: A novel temporal error concealment framework in H.264/AVC. In: IEEE International Conference on Multimedia and Expo (ICME), pp. 1–6 (2013)
10. Zheng, Y.-J., Zhang, Y.H., Wang, Z.-W., et al.: Edge detection algorithm based on the eight direction Sobel operation. Comput. Sci. **40**, 354–356 (2013)
11. Arnold, J.F., Frater, M.R., Zhang, J.: Corrupted resilience in the MPEG-2 video coding standard for cell based networks–a review. Sig. Process. Image Commun. **14**, 607–633 (1999)
12. Qaratlu, M.M., Ghanbari, M.: Intra-frame loss concealment based on directional extrapolation. Sig. Process. Image Commun. **26**, 304–309 (2011)
13. Kumar, S., Xu, L., Mandal, M.K., et al.: Error resiliency schemes in H.264/AVC standard. J. Vis. Commun. Image Represent. **17**, 425–450 (2006)
14. Ding, Z.H., Wang, G., Liu, L.Z.: New temporal error concealment method base on motion object. Appl. Res. Comput. **28**(10), 3996–3997 (2011)

Calibration Method to the Temperature Measuring System Based on Color CCD Camera

Tianhe Yu[1](✉), Yongjin Zhang[1], and Jingmin Dai[2]

[1] Harbin University of Science and Technology, Harbin 150080, China
ythaa@163.com
[2] Harbin Institute of Technology, Harbin 150001, China

Abstract. Temperature field measurement technology based on color charge-coupled device (CCD) image sensor is a new temperature measuring method with advantages of all the non-contact temperature measuring method. It can give the distribution of temperature field, and it is one of the hot research topics in the field of high temperature detection. The colorimetric temperature measurement method is used to conduct the calibration experiment in this paper. And the errors and the uncertainty of the temperature measurement system are analyzed. The results show that the errors and uncertainty are low, and the temperature measurement system can be used for actual distribution of the temperature field measurement.

Keywords: Scanning pyrometer · Color CCD · Digital image processing · Temperature measurement

1 Introduction

As the charge-coupled device (CCD) imaging technology develops in recent years, CCD is applied to the high temperature field measurement gradually. Common industrial CCD is not developed for radiation temperature measurement specifically, and its dynamic range is too narrow to meet the requirements of high temperature measurement for temperature measurement range, which makes the application of radiation temperature measurement based on CCD technology limited [1]. High-speed CCD camera with the characteristics of shorter exposure time can promote a single measurement range of the image and record the instantaneous temperature field distribution under the non-contact [2, 3]. Before put into use, the temperature measurement system must carry out calibration, or it is meaningless. The same as algorithm implementation, calibration technology is very important. Especially in high temperature, the precision of the instrument is largely limited to the calibration technology. So the calibration method laid a foundation for high temperature field measurement in this paper.

© Springer Science+Business Media Singapore 2016
T. Tan et al. (Eds.): IGTA 2016, CCIS 634, pp. 44–50, 2016.
DOI: 10.1007/978-981-10-2260-9_6

2 The CCD Imaging Principle

CCD is the integrated photoelectric conversion device of photosensitive element, the input structure and output structure and other parts. Its outstanding characteristic is that charge can be regarded as a signal carrier because it can be quickly calculated by computer processing [4]. When the incident light on the CCD photosensitive unit, photosensitive unit will produce photoelectric Q, which is proportional to photon rate Δn_0, illumination time T_c, receives unit area A.

$$Q = \eta q \Delta n_0 A T_c \qquad (1)$$

Where η is the quantum efficiency of materials, and q is the electronic charge. The photoelectric conversion characteristic of CCD image sensor is shown in Fig. 1. Where abscissa is illumination $lx.s$ and ordinate is output voltage V_0, meeting the following formula in the unsaturated zone [5].

$$f(s) = d_1 s^\tau + V_D \qquad (2)$$

Where $f(s)$ is the output voltage (V); s is exposure $(lx.s)$; τ is the photoelectric conversion coefficient and approximately equal to 1; V_D is the output voltage when there is no light for CCD; d_1 is the slope of the line which expresses light responsivity of CCD. The exposure S_E of the inflection point G of characteristic curve is called saturated exposure and the output voltage V_{SAT} is called saturated output voltage. When the exposure is above the S_E, CCD output signal is no longer increasing. It is necessary to make sure that the CCD is in the unsaturated zone if you want to make the CCD camera to complete temperature measurement [6].

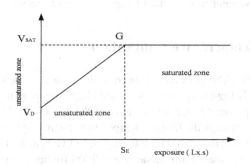

Fig. 1. CCD photoelectric conversion characteristic

3 Colorimetric Thermometry Based on Color CCD

When use colorimetric temperature measurement method, we need idealized assumptions for the model. Assumption 1: the measured object is gray body and cosine radiator; Assumption 2: the video object is plane; Assumption 3: the temperature of the same pixel point is the same; Assumption 4: measured temperature between $800 \sim 3000$ K, the wavelength is in $300 \sim 800$ nm, and the situation meets Wayne formula. According to the Planck formula, blackbody radiation can be expressed as:

$$E(\lambda, T) = \pi I(\lambda, T) = \varepsilon_\lambda \frac{c_1}{\lambda^5} \left(e^{\frac{c_2}{\lambda T}} - 1 \right)^{-1} \tag{3}$$

Where $E(\lambda, T)$ is radiant energy; $I(\lambda, T)$ is radiation intensity; ε_λ is Blackbody radiation rate; T is degree Kelvin; λ is wavelength; c_1 is the first radiation constant $3.742 \times 10^{-16} W \cdot m^2$; c_2 is the second radiation constant $1.438833 \times 10^{-2} m \cdot K$. From assumption three, we can get the following formula by using Wayne formula to simplify Planck formula [7].

$$M(\lambda, T) = \frac{\varepsilon(\lambda, T) c_1}{\lambda^5 e^{c_2/\lambda T}} \tag{4}$$

$$T = \frac{c_2 \left(\frac{1}{\lambda_b} - \frac{1}{\lambda_r} \right)}{ln \frac{R}{B} + 5 ln \frac{\lambda_r}{\lambda_b} + K_{rb}} \tag{5}$$

Where λ_r, λ_b represent the wavelength of red and blue; R, B represent the gray levels of pixel of red and blue; K_{rb} is a constant. So you can get the current temperature value T according to the formula (5).

Colorimetric temperature measurement method can be used to measure the temperature field distribution, even if we do not know the exact spectral emissivity of the measured object, but only know the ratio between spectral emissivity of two wavelengths. Because the measurement of precision value of spectral emissivity will be more difficult than the measurement of ratio between spectral emissivity, colorimetric method is more convenient in the actual temperature field measurement.

4   Method to Temperature Calibration

WJL-11 Horizontal blackbody furnace is used in the system, which can provide up to 1073.16 K–3373.16 K high temperature standard blackbody radiation source. Scale by the standard optical pyrometer, the temperature of the blackbody furnace is controlled and collected by the blackbody furnace temperature control system. FastCAM Mini UX50 color high-speed camera produced by Japanese PHOTRON Company is used in the system. Its full pixel maximum frame rate is 2000 frames per second, unsaturated maximum frame rate is 160000 frames per second, and RGB gray level is 4096. Calibration experiment device is shown in Figs. 2 and 3.

Here are the experimental steps: (1) Choose a dark room for the experiment; avoid other visible light in the experiment. (2) Keep the CCD camera and blackbody furnace located on the same axis. Connect the CCD camera to the computer. Adjust the aperture of the camera. (3) Close the light, open the blackbody furnace and set the required calibration temperature according to the blackbody furnace operation manual.

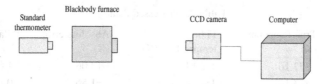

Fig. 2. The schematic diagram of calibration experiment device

Fig. 3. The photo of calibration experiment device

After the temperature is stable, start the CCD camera and computer image acquisition software. (4) Set the exposure rate t (20000 μs $\geq t \geq$ 6.25 μs) and collect data.

Setting the exposure time is 500 μs when the temperature is below 1673.2 K, and exposure time is 10 μs when the temperature is between 1673.2 K and 2073.2 K. Use the least squares fit between the measured grey value and the true temperature value. Calibration data is shown in Table 1.

Table 1. Calibration data

Exposure time	True temperature (K)	R	B
500 μs	1273.16	17.44	12.37
	1373.16	33.31	14.63
	1473.16	71.50	19.35
	1573.16	149.84	33.42
10 μs	1773.16	67.56	42.60
	1873.16	103.76	58.96
	1973.16	146.05	73.51
	2073.16	201.60	85.17

The R/B in formula (5) to calculate the temperature of the fitting values, data processing is shown in Table 2.

Table 2. Processed data

Exposure time	True temperature (K)	Fitting temperature (K)	Absolute error (K)	Relative error (%)
500 μs	1273.16	1260.1	−13.06	−1.03
	1373.16	1371.6	−1.56	−0.11
	1473.16	1499.0	26.04	1.77
	1573.16	1569.4	−3.76	−0.24
10 μs	1773.16	1797.9	24.74	1.40
	1873.16	1863.5	−9.66	−0.52
	1973.16	1947.2	−25.96	−1.31
	2073.16	2081.6	8.44	0.41

The above data shows that the calibration relative error of the CCD colorimetric thermometry is within 2 %. The temperature fitting curve is shown in Figs. 4 and 5.

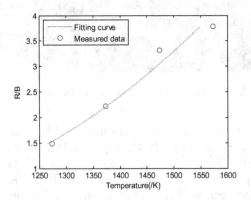

Fig. 4. Temperature fitting curve of 500 μs

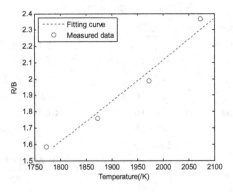

Fig. 5. Temperature fitting curve of 10 μs

5 Error and Uncertainty Analysis

Errors and uncertainty analysis are as follows:

(1) We can get the error formula (6) by using Wayne formula to simplify Planck formula.

$$\frac{M_{Wayne(\lambda,T)} - M_{planck(\lambda,T)}}{M_{planck(\lambda,T)}} = e^{-e^{\frac{c_2}{\lambda T}}} \tag{6}$$

Spectral range is 380 nm~780 nm; Measuring temperature range is 1000 K~3000 K and the maximum relative error of the system is 0.014 %.

(2) In the experiment, we assume that the measured object is gray body, making $\varepsilon(\lambda_r, T)$, $\varepsilon(\lambda_g, T)$, $\varepsilon(\lambda_b, T)$ approximately equal [8]. So resulting in the error is about 0.2 %.

(3) The measuring error caused by the non ideal CCD response wavelength bandwidth is 0.3 %.

(4) The accuracy of blackbody furnace temperature control system.

(5) Quantization error of R, G, B brightness value:

$$\frac{1}{2} \times \frac{1}{4096} \times 100\% \approx 0.012\%$$

(6) CCD camera would produce thermion noise, which is additive white noise, and the median filter can be used.

The uncertainty U_1 is caused by using Wayne formula to simplify Planck formula; the uncertainty U_2 is caused by the quantization of R, G, B brightness value; the uncertainty U_3 is caused by the non ideal CCD response wavelength bandwidth; the uncertainty U_4 is caused by the calibration system model. So we can get the total uncertainty as follows:

$$U = \sqrt{U_1^2 + U_2^2 + U_3^2 + U_4^2} \tag{7}$$

The data into the formula (7):

$$U = \sqrt{(0.014^2 + 0.012^2 + 0.3^2 + 1.77^2)}\% = 1.80\%$$

6 Conclusions

In previous work, the highest temperature is about 1500 K, and the error increased with the temperature increasing, over 2 %. On the basis of artificial blackbody radiation heat source, in this paper, the colorimetric temperature measurement method is used to conduct the calibration experiment and data processing for CCD measuring system. The errors of the CCD temperature measurement system and the uncertainty were analyzed, and the errors are not more than 2 %, the uncertainty is about 1.80 %. It indicated that the CCD temperature measurement system can be used for high temperature field measurement.

References

1. Simonini, S., Elston, S.J., Stone, C.R.: Soot temperature and concentration measurements from color charge coupled device camera images using a three-color method. Proc. Inst. Mech. Eng. **215**, 1041–1052 (2009)
2. Zhuoyong, Y., Qinghua, G.: The calibration method of color CCD temperature measurement system based on image processing. Comput. Appl. Chem. **24**(11), 1454–1456 (2007). (in Chinese)
3. Yuan, S., Xiaoqi, P.: The high temperature field of radiation temperature measurement method based on color CCD. J. Instrum. **32**(11), 2579–2584 (2011). (in Chinese)
4. Wei, J.: Research and development of high-temperature field measurement and burner design of oxygen-fuel combustion. Dissertation for Master degree, Zhejiang University (2015)
5. Zhaofei, Y., Yang, S.: Algorithm improvement based on the colorimetric temperature measurement. Servo Control **5**, 60–61 (2013)
6. Jie, H., Ke, Z.: Calibration of CCD temperature measurement system based on RGB digital filtering in laser cladding. J. Optoelectron. Laser **24**(5), 968–972 (2013). (in Chinese)
7. Kai, G.: Research on the system of high temperature field measurement of melt surface based on CCD image sensor. Dissertation for Master degree, Hangzhou Dianzi University (2013)
8. Kaidi, C.: Research on temperature field measurement system based on CCD image sensor. Dissertation for Master degree, Harbin Industrial University (2010)

A High-Capacity Image Data Hiding Based on Extended EMD-2 Reference Matrix

Xue-Jing Li, Yu-Qi Feng, and Wan-Li Lyu[(✉)]

Key Laboratory of Intelligent Computing and Signal Processing
of Ministry of Education, School of Computer Science and Technology,
Anhui University, Hefei 230039, China
xjalcatraz@outlook.com, luckymonicafe@gmail.com,
wanly_lv@163.com

Abstract. Numerous steganography algorithms have been proposed to protect messages put into images. LSB, which is an exceedingly prominent means in this field, has been proven to work if the least significant bit of the cover image is replaced with the binary secrets stream. Inspired by LSB, a series of simple but effective methods were proposed, such as LSB-MR, EMD (exploiting modification direction), Sudoku, EMD-2, Turtle Shell, and so on. Nonetheless, an image steganography with larger payload is tremendously needed nowadays. A novel high capacity image data hiding algorithm based on extended EMD-2 and Sudoku hybrid reference matrix is proposed in this study. In this method, each cover pixel pair carries two secret 9-ary notational system numbers. The experiment result shows the embedding rate of the method is up to 3.16 *bpp*, which is higher than the related schemes and the visual quality desired.

Keywords: Data hiding · Image steganography · Modification direction · Embedding capacity

1 Introduction

Generally, the carriers of digital steganography include character, still image, dynamic video, voice, and so on. In addition, the data hiding of digital images has been more popular in recent years due to the increasing transmission of pictures [1, 2]. The technology was increasingly used to protect military information, but now is applied to most areas of people's life, especially to messages transmitted via the Internet [3]. The basic criteria to evaluate an image data hiding algorithm are ER (embedding rate) and PSNR (peak signal-to-noise ratio). Embedding capacity is estimated by ER while PSNR evaluates the visual quality of steganographic images. Furthermore, image quality interacts with the embedding payload [4]. A high capacity image steganography algorithm tends to gain a relatively poor image visual quality; hence it is a main focus where researchers seek new schemes, such as [5–7].

The classic algorithm LSB (the least significant bit replacement method) [8] was proposed by Turner in 1989, replacing the least significant bits to hide secret bits simply and efficiently. Nevertheless, the substitution bits can be detected through uncomplicated analysis. Then, a series of schemes are put forward, which are motivated

© Springer Science+Business Media Singapore 2016
T. Tan et al. (Eds.): IGTA 2016, CCIS 634, pp. 51–61, 2016.
DOI: 10.1007/978-981-10-2260-9_7

by LSB substitution. Mielikainen proposed the LSB-MR (LSB matching revisited) algorithm in 2006 [9]. Although the hiding capacity in LSB-MR is much as LSB, the modification equation $f(p_1, p_2) = LSB(p_1/2 + p_2)$ is changed, aiming to enhance security. In this method, two pixels (p_1, p_2) act as an embedding unit to hide two bits of secret messages, only one pixel of the embedding unit needs to be modified.

Subsequently, Zhang and Wang brought up an improved scheme named EMD (exploiting modification direction) [10], where each digit in the $(2n + 1)$-ary notational system is embedded by modifying, at most, one in the group of n cover pixels to obtain a higher embedding efficiency. The embedding payload is up to $\log_2(2n + 1)/n$ *bpp*. Chang et al. proposed put forward a novel Turtle Shell based method for image data hiding [11] whose embedding capacity is proved to be 1.50 *bpp*. In 2008, a new data hiding algorithm was proposed by Chang et al., named Sudoku [12]. The directions of modification have more selections compared to EMD, in order to obtain high embedding payload with minimal distortion. This method can hide a digit in the base-9 numeral system using two cover pixels, so the ER is up to $\log_2 9/2$ *bpp*. Soon after this algorithm became well-known, in 2010, Kim et al. put forward the EMD-2 method [13] allowed to modify at most two of n pixels in a base-$(10n - 13)$ $(n > 2)$ numeral system; namely, there are two values of pixels that can be increased or decreased by 1. So the embedding capacity increases to $\log_2(10n - 13)/n$ *bpp* $(n > 2)$. Later, a mass of algorithms come forward, but the embedding rate is limited to 1.58 *bpp*.

In this paper, a novel high-capacity image data hiding scheme called E-EMD2 (Extended EMD-2), which has the desired visual quality is discussed. This algorithm is based on an extended EMD-2 and Sudoku hybrid reference matrix M^*, more momentously, the embedding capacity is much higher than anyone mentioned. The hybrid key matrix M^*, whose abscissa and ordinate values range from 0 to 255, is generated by several unique Sudoku grids, which will be expounded on in Sect. 3 at great length. Every paired pixel can locate an appropriate element by guiding two 9-ary notational system digits to be embedded into matrix in the M^* meanwhile. Therefore, we can utilize a pair of cover image pixels to hide the secret image data twice to enhance the embedding payload, which increases up to $\log_2 9$ *bpp*. To exemplify our point, numerous experiments have been performed and corresponding results show the merits of this algorithm compared with others, which concretely reflect the high capacity with the desired visual quality.

The rest of the paper is organized as follows. Section 2 briefly introduces the related schemes including EMD, Sudoku and EMD-2, and Sect. 3 is the proposed method described in detail. The experiment results and conclusion will be stated in Sects. 4 and 5, respectively.

2 Related Work

2.1 EMD Method

A novel steganography method EMD, put forward by Zhang and Wang [10], converts secret messages into a sequence of digits in a $(2n + 1)$-ary notational system before the embedding procedure. In addition, every base-$(2n + 1)$ digit is carried by n pixels.

In this method, at most one pixel needs to alter its value by increasing or decreasing 1. So there are $(2n+1)$ possible ways to modify each cover pixel pair, including one way without modification. Additionally, the embedding and extraction formula f_1 is described by Eq. (1).

$$y = f_1(p_1, p_2, \cdots, p_n) = \left[\sum_{i=1}^{n} p_i \times i \right] mod(2n+1) \tag{1}$$

In Eq. (1), y is calculated by the sum of weights module $(2n+1)$, and pixels in the cover image are divided into a series of groups where $(p_1, p_2, \cdots, p_n)$ are gray values of pixels in a group, i.e., p_i is the i - th pixel.

The embedding procedure is described as follows. If a $(2n+1)$-ary numeral system secret digit $d = y$, then there is no embedding modification of directions that needs to be done, else compute $t = (d - y)mod(2n+1)$. Afterwards, increase the value of p_t by 1 while t is no more than n, otherwise, decrease the value of p_{2n+1-t} by 1.

By means of formula f_1, the receiver can easily retrieve the secret digit d. In the extraction procedure, when all of the secret digits have been calculated, they will be combined into a base-$(2n+1)$ notational system embedding sequence, which is converted from the original secret messages.

Experiment results prove the ER of the EMD method is up to 1.59 bpp when $n = 1$ and 1.16 bpp when $n = 2$. In a nutshell, the embedding payload and security have great improvement when compared with the LSB method.

2.2   Sudoku Method

Sudoku, another image data hiding algorithm proposed by Chang et al. [12], improves the EMD method in embedding capacity. This scheme's reference matrix is generated by a logic-based number placement Sudoku puzzle where every 9×9 grid is filled with the digits from 0 to 8. In a nutshell, the principal idea of this proposed method is to modify a pair of cover pixels according to the secret digit's candidate positions in a key matrix with minimum distortion.

The concrete embedding and extraction procedures are exhibited as follows. First and foremost, we calculate three sets of candidate elements CE_H, CE_V and CE_B, which are separately defined as the following regulations. For each cover pixel pair (p_i, p_{i+1}), the corresponding row and column elements in the Sudoku matrix, whose center digit is $M(p_i, p_{i+1})$, are unrepeated digits from 0 to 8. $M(p_i, p_{i+1})$ is the location of the two contiguous cover pixels, p_i and p_{i+1}, in the Sudoku reference matrix. Therefore, they compose the element sets CE_H and CE_V, which is presented in Eq. (2), where k is selected from $\{-4, -3, -2, -1, 0, 1, 2, 3, 4\}$.

$$\begin{cases} CE_H = \{M(p_i, p_{i+1} + k)\} \\ CE_V = \{M(p_i + k, p_{i+1})\} \end{cases} \tag{2}$$

$$CE_B = \begin{bmatrix} M(x_b, y_b) & M(x_b, y_b + 1) & M(x_b, y_b + 2) \\ M(x_b + 1, y_b) & M(x_b + 1, y_b + 1) & M(x_b + 1, y_b + 2) \\ M(x_b + 2, y_b) & M(x_b + 2, y_b + 1) & M(x_b + 2, y_b + 2) \end{bmatrix} \qquad (3)$$

Ultimately, CE_B is defined as the surrounding elements set shown as Eq. (3), in the center of which is digit $M(p_i, p_{i+1})$. In Eq. (3), $x_b = 3 \times p_i/3$ while $y_b = 3 \times p_{i+1}/3$. Then, we will select three candidate elements from CE_H, CE_V, and CE_B, whose values equal the secret digit. After comparison, the ultimate modified location with minimum distortion is confirmed.

In summary, the embedding payload (i.e., 1.58 bpp) and security are both significantly improved due to the various Sudoku matrixes, while the visual quality of steganographic images is also satisfying with nearly 45 db on average.

2.3   EMD-2 Method

To enhance the embedding capacity and to relatively improve image quality, Kim et al. put forward an exceedingly efficient information hiding scheme named EMD-2 scheme [13] in 2010. It allows for modification, at most, of two pixels' value by increasing or decreasing 1 in order to embed every secret digit transformed into $(2w + 1)$-ary notational system. In addition, w equals 4 when n = 2, otherwise, the w value is $8 + 5(n - 3)$ while $n > 2$. Equation (4) is used to describe the embedding and extraction formula f_2.

$$y = f_2(p_1, p_2, \cdots, p_n) = \left[\sum_{i=1}^{n} p_i \times b_i \right] mod(2w + 1) \qquad (4)$$

In Eq. (4), $(p_1, p_2, \cdots, p_n)$ is an n-dimension vector P_n composed of n pixels in a cover image, while b_i is defined as following Eq. (5).

$$[b_1, b_2, \cdots, b_i, \cdots, b_n] = \begin{cases} [1, 3] & n = 2 \\ [1, 2, \cdots, 6 + 5(n - 3)] & n > 2 \end{cases} \qquad (5)$$

If secret digit $d = y$, then none of the pixel value modifications need to be done. Else, we need to compute $t = (d - y)mod(2w + 1)$ and then select appropriate $t's$ n-dimension basis vector $P_t = (t_1, t_2, \cdots, t_i, \cdots, t_n)$ which makes Eq. (6) hold, where the conceivable options of t_i are selected from $\{1, 0, -1\}$. Eventually, the n-dimension pixels modified vector P_n' can be obtained by calculating the sum of P_n and P_t.

$$t = \left[\sum_{i=1}^{n} t_i \times b_i \right] mod(2w + 1) \qquad (6)$$

The receiver can expediently figure out the formula f_2 with the modified pixels' value and combine them into the original secret message. To summarize, this method has great amelioration in carrying payload compared with EMD. Nevertheless, the embedding rate is limited to 1.58 bpp while n = 2.

3 Proposed Scheme

As there are limited modification directions in previous reference matrixes, the payload of embedding secrets is not satisfied. Here, we present a novel high capacity image steganography method at great length, which is based on an extended EMD-2 and Sudoku hybrid reference matrix M^*. Aiming at obtaining the higher embedding payload with a desired image visual quality, we make full use of the proposed matrix M^* generated by 9-ary notational system via modifying paired pixels twice. Namely, this two-dimensional key matrix M^* needs to guide two base-9 numeral digits to be embedded into the paired pixels.

3.1 Reference Matrix

The high-capacity proposed algorithm utilizes an extended EMD-2 and Sudoku hybrid two-dimensional reference matrix M^* whose abscissa and ordinate values range from 0 to 255. The entire matrix consists of several 9-ary digital system 27×9 grids, where every 3×3 sub-grid encompasses all base-9 digits from 0 to 8 and any nine adjacent sub-grids can constitute a 9×9 Sudoku puzzle. More momentously, the middle digits of the 3×3 sub-grids in every Sudoku puzzle are nine unrepeated continuous base-9 numeral digits. All of the 3×3 sub-grids' middle figures compose the EMD-2 two-dimensional key matrix once again. The formative 256×256 reference matrix M^* is shown in Fig. 1.

Definition 1. The concrete location of a cover pixel pair $\left(p_x, p_y\right)$ in key matrix M^* can be computed according to Eq. (7), where formulas F and R are defined as $F(x) = x/3$ and $R(x,y) = x \bmod y$, respectively.

$$M(p_x, p_y) = R\big([F(R(p_y, 27), 3) + R(p_x, 9) + 3R(p_y, 3) - 1], 9\big) \tag{7}$$

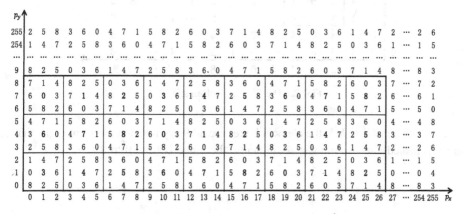

Fig. 1. The 256×256 reference matrix M^*

Definition 2. Every 3×3 sub-grid can be regarded as a box denoted by $B(b_x, b_y)$, which contains nine $M(p_x, p_y)$ elements and $p_x \in \{3b_x, 3b_x + 1, 3b_x + 2\}$ and $p_y \in \{3b_y, 3b_y + 1, 3b_y + 2\}$. We utilize the center digit of each box to indicate its value, i.e., $B(b_x, b_y) = M(3b_x + 1, 3b_y + 1)$, as the overstriking character shown in Fig. 1. For instance, $B(0,0) = M(1,1) = 3$ while $B(1,2) = M(4,7) = 8$. To summarize, every cover pixel pair (p_x, p_y) pertains to a 3×3 box named $B(b_x, b_y)$ where b_x and b_y can be computed as Eq. (8).

$$\begin{cases} b_x = p_x/3 \\ b_y = p_y/3 \end{cases} \tag{8}$$

Definition 3. All center elements in the boxes constitute a two-dimensional EMD-2 reference matrix R^*, as indicated in Fig. 2. Hence, the circumambient boxes for each $B(b_x, b_y)$ compose a new 3×3 cell defined as Eq. (9), where b_x and b_y are calculated anteriorly by Eq. (8).

$$C(b_x, b_y) = \begin{bmatrix} B(b_x - 1, b_y - 1) & B(b_x - 1, b_y) & B(b_x - 1, b_y + 1) \\ B(b_x, b_y - 1) & B(b_x, b_y) & B(b_x, b_y + 1) \\ B(b_x + 1, b_y - 1) & B(b_x + 1, b_y) & B(b_x + 1, b_y + 1) \end{bmatrix} \tag{9}$$

b_y													
84	3	4	5	6	7	8	0	1	2	3	4	⋯ 8	0
83	0	1	2	3	4	5	6	7	8	0	1	⋯ 5	6
⋯	⋯	⋯	⋯	⋯	⋯	⋯	⋯	⋯	⋯	⋯	⋯	⋯	⋯
7	6	7	8	0	1	2	3	4	5	6	7	⋯ 2	3
6	3	4	5	6	7	8	0	1	2	3	4	⋯ 8	0
5	0	1	2	3	4	5	6	7	8	0	1	⋯ 5	6
4	6	7	8	0	1	2	3	4	5	6	7	⋯ 2	3
3	3	4	5	6	7	8	0	1	2	3	4	⋯ 8	0
2	0	1	2	3	4	5	6	7	8	0	1	⋯ 5	6
1	6	7	8	0	1	2	3	4	5	6	7	⋯ 2	3
0	3	4	5	6	7	8	0	1	2	3	4	⋯ 8	0
	0	1	2	3	4	5	6	7	8.	9	10	⋯ 83	84 b_x

Fig. 2. The 85×85 sub-matrix R^*

For each cell $C(b_x, b_y)$, the element boxes are all 9-ary notational system digits that are unrepeated and continuous; additionally, the range is from 0 to 8.

3.2   The Embedding Phase

In the reference hybrid matrix M^*, each 3×3 box is constituted of base-9 digits and the nine adjacent boxes can compose a Sudoku puzzle. Furthermore, all of the middle numbers of the boxes generate a new sub-matrix R^*, which is a EMD-2 two-dimension key matrix. Initially, the size of the designated gray-level cover image I and stego image I' are similarly $H \times W$, which are the height and width of I, respectively. The embedding algorithm is indicated as following steps.

> *Input:* Cover grayscale image I, secret digit stream S, and reference matrix M^*.
> *Output:* Steganographic grayscale image I'.
> *Step 1.* Convert the binary secret stream $S = (b_1, b_2, \cdots, b_L)$ into 9-ary notational system digits, i.e., $(b_1, b_2, \cdots, b_L)_2 = (s_1, s_2, \cdots, s_{H \times W})_9$ where $L = H \times W \times \log_2 9$. Then carry out Step 2.
> *Step 2.* Initialize $i = 1$ and then proceed to Step 3.
> *Step 3.* Locate the specific element $M(p_i, p_{i+1})$ in the reference matrix M^* for each cover pixel pair (p_i, p_{i+1}), which computing method is in accordance with Eq. (7). Moreover, according to Definition 2, the located element $M(p_i, p_{i+1})$ pertains to a box $B(b_x, b_y)$ where $b_x = p_i/3$ and $b_y = p_{i+1}/3$. Afterwards, move to Step 4.
> *Step 4.* Read the converted secret digit stream $(s_i, s_{i+1})_9$. If $s_i = B(b_x, b_y)$, no modification of directions is required; else, select the appropriate box $B\left(b'_x, b'_y\right)$ whose value equals s_i, according to Eq. (9). Continue to Step 5.
> *Step 5.* Judge the value of s_{i+1}, if $B\left(b'_x, b'_y\right) = s_{i+1}$, maintain the status quo. Otherwise, choose the applicable element $M\left(p'_i, p'_{i+1}\right)$ in the 3×3 box $B\left(b'_x, b'_y\right)$, where $s_{i+1} = M\left(p'_i, p'_{i+1}\right)$. Ultimately, $(s_i, s_{i+1})_9$ is embedded into the cover pixel pair (p_i, p_{i+1}) simultaneously, which satisfies Eq. (10). Next, move to Step 6.

$$
\begin{cases}
s_i = B\left(b'_x, b'_y\right) \\
s_{i+1} = M\left(p'_i, p'_{i+1}\right)
\end{cases}
\tag{10}
$$

> *Step 6.* Set $i = i + 2$ and repeat Steps 3 to 5 through the end of the secret stream.

Instance 1. Embedding the secret stream

Presume the original binary secret stream S is $(1111)_2$ and the cover grayscale pixel pair (p_i, p_{i+1}) is $(6, 7)$. First and foremost, the binary secret messages S need to be converted into base-9 numeral system digits, i.e. $(s_i, s_{i+1}) = (16)_9$. Ultimately, we locate an accurate point $M(6, 7) = 1$ in the reference matrix M^* according to Eq. (7). In addition, $M(6, 7)$ belongs to box $B(2, 2)$, which can be computed by Eq. (8). Because the value of $B(2, 2)$ is equal to $M(7, 7) = 2 \neq s_i$, we thus seek through the 3×3 cell $C(2, 2)$ in sub-matrix R^* to obtain the proper box element, which is $B(2, 1) = M(7, 4) = 1 = s_i$. After modifying the cover pixels for the first time, the current location in the key matrix M^* is $M(7, 4) = 1$, which isn't identical to s_{i+1}. Therefore, check the other eight elements around $M(7, 4)$ in box $B(2, 1)$ to seek out a final position $M(p'_i, p'_{i+1})$ that satisfies equality $s_{i+1} = M(p'_i, p'_{i+1}) = 6$. Ultimately, the stego image I' is obtained by recomposing the cover pixels' value to $M(6,3)$ in order to conceal the secret digits $(16)_9$.

3.3   The Extraction Phase

Similarly, the secret messages S can be exactly retrieved from the received steganographic image I' by means of the following extraction algorithm. Since the size of the stego grayscale image I' is also $H \times W$ defined as above, the extracted secret stream S is no more than $H \times W \times \log_2 9$.

Obtain stego pixel pair (p'_i, p'_{i+1}) from grayscale steganographic image I' and calculate current location $M(p'_i, p'_{i+1})$ by using Eq. (7) to identify the hidden secret digit s_{i+1}. Compute the box $B(b'_x, b'_y)$ that $M(p'_i, p'_{i+1})$ pertains to, in accordance with $b'_x = p'_i/3$ and $b'_y = p'_{i+1}/3$, so that $s_i = B(b'_x, b'_y)$. Hence, the two embedded base-9 secrets are extracted similarly as in Eq. (10). Until all the stego pixels have been traversed and the extraction tasks are finished, we convert the extracted 9-ary numeral system digits into the original binary secret stream S, i.e., $(s_1, s_2, \cdots, s_{H \times W})_9 = (b_1, b_2, \cdots, b_L)_2$ in which L is equal to $H \times W \times \log_2 9$.

Instance 2. Extracting the secret stream

Assume the obtained pair of stego pixels (p'_i, p'_{i+1}) is $(6,3)$, and the values of $M(p'_i, p'_{i+1})$ and corresponding $B(b'_x, b'_y)$, where $b'_x = 2$ and $b'_y = 1$, both can be simply calculated according to Eqs. (7) and (8), i.e., $M(6,3) = 6$ while $B(2,1) = 1$. We extract the embedded secret 9-ary digits satisfied by Eq. (10), so $(s_i, s_{i+1})_9 = (16)_9$. After converting this into a binary numeral stream, the original secret messages are presented as $(b_i, b_{i+1})_2 = (s_i, s_{i+1})_9 = (16)_9 = (1111)_2$.

4   Experimental Results

To certify the performance of the proposed method, we used eight grayscale cover images of the common size 512×512, and all experiments were performed using MATLAB R2014a software.

In this experiment, the embedding payload rate (ER) and the peak signal to noise ratio (PSNR) are two criteria used to evaluate the implementation result, which represents the payload capability and image visual quality, respectively. The PSNR of an $H \times W$ grayscale image is calculated by Eq. (11), where x_{ij} indicates the value of cover image's pixel and $\bar{x}_{ij}$ denotes the steganographic image pixel's value.

$$PSNR = 10 \times \log_{10} \frac{255^2}{\frac{1}{H \times W} \times \sum_{i=1}^{H} \sum_{j=1}^{W} (x_{ij} - \bar{x}_{ij})^2} \tag{11}$$

Additionally, the ER of an $H \times W$ cover image is described as Eq. (12) at length. Here, $\|S\|$ is a statistical value denoting the total sum of the embedded secret digits.

$$ER = \frac{\|S\|}{H \times W} \tag{12}$$

As a result, the ER of all hiding methods above can be simply computed using Eq. (12). Because the EMD method can hide a base-$(2n+1)$ numeral system digit in n pixels, $ER_{EMD} = log_2(2n+1)/n$ bpp, i.e., while $n = 2$, the ER of EMD is merely equal to 1.16 bpp. The Turtle Shell Method enhances the hiding capacity compared to EMD since $ER_{Turtle\,Shell} = log_2 8/2 = 1.50$ bpp. $ER_{Sudoku} = log_2 3$ bpp, which is nearly up to 1.58 bpp. The hiding capacity of proposed algorithm is greater than the former, as it can embed two digits in base-9 into two pixels simultaneously. Therefore, $ER_{E-EMD2} = log_2 9$ bpp, which is approximately equal to 3.16 bpp. It is obvious that our method has been proven to provide the best results.

The visual quality of the experimental images implemented by this proposed algorithm is shown as in Fig. 3. In summary, there are eight steganographic grayscale images to exemplify the ER and the corresponding PSNR of the proposed method in this study. The following Table 1 shows the PSNR and the corresponding embedding rate of different steganography algorithms. Experiment results show the ER of our proposed method is up to 3.16 bpp, while the PSNR average approaches 39.62 db.

The above experiment results indicate that the embedding payload capability of this proposed scheme is much higher than other related works. Meanwhile, it still offers an acceptable visual quality. On account of the concession we made in image quality, the novel method stands out in obtaining a much higher payload in the embedding rate when compared to other published works previously mentioned.

Group a. Tiffany, Baboon, Zelda and Barbara

Group b. Bridge, Goldhill, Lena and Pepper

Fig. 3. Steganographic images after embedding secrets with the proposed algorithm using Tiffany, Baboon, Zelda, Barbara, Bridge, Goldhill, Lena and Pepper grayscale images

Table 1. Comparisons of ER and corresponding PSNR of the proposed scheme and related reference-matrix-based schemes

Images	EMD [10]		Turtle Shell [11]		Sudoku [12]		Proposed	
	PSNR (db)	ER (bpp)	PSNR (db)	ER (bpp)	PSNR (db)	ER (bpp)	PSNR (db)	ER (bpp)
Tiffany	52.11	1.16	49.41	1.50	45.02	1.58	39.61	3.16
Baboon	52.11	1.16	49.39	1.50	44.68	1.58	39.63	3.16
Zelda	52.12	1.16	49.40	1.50	44.96	1.58	39.62	3.16
Barbara	52.11	1.16	49.40	1.50	44.77	1.58	39.61	3.16
Bridge	52.12	1.16	49.42	1.50	44.62	1.58	39.62	3.16
Goldhill	52.11	1.16	49.38	1.50	44.84	1.58	39.61	3.16
Lena	52.12	1.16	49.42	1.50	44.97	1.58	39.63	3.16
Pepper	52.12	1.16	49.40	1.50	44.67	1.58	39.62	3.16

5   Conclusions

A novel high-capacity image steganography based on the extended EMD-2 and Sudoku hybrid reference matrix is reviewed in this study, which concurrently embeds two base-9 notational system digits into paired pixels. From the above experiment results, we have concluded that the proposed method can obtain a large payload and a relatively desired image visual quality; more specifically, the ER and corresponding PSNR are 3.16 *bpp* and 39.62 *db*, respectively.

Acknowledgements. This research work is supported by Provincial Training Projects of Innovation and Entrepreneurship for Undergraduates of Anhui University, which is under Grant No. J1018515315. The corresponding experiment results is with the help of key laboratory of intelligent computing and signal processing of ministry of education.

References

1. Bender, W., Gruhl, D., Morimoto, N., Lu, A.: Techniques for data hiding. IBM Syst. J. **35**, 313–336 (1996)
2. Zielinska, E., Mazurczyk, W., Szczypiorski, K.: Trends in steganography. Commun. ACM **57**(3), 86–95 (2014)
3. Ker, A.D.: Improved detection of LSB steganography in grayscale images. In: Fridrich, J. (ed.) IH 2004. LNCS, vol. 3200, pp. 97–115. Springer, Heidelberg (2004)
4. Fridrich, J., Soukal, D.: Matrix embedding for large payloads. IEEE Trans. Inf. Forensics Secur. **1**(3), 390–394 (2006)
5. Chao, R.M., Wu, H.C., Lee, C.C.: A novel image data hiding scheme with diamond encoding. EURASIP J. Inf. Secur. **2009**, 1–9 (2009)
6. Hong, W., Chen, T.S.: A novel data embedding method using adaptive pixel pair matching. IEEE Trans. Inf. Forensics Secur. **7**(1), 176–184 (2012)

7. Hong, W.: Adaptive image data hiding in edges using patched reference table and pair-wise embedding technique. Inf. Sci. **221**(1), 473–489 (2013)
8. Turner, L.F.: Digital data security system. Patent IPN, WO89/08915 (1989)
9. Mielikainen, J.: LSB matching revisited. IEEE Sig. Process. Lett. **13**(5), 285–287 (2006)
10. Zhang, X., Wang, S.: Efficient steganographic embedding by exploiting modification direction. IEEE Commun. Lett. **10**(11), 781–783 (2006)
11. Chang, C.C., Liu, Y., Nguyen, T.: A novel turtle shell based scheme for data hiding. In: 10th International Conference on Intelligent Information Hiding and Multimedia Signal Processing (IIHMSP-2014), Kitakyushu, Japan, pp. 89–93 (2014)
12. Chang, C.C., Chou, Y.C., Kieu., T.D.: An information hiding scheme using Sudoku. In: Proceedings of 3rd International Conference on Innovative Computing, Information and Control, pp. 17–21 (2008)
13. Kim, H.J., Kim, C., Choi, Y., Wang, S., Zhang, X.: Improved modification direction methods. Comput. Math Appl. **60**(2), 319–325 (2010)

Improved Design of UEP-LDPC Encoder Using Two-Stage Dynamic Programming in Image Transmission

Xiangran Sun[✉] and Han Ju

Information Engineering School,
Communication University of China, Beijing, China
sunxr@cuc.edu.cn

Abstract. Irregular low-density parity-check (LDPC) codes can provide an unequal error protection (UEP) capability naturally by unequal degree distribution. In this paper we propose a new architecture of UEP-LDPC encoder based on the method of Richardson and Urbanke in image transmission. In order to reduce processing complexity and hardware consumption, we also present a novel two-stage dynamic programming algorithm to perform matrix triangulation instead of traditional approach. Experiment results show the optimization architecture and algorithm can provide high UEP capability and reduce encoding complexity significantly.

Keywords: UEP · LDPC · Encoder · Two-stage dynamic programming

1 Introduction

Low-density parity-check (LDPC) codes, first introduced by Gallager in 1962 [1], have amazing influence with near Shannon limit performance. LDPC codes have been widely used in many communication scenarios, such as digital multimedia communication systems and transport of image data. It is not necessary to provide uniform protection for all transport data and is not flexible for these systems. Unequal error protection (UEP) is a well-known technique in multimedia communication, which can perform the efficiency compared to an equal error protection scheme significantly, since it provides more protection for the more important bits by sacrificing some performance of the less important bits.

For irregular LDPC codes, due to different connection degrees of bit nodes, they can provide inherent unequal error protection capability over different channels [2, 3]. Because the bit nodes with high connection degrees can be decoded more accurately, the important data are associated with the high degree bit nodes. Irregular UEP-LDPC codes achieve good UEP capacity depending on the variable and check node degree distributions. Irregular non-structured LDPC codes are used to take an active role in image transmission. In [8], a novel method for designing UEP-LDPC decoder was investigated. Sandberg [9] proposed optimized rate-compatible UEP-LDPC codes for networks application. Many researches have focused on the application of UEP-LDPC codes in communication systems.

© Springer Science+Business Media Singapore 2016
T. Tan et al. (Eds.): IGTA 2016, CCIS 634, pp. 62–68, 2016.
DOI: 10.1007/978-981-10-2260-9_8

LDPC codes are a class of linear group code and have low-density parity-check matrix, so LDPC encoded codeword is the product of generation matrix and information bits. Although parity-check matrix of LDPC codes is always very sparse, the generation matrix is not sparse in general and results in the complexity of the encoding directly. Because the quadratic complexity to code length in the LDPC encoding based on the generation matrix, it is impossible to implement with low-cost hardware and in required time. Lots of attempts have been made to design LDPC encoder with linear complexity to code length. Richardson and Urbanke [4] figure out that linear time encoding is achievable through careful linear manipulation of LDPC codes and also present an approach (named as RU method) based on greedy algorithm to preprocess the parity-check matrix.

In this paper, for UEP-LDPC codes in image transmission, we present a novel approach based on RU method, which employ two-stage dynamic programming algorithm to transform the parity-check matrix into the approximate lower triangular (ALT) matrix. It can significantly improve the performance of LDPC encoding and reduce the consumption of the hardware encoder. We also design the architecture of LDPC encoding corresponding to our proposed algorithm for UEP-LDPC codes.

The remainder of the paper is organized as follows. In the next section the degree distribution of UEP-LDPC codes is described and the conclusion about error protection is introduced. Section 3 describes the encoding method for UEP-LDPC codes based on RU method. Next, our proposed dynamic programming algorithm to perform the sparse matrix to the ALT matrix is presented and the results corresponding to different algorithms are compared. In Sect. 5, the design of the architecture of our proposed UEP-LDPC encoding is give. Section 6 concludes the paper.

2 Irregular UEP-LDPC Codes

Irregular LDPC codes have different connection degrees of the code node, so they own the immanent capability of unequal error protection. An irregular LDPC code can be described by the degree distribution pair (λ, ρ) [5]. But for the UEP application, we define the LDPC code ensemble in the following way. We classify the bits of an LDPC codeword into T blocks according to different Error Protection Level (EPL) t. Let the fraction of bits with different EPL be defined τ_t, the fraction sequence is $\tau = (\tau_1, \tau_2, \cdots, \tau_T)$, satisfied by $\sum_{t=1}^{T} \tau_t = 1$.

Under normal conditions, the same degree is mapped to the same EPL t bits. And the greater degree is corresponding to the higher EPL. In order to implement the important protection, the information bits of a LDPC codeword are associated with the greater degree bit nodes. In contrast, the parity-check bits are linked to the smallest degree bit nodes. Using above description, we have $d = (d_1, d_2, \cdots, d_T)$ as the bit node degree sequence, in which d_t, is the degree of the EPL t bits in the decreasing order. Then the fraction of edges emanating from bit node degree d_t is given by

$$\lambda_t = (\tau_t d_t) \Big/ \left(\sum_{i=1}^{T} \tau_i d_i \right).$$

As has been pointed out by [5], a good LDPC code would be that all the check nodes have equal degree or nearly degree. Assuming that all the check nodes have the same degree d_c. Let R be the code rate, d_c must satisfy the following constraint

$$\lambda_t = \frac{1}{1-R} \sum_{i=1}^{T} \tau_i d_i \qquad (1)$$

So it is an import conclusion that the pair (λ, ρ) can be determined by (R, τ, d), which can describe UEP-LDPC codes more concisely. Many researchers have investigated lots of approaches to design UEP-LDPC codes which achieve good performance in image transmission, so we can use good irregular LDPC codes. In a given LDPC code, the code rate R and the sequence of τ are initially known. Moreover the degree sequence d and the parity matrix are also determined. Our strategy is considered to take into account the different error sensitivities of the codeword. We investigate an optimized algorithm to map information bits and check bits to different degree bit nodes, which achieves the flexibility and good BER performance for bits of protection level one.

3   UEP-LDPC Encoder Based on RU Method

Without loss of generality, an LDPC encoding can be described by solving parity equations:

$$\mathbf{H} \cdot c^T = 0^T \qquad (2)$$

where $\mathbf{H}$ is the parity matrix of LDPC codes, $c = \{c_0, c_1, \cdots, c_n\}$ is encoded codeword, n is the length of LDPC code bits, which is consisted of parity code bits $p = \{p_0, p_1, \cdots, p_{n-k}\}$ and information code bits $s = \{s_0, s_1, \cdots, s_{k-1}\}$, k is the length of information code bits.

In general parity matrix $\mathbf{H}$ of LDPC code is not systematic, so it is not suitable for encoding process and implementation. Assuming that c_{sys} is defined to represent the systematic code corresponding to encode codeword c, given by $c_{sys} = [p|s]$. The code can be expressed as $c = c_{sys} \cdot \mathbf{V}$, where $\mathbf{V}$ is the permutation matrix and the weight of rows and the weight of columns are one. The matrix $\mathbf{V}$ has two function, one is to turn codeword c into systemic codeword c_{sys}, the other is to adjust the order of code word in order to make code bits corresponding to different degree bit nodes.

From (2) we can get $\left(\mathbf{H}\mathbf{V}^T\right) \cdot c_{sys}^T = 0^T$ in which $\mathbf{V}^T$ is transposed matrix from $\mathbf{V}$. $\mathbf{V}^T$ can be separated to two parts, so parity equations is defined by

$$(\mathbf{H}\mathbf{V}_P) \cdot p^T + (\mathbf{H}\mathbf{V}_S) \cdot s^T = 0^T \qquad (3)$$

We design optimized RU method for irregular LDPC codes which only processes the matrix $\mathbf{H}\mathbf{V}_P$ corresponding to parity code. The major job is to make the matrix into an ALT form by performing row and column permutations in preprocessing.

We execute the preprocessing in software since it needs to be performed only once for the given matrix. So it does not cost the encoding time and resource of the actual hardware encoder.

Let us define an ALT matrix $\mathbf{H}_{ALT}$, given by $\mathbf{H}_{ALT} = \mathbf{L}_N \cdot (\mathbf{HV}_P) \cdot \mathbf{R}_M$ where $\mathbf{L}_N$ denotes that the matrix $\mathbf{HV}_P$ is multiplied by permutation matrices on its left which is equal to realign the rows. Similarly, $\mathbf{R}_M$ denotes that the matrix is multiplied by permutation matrices on its right which is equal to realign the columns. So the matrix $\mathbf{HV}_P$ is given by $(\mathbf{HV}_P) = \mathbf{L}_N^{-1} \cdot \mathbf{H}_{ALT} \cdot \mathbf{R}_M^{-1}$.

From (3) we get $\mathbf{H}_{ALT} \cdot (\mathbf{R}_M^{-1} \cdot p^T) = -\mathbf{L}_N \cdot (\mathbf{HV}_S) \cdot s^T$. If define $p_R^T = \mathbf{R}_M^{-1} \cdot p^T$ and $\mathbf{H}_S = \mathbf{L}_N \cdot (\mathbf{HV}_S)$, parity equation is equal to:

$$\mathbf{H}_{ALT} \cdot p_R^T = -\mathbf{H}_S \cdot s^T \tag{4}$$

We describe the ALT matrix $\mathbf{H}_{ALT}$ by $\begin{bmatrix} \mathbf{A} & \mathbf{T} \\ \mathbf{B} & \mathbf{C} \end{bmatrix}$, where $\mathbf{T}$ is a $(j - g)$ by $(j - g)$ lower triangle matrix with ones along the diagonal, where g is the gap of the lower triangular matrix and is the length of parity code bits. Further all the matrices are sparse.

If define $p_R = [p_1 \quad p_2]$ and $\mathbf{H}_S = \begin{bmatrix} \mathbf{H}_{S1} \\ \mathbf{H}_{S2} \end{bmatrix}$, multiply $\begin{bmatrix} \mathbf{I} & \mathbf{0} \\ -\mathbf{CT}^{-1} & \mathbf{I} \end{bmatrix}$ from the left and right of (4), we get

$$\begin{bmatrix} \mathbf{A} & \mathbf{T} \\ -\mathbf{CT}^{-1}\mathbf{A} + \mathbf{B} & \mathbf{0} \end{bmatrix} \cdot [p_1 p_2]^T = -\begin{bmatrix} \mathbf{H}_{S1} \\ -\mathbf{CT}^{-1}\mathbf{H}_{S1} + \mathbf{H}_{S2} \end{bmatrix} \cdot s^T \tag{5}$$

If define $\mathbf{G} = \left(-\mathbf{CT}^{-1}\mathbf{A} + \mathbf{B}\right)^{-1} \cdot (\mathbf{CT}^{-1}\mathbf{H}_{S1} - \mathbf{H}_{S2})$, p_1 can be calculated by

$$p_1^T = \mathbf{G} \cdot s^T \tag{6}$$

and p_2 can be calculated by

$$p_2^T = -\mathbf{T}^{-1} \cdot \left(\mathbf{A} \cdot p_1^T + \mathbf{H}_{S1} \cdot s^T\right) \tag{7}$$

In order to implemented high efficiency and low complexity LDPC encoder, the core content is to change $\mathbf{HV}_P$ to an ALT matrix $\mathbf{H}_{ALT}$ by rows and volumes permutation with an algorithm. The purpose is to decrease the gap g and acquire as large lower triangular matrix $\mathbf{T}$ as possible. At the same time the algorithm satisfy the basic request of error protection by UEP-LDPC codes. In the next section our novel algorithm is introduced for the application in image transmission.

4 Approximate Lower Triangulation Based on Two-Stage Dynamic Programming Algorithm

The criterion of the performance of LDPC encoder based on RU method is discussed in [4]. The key of RU method is to change the matrix $\mathbf{HV}_P$ into an ALT matrix with small a gap g as possible. It can decrease the complexity for computing the check bits by (6). For high UEP capacity of UEP-LDPC codes, it is important to make the matrix $\mathbf{HV}_S$ in (3) as large degree distribution as possible. We find out an efficient method based on two-stage dynamic programming that could achieve above two targets. The encoding of LDPC codes based on RU method carry out row and column permutations with the matrix using greedy algorithm at earliest. But greedy algorithm can't achieve the globally optimal solution in most cases. Due to ignore the importance of the choice of check bits, dynamic programming algorithm can't get better result too. So we presents two-stage dynamic programming algorithm to perform the triangulation of the matrix $\mathbf{HV}_P$.

We introduce two-stage dynamic programming algorithm for UEP-LDPC encoder based on RU methods as follow. Assume there is a node degree d_M corresponding to both the part of information bits and the part of check bits, which is totally $n \cdot \tau_M$ bits, it means that there are $n \cdot \tau_M$ rows in the matrix $\mathbf{V}$ that are undetermined. Furthermore there are $n \cdot \tau_M$ columns in the matrix $\mathbf{V}_P$ and $\mathbf{V}_S$ are undetermined correspondingly. The determination of the matrix $\mathbf{V}_P$ and $\mathbf{V}_S$ should balance the bits degree and the complexity of encoder.

(1) Assign the degree sequence d to information bits and check bits and find the cross d_M and $n \cdot \tau_M$ rows in the matrix $\mathbf{V}$.

(2) Exchange two rows in $\mathbf{V}_P$ and $\mathbf{V}_S$ which are included in $n \cdot \tau_M$ rows of $\mathbf{V}^T$.

(3) Calculate the sum of all rows of degree one in the matrix $\mathbf{HV}_P$, which is defined by α, go to step 2. Until the exchange is finished, get $\mathbf{HV}_P$ corresponding to the maximum α_{MAX}.

(4) Find the rows of degree one in the matrix $\mathbf{HV}_P$. If no row exists, get the modified matrix $(\mathbf{HV}_P)_M$ by removing the left most column of $\mathbf{HV}_P$. Go to step 4, update $(\mathbf{HV}_P)_M$.

(5) Select each "1" in the selected rows of $(\mathbf{HV}_P)_M$ as a candidate node. For each candidate node compute the sum of all rows of degree one in the residual matrix by deleting the row and column corresponding to the candidate node. Then find the candidate nodes which corresponds to the same maximum sum, mark the nodes as key nodes. Let us define a key node $\beta_i^{(0)}$ and the key nodes constitute a set of $\beta = \left\{ \beta_i^{(0)} | i = 1 \ldots N_{MAX} \right\}$, where N_{MAX} is the number of the key nodes.

(6) Delete the row and column of the matrix $(\mathbf{HV}_P)_M$ corresponding to the key node $\beta_i^{(0)}$ separately, the residual matrix is given by $(\mathbf{HV}_P)_R^{\left(\beta_i^{(0)}\right)}$. It is obvious that each key node is corresponding to a different residual matrix. Take each "1" in the rows of degree one in $(\mathbf{HV}_P)_R^{\left(\beta_i^{(0)}\right)}$ as a candidate node. Compute the sum of all rows of degree one in the residual matrix by removing the row and column corresponding to the candidate node. If no row of degree one, go to step 7. Otherwise find the candidate nodes which corresponds to the same maximum sum, name the nodes as progress nodes. Let us define a progress node $\beta_i^{(1)}$ and a nodes sequence γ_i, the vector is composed with the key node $\beta_i^{(0)}$ and the progress node $\beta_i^{(1)}$. At the same time, eliminate the other key nodes, and repeat step 6.

(7) Perform the row and column permutation with $(\mathbf{HV}_P)_M$ according to the path recorded in γ_i, transform the matrix into ALT form.

(8) Operate $(\mathbf{HV}_P)_M$ again by removing the triangular part. The residual matrix is empty, the algorithm terminates. Otherwise, remove a column of $(\mathbf{HV}_P)_M$ and go to step 5.

We use irregular rate-1/2 UEP-LDPC codes of length n = 2048 and n = 8192, which are named by Code-1 and Code-2 given in [6]. According to greedy algorithm, dynamic programming algorithm and our two-stage dynamic programming algorithm, we triangulate the matrices and achieve the gaps which are listed in Table 1.

Table 1. The gap of the lower triangular matrix by classic greedy algorithm, dynamic programming algorithm and our proposed two-stage dynamic programming algorithm

N	Greedy algorithm	Dynamic programming algorithm	Our algorithm
n = 2048	133	127	98
n = 8192	475	453	317

It can figure out that the gap with new algorithm offers smaller value than greedy algorithm and dynamic programming algorithm from Table 1. It can also conclude that the method based on two-stage dynamic programming can not only satisfy the request of UEP, but also can find good lower triangular matrix.

5 Architecture of UEP-LDPC Encoder

The overview of our UEP-LDPC encoding architecture is shown in Fig. 1. Our approach for UEP-LDPC encoding consists of software and hardware.

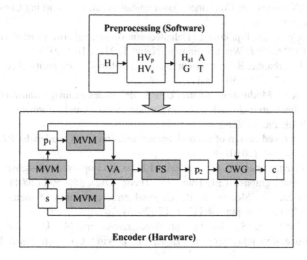

Fig. 1. Overview of the architecture of UEP-LDPC encoding software and hardware.

The preprocessing is operation with the matrices of LPDC codes, which is performed by software programs totally. It generates the matrices used in the LDPC encoder which are stored in the hardware encoder. The encoder is implemented on FPGA device and outputs the encoded codeword. The original parity-check matrix $\mathbf{H}$ is preprocessed with the optimized RU method to generate the matrices needed by the hardware encoder. The preprocessing is performed only once for the given matrix $\mathbf{H}$ based on our proposed optimized RU method. The hardware encoder is to compute the parity-check bits consisted of two parts p_1 and p_2, according to Eqs. (6) and (7). The main operations performed in the encoder are matrix-vector multiplication (MVM), forward-substitution (FS), vector addition (VA) and codeword generation (CWG). Codeword generation implements the bit permutations. The matrices required by the operations is accomplished in the preprocessing step and stored in the hardware.

6 Conclusion

In this paper, an optimized architecture of irregular UEP-LDPC encoder based on RU method in image transmission is presented. Two-stage dynamic programming algorithm was proposed to balance the protection capacity of LDPC codes and the hardware complexity of LDPC encoder. Experiment results showed that our novel algorithm could achieve a smaller gap of approximate lower triangulation matrix compared with classical greedy algorithm. Moreover it reduced encoding complexity and hardware consumption for UEP-LDPC codes.

References

1. Gallager, R.G.: Low-Density Parity-Check Codes, pp. 21–28. Мир, Cambridge (1966)
2. Yang, X., Yuan, D., Ma, P., et al.: New research on unequal error protection (UEP) property of irregular LDPC codes. In: Consumer Communications and Networking Conference 2004, pp. 361–363 (2004)
3. Poulliat, C., Declercq, D., Fijalkow, I.: Enhancement of unequal error protection properties of LDPC codes. EURASIP J. Wirel. Commun. Netw. 1, 211–216 (2007)
4. Richardson, T.J., Urbanke, R.L.: Efficient encoding of low-density parity-check codes. IEEE Trans. Inf. Theor. 47, 638–656 (2001)
5. Ma, P., Kwak, K.S.: Modulation-assisted UEP-LDPC codes in image transmission. In: Proceedings of 9th International Conference on Communications and Information Technologies, pp. 230–233. IEEE Press (2009)
6. Sandberg, S.: Improved design of unequal error protection LDPC codes. EURASIP J. Wirel. Commun. Netw. 2, 1–8 (2010)
7. Luby, M.G., Mitzenmacher, M., Shokrollahi, M.A., et al.: Improved low-density parity-check codes using irregular graphs. IEEE Trans. Inf. Theor. 47(2), 585–598 (2001)
8. Condo, C., Masera, G., Montuschi, P.: Unequal error protection of memories in LDPC decoders. IEEE Trans. Comput. 64(1), 11–17 (2015)
9. Khattak, R., Sandberg, S.: Jointly optimized rate-compatible UEP-LDPC codes for half-duplex co-operative relay networks. EURASIP J. Wirel. Commun. Netw. 2014(1), 1–16 (2014)

Rich and Seamless Texture Mapping to 3D Mesh Models

Jie Shu, Yiguang Liu$^{(\boxtimes)}$, Jie Li, Zhenyu Xu, and Shuangli Du

Vision and Image Processing Laboratory, College of Computer Science,
Sichuan University, Chengdu 610065, People's Republic of China
liuyg@scu.edu.cn

Abstract. Texture of reconstructed models are typically recovered by mapping detailed fragments to its surface, however, the visibility of the seams are often appear at the board of patches, due to inaccuracy mesh model and registration, lighting various and surface reflections etc. To address this problem, we apply a preprocessing step to every face in the mesh model by removing its candidate fragments, which are obviously different from others. Then, selecting fragment for every face is treated as a Markov random field energy optimization (MRF) problem, consist of the proposed data and smooth terms. Finally, poisson editing is employed to adjust the color information of vertices and edges of every fragments for better color consistency among fragments. Experimental results show that our method is able to produce seamless textured models with rich color information, compared with the state of the arts.

Keywords: Texture · 3D graphics and realism

1 Introduction

Texture is a crucial part of a geometric model, which has a significant impact on its realism. In this paper, we try to generate seamless texture with rich color information form a set of calibrated images. In general, one image can not cover the entire texture information of a 3D model, thus an image sequence is required. Given the image sequence, texture mapping can be done simply by binding the "best" fragments to the faces of the model according to the viewing angle. In an ideal scenario, where the geometric model and the camera parameters are accurate and all images share the same lighting condition, the resulting texture is seamless. However, this straightforward method is ineffective in practice due to inaccurate calibration and dramatically different lighting conditions. As a result, seams which strongly influence the outlook of the model appear at the border of each patch (the fragments which have the same label are located next to each other in the 3D mesh structure).

There are some impressive works focusing on eliminating such seams. Adam Baumberg [1] performs weighted averaging of fragments over the whole mesh. However, they fail to consider the significant connection between overlapping

© Springer Science+Business Media Singapore 2016
T. Tan et al. (Eds.): IGTA 2016, CCIS 634, pp. 69–76, 2016.
DOI: 10.1007/978-981-10-2260-9_9

regions and the size of feature points in different frequency bands. As a result, this method may break up the inner structure of the texture just because of the high frequency features such as edges and lines across the regions are textured from different misregistered images. Chen et al. [3] extend this work to blend texture in the overlapping regions in different frequency bands. However, this method always causes ghosting and blurring because of geometric misalignments, and it is inevitable to loss details because the images are resampled into a common coordinate frame. Lempitsky [9] proposes an innovative texturing method which formulates the problem of assigning view for each face as a Markov Random Field (MRF) energy optimization. They take both texture smoothness and details into account. Then a seam levelling procedure is applied to eliminate the residual seams between patches. This method prefers the smaller angle between viewing direction and the face normal, however, it cannot work well with occlusions and various lighting conditions. Garcia-Dorado et al. [7] reconstruct and texture entire cities while these buildings have chucks of the same color.

In this paper, we propose a texture mapping method, which can produce textured models without notable seams. And, these models cover rich color information. First, a visible preprocessing step for solving self-occlusion is proposed. Then fragment is assigned to each face to produce an initial textured model by minimize the Markov random field energy. Finally, color adjustment is applied in an artful way to eliminate the residual seams.

2   MRF-Based Fragments Selecting

2.1   Process Overview

First, a few dozens of images are taken as input in a free style around the subject object. Then, these images are calibrated using structure-from-motion [2,5,11]. Finally, the object is reconstructed by current popular stereo techniques [4,6] and is further post-processed yielding a triangular mesh model [8]. The notations used are summarized as follows: K images $I = \{l_1, l_2...l_k\}$ (namely views) are imputed. The mesh model M include a set of triangles (namely faces) F, where $F = \{F_1, F_2....F_n\}$, n is the number of the faces in the model. For face F_i correspond to some fragments $\{f_{ij}, ...f_{im}\}$ while the face could be seen by $\{l_j, ...l_m\}$, where $0 \leq j \leq m, 0 \leq m \leq k$.

2.2   Preprocessing

To reduce the face's improper candidate fragments from the its correspond fragments set, we take a preprocessing step. Occlusions, such as pedestrians and cars, may not be reconstructed in the mesh model, but these scenes may appear in the candidate options of the faces due to the inaccuracy camera parameters. If these scenes are mapped to the surface of the model, it will be a disaster. We assume that for a specific face most views can see the correct color, a few may see the wrong color (i.e., an occluder). To address this problem, let us first assume that face F_i correspond to fragments $f = \{f_1, f_2...f_t\}$, where $0 \leq t \leq k$, then the processing steps are presented as following steps (Fig. 1):

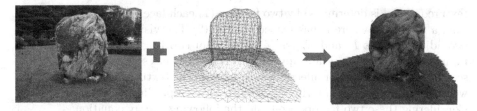

Fig. 1. Overview of the method. Given a set of images and a triangle mesh model, we compute a seamless texture for it. The examples shown in this paper use customer camera for the source imagery. The model is gotten by the Bundle, PMVS, and Poisson triangulation. The output is a texture map for the given object.

1. compute the mean color of each fragment which could see the face F_i to get $G = \{g_1, g_2...g_t\}$.
2. compute the mean value g of G.
3. compute the Euclidean distances between every element in G and g, discard the option in f when its value is the biggest. Update G, f, g.
4. repeat 2~4 until the number of elements in G is below 4, or the distances all drop to 1e−6 (Fig. 2).

Fig. 2. Preprocessing. The red rectangle shows that these scenes do not appear in the origin images (these faces do not have candidate options). The yellow rectangle shows that the preprocessing step (the right yellow rectangle) could eliminate erroneous candidate fragments (the left yellow rectangle). (Color figure online)

2.3 View Selecting

View selecting, a labelling procedure, tries to assign a "best" view to each face. This stage is for producing a good initial textured model. The quality of the textured model is determined by two factors: (1) each face F_i should be textured from a fragment, where it has better quality. (2) The visibility of the seams. If two adjacent faces F_i and F_j are textured from two fragments where they are from different views, a seam appear between these faces. The visitable of the seams is the second factor affecting the quality of the textured model. Unlike [9], we choose difference data term and smooth term to produce better appearance. Considering these two factors, we build the following energy equation:

$$E(M) = \sum_{F_i \subseteq F, l_j \subseteq I} E_{data}(F_i, l_j) + \sum_{l_i \subseteq I, l_i \subseteq I} E_{smooth}(l_i, l_j) \tag{1}$$

Data Term. We define the data term in this form

$$E_{data}(F_i, l_j) = -H(Pr_{l_j}(F_i)) \tag{2}$$

where Pr_k is a projection operator for the view k and $H(x)$ is the entropy of the fragment x ($P_{ij} = f(i, j)/N^2$, assume i is the color of the pixel, and j is the color of the neighbor pixel ($0 \leq i \leq 255, 0 \leq j \leq 255$). f(i,j) is the frequency of (i,j) appear in the fragments. N is the number of pixels in the fragment. $H(x) = \sum_{i=0}^{255} P_{ij} log P_{ij}$, x is the fragment where the face project to.). This term correspondence to the quality of fragments used in the textured model. This term prefer the energy which is smaller for the fragments with better quality.

Smooth Term. We take smooth term as

$$E_{smooth}(l_i, l_j) = \lambda N \tag{3}$$

where N is the number of patches, λ is the coefficient. This term corresponds to the seams between patches. This term prefer more adjacent faces which coming from the same view. Loopy belief propagation is applied to minimize Eq. 1 (namely the MRF energy). Experiments demonstrate this method can produce a good performance textured model.

3   Color Adjustment

Models obtained from the view selecting phase (e.g. Fig. 3) contain many fragments with color discontinuities. These color discontinuities need to be adjusted to minimize seams visible.

Seams will appear in such case where adjacent faces are textured by different views (see Fig. 4). It is no doubt that these seams will seriously affect the visualization of the initial textured model. At this part, we adjust every vertex in the fragments and further apply [10] to eliminate such seams. I' is a copy set of the origin images I. As Fig. 4 shows, A can duplicate into two vertices: vertex V_{left} belongs to the face to the left and V_{right} belongs to the face to the right. We add an extra color V to the smaller color of V_{left} and V_{right} (e.g. if $V_{left} < V_{right}$, $V + V_{left} = v_{right}$). Every pixel at the edge between A and E, like D, can also duplicate into two vertices: V_b belonging to the face to the left, V_r belonging to

Fig. 3. Models are textured from different images with pure color, each color represent a view. (Color figure online)

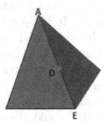

Fig. 4. Share vertex. Vicinity faces share same vertices while textured from different images.

the face to the right. We adjust the color V_e of E: $V_e = 1/2(V_b + V_r)$. What we do about color adjustment is rewriting the color of pixels in I'.

Poisson Editing: All visible seams can not be eliminated even tackled with the above color adjustment. Thus we additionally perform poisson image editing [10] to eliminate the residual seams. Since the color of vertices and edges are rewritten in I', what we do here is to keep the inner gradients of I' close enough to I which is the guidance of vector field. Therefor we compute an addition color g for every pixel in image I' by the equation:

$$\int_{I'} (\nabla g)^2 dx = min \qquad (4)$$

This function (4) is a typical Laplacian problem. We fix the color of these pixels which have been adjust in the step of color adjustment to 0. These pixels can be regarded as the boundary condition to (4) which is a typical Laplacian problem.

4   Experiments

In this section, we demonstrate the ability of our method to generate seamless textured models under a large variety of conditions. To obtain an image sequence, we take a few dozens of images around the subject object and further create a

Table 1. Summary of datasets

Dataset name	Number of images	Size	Number of faces
TreeStump	14	1024*685	17493
Stone	39	2848*2136	49090
Kermit	11	640*480	26103

mesh model by using [6,8,11]. Table 1 describes the detailed information about the input images and the mesh model.

At first, we conduct an experiment to compare the result between MVE and our method (MVE is developed by [12], and it can be regarded as the one of the top methods now (see Figs. 5, 6 and 7). In Fig. 5 we show the whole appearance of both methods (the left one is produced by MVE, and the right one is ours.). We can obviously observe that: (A) the right one shows a more completed outlook than the left one. (B) the right one preserves better color information in detail. In Fig. 6 we show the details between MVE and our method (the above is produced by MVE, and the below one is ours). We can see the most obvious difference (marked in the two images as 1, 2, 3): (A) the below one keeps better inner instruction than the above one (see the yellow rectangle 1). (B) the below one does not texture with wrong fragments (see the yellow rectangle 2). (C) the below one keeps better color continuity than the above one (see the yellow rectangle 3). We show another comparative example in Fig. 7.

Figure 8 shows the result of our method. The left two columns are the origin images (Note that the source images are not all displayed), the right two columns are the textured models. These input images cover rich color information (the images distribute the color information randomly). The Chinese characters on

Fig. 5. Left: textured model produced by MVE. **Right:** textured model produced by the proposed method.

Fig. 6. Difference details of both methods (Color figure online)

Fig. 7. Difference details of both methods

Fig. 8. Stone. **Left two columns:** origin images. **Right two columns:** seamless and rich textured model (Color figure online)

Fig. 9. Tree. **Left two columns:** origin images. **Right two columns:** seamless and rich textured model

the surface are exactly aligned. These models are the final results where they have gone though these steps: preprocessing, selecting fragments, color adjustment, poisson editing. We can see that these models with no seams over the surface. Figure 9 shows another example result of our method.

5   Conclusion

In this paper, we have proposed a texture mapping method to produce seamless textured models. To achieve this, a preprocessing step has been proposed to eliminate erroneous candidate fragments. Then, a MRF energy optimization method has been employed to handle the problem of assigning fragments, which takes both the quality of the fragments and color continuous of the seams between the fragments into consideration. Finally, every pixel in the origin images has been adjusted as the boundary condition to the Laplace equation. Good performance of the method has been demonstrated experimentally on the real world data under various lighting conditions with texture which have rich color information and inaccurate camera parameters.

Acknowledgments. We thank the editors and anonymous reviewers for their insights. Also, we thank Pengfei Wu for modifying this paper. This work is supported by NSFC under grants 61571313, funding from Sichuan Province (2014HH0048) and the Science and Technology Innovation seedling project of Sichuan (2014-046).

References

1. Baumberg, A.: Blending images for texturing 3D models. In: BMVC, vol. 3, pp. 5. Citeseer (2002)
2. Chen, T., Liu, Y., Li, J., Wu, P.: Fast narrow-baseline stereo matching using CUDA compatible GPUs. In: Tan, T., Ruan, Q., Wang, S., Ma, H., Di, K. (eds.) IGTA 2015. CCIS, vol. 525, pp. 10–17. Springer, Heidelberg (2015)
3. Chen, Z., Zhou, J., Chen, Y., Wang, G.: 3D texture mapping in multi-view reconstruction. In: Bebis, G., et al. (eds.) ISVC 2012, Part I. LNCS, vol. 7431, pp. 359–371. Springer, Heidelberg (2012)
4. Cui, P., Liu, Y., Wu, P., Li, J., Yi, S.: An effective multiview stereo method for uncalibrated images. In: Zha, H., Chen, X., Wang, L., Miao, Q. (eds.) CCCV 2015, Part I. CCIS, vol. 546, pp. 124–133. Springer, Heidelberg (2015)
5. Frahm, J.-M., et al.: Building Rome on a cloudless day. In: Daniilidis, K., Maragos, P., Paragios, N. (eds.) ECCV 2010, Part IV. LNCS, vol. 6314, pp. 368–381. Springer, Heidelberg (2010)
6. Furukawa, Y., Ponce, J.: Accurate, dense, and robust multiview stereopsis. IEEE Trans. Pattern Anal. Mach. Intell. **32**(8), 1362–1376 (2010)
7. Garcia-Dorado, I., Demir, I., Aliaga, D.G.: Automatic urban modeling using volumetric reconstruction with surface graph cuts. Comput. Graph. **37**(7), 896–910 (2013)
8. Kazhdan, M., Hoppe, H.: Screened poisson surface reconstruction. ACM Trans. Graph. (TOG) **32**(3), 29 (2013)
9. Lempitsky, V., Ivanov, D.: Seamless mosaicing of image-based texture maps. In: 2007 IEEE Conference on Computer Vision and Pattern Recognition, CVPR 2007, pp. 1–6. IEEE (2007)
10. Pérez, P., Gangnet, M., Blake, A.: Poisson image editing. ACM Trans. Graph. (TOG) **22**, 313–318 (2003). ACM
11. Snavely, N., Seitz, S.M., Szeliski, R.: Photo tourism: exploring photo collections in 3D. ACM Trans. Graph. (TOG) **25**, 835–846 (2006). ACM
12. Waechter, M., Moehrle, N., Goesele, M.: Let there be color! Large-scale texturing of 3D reconstructions. In: Fleet, D., Pajdla, T., Schiele, B., Tuytelaars, T. (eds.) ECCV 2014, Part V. LNCS, vol. 8693, pp. 836–850. Springer, Heidelberg (2014)

A Novel Interaction System Based on Management of Students' Emotions

Yunyun Wei[1(✉)] and Xiangran Sun[2]

[1] School of Architecture and Design, Beijing Jiaotong University, Beijing, China
yunyunwei@outlook.com
[2] Information Engineering School, Communication University of China, Beijing, China
sunxr@cuc.edu.cn

Abstract. Traditional classroom education has the distinctive features of inter-activity and promptness, and cannot be replaced by distant education nowadays. Computer becomes essential equipment in classroom and plays a core role in modern education. In this paper we make effort on human-computer interaction to improve the efficiency of student learning and the performance of teacher. An interaction system based on management of students' emotions is presented to prompt the experience of interactive teaching and learning. As analyzing the relationship of emotion and learning, we suggest educational methods corresponding to our proposed system. We also design and implement the interaction system with the algorithm of emotion recognition and emotion management.

Keywords: Human-computer interaction · Education · Emotion recognition · Emotion management

1 Introduction

In recent years the rapid growth of technology has sparked revolution in the whole world, including human-computer interaction, cloud computing and emotion recognition. Especially the use of state-of-the-art computer technologies makes many significant achievements for modern education nowadays and plays an important role in traditional education environment. Rapid developments have brought new trends and opportunities to improve the quality of classroom education and enhance interaction between teacher and student.

Interactivity is a key factor of the efficiency of teaching and learning in traditional classrooms. The improvement of interaction in classroom can make student get more achievement on learning significantly [1, 2]. From the perspective of education, traditional teacher-student interaction behavior in classroom is not only the speech and gesture of teacher and students, but also many modes, such as teaching content and resources, activities and games, emotion and affection. Moreover it is the same important to take into consideration student-student interaction, such as competition and cooperation, emotion and affection. Due to the development of computer technology, computer is becoming more popular in modern classroom education. Traditional teacher-student and student-student interaction behavior in classroom is turning out to be more

© Springer Science+Business Media Singapore 2016
T. Tan et al. (Eds.): IGTA 2016, CCIS 634, pp. 77–84, 2016.
DOI: 10.1007/978-981-10-2260-9_10

comprehensive four-dimensional observation interaction system. Computer is taken as the center of classroom education, so human-computer interaction is the most important issue for educators and researchers. In recent years more and more human-computer interface systems have been developed to provide the convenience of classroom education and improve the quality of teaching and learning.

More and more examples can conclude that emotions influence the results of students' learning obviously. Not only the teaching methodologies and the activities in classroom can affect learning, but also student's emotion actually plays important role in learning process. The research of Colin Beard found out that a significant effect of the student can change emotions on students' engagement in learning [3]. Suzuki found that emotional clues prompt a deeper learner engagement and make students use their knowledge to argue the issues [4]. A study made by Robert Sylvester figured out that positive emotion of students can enhance the learning process and negative emotion can reduce the effect of learning [5]. A research conducted by Candy Lawson showed that emotion arise from memories and reactions to current events [6]. Hence, managing students learning means managing emotions. So emotion recognition and emotion management involved in computer technology will become an major module in electronic education and learning system.

Cloud Computing is applied to everywhere nowadays such as web-service, e-commerce, education. The feature of cloud computing is the integration of massive information and computing resources for users by providing services, and is significant convenience to access information for users anywhere. It can collect and store massive information data in cloud server and have powerful ability of analysis and synthesis to give users helpful advises. The platform of cloud education based on cloud computing not only can record learning inhabits and experience for each student, but also can support teachers to design interactive instructions and improve the teaching results.

In order to promote a more efficient and interactive education among teacher and student in classroom, we design an intelligent classroom education system based on human-computer interaction with emotion recognition and management, which using the technology of cloud computing and decision support system. This paper is organized as following: Sect. 2 gives an outline of the influences of emotion in traditional classroom education. We propose some educational methods applied to our designed system which can influence students' emotion in Sect. 3. In Sect. 4, the architecture of our proposed intelligent education system is introduced, and detailed methods of the system are described at the same time. Next, the method of emotion recognition in our system is described and the result of the experiment is shown. Finally Sect. 6 concludes with some conclusions and presented future work.

2   Emotional Interaction of Traditional Classroom Education

From the perspective of pedagogy and psychology, the interaction between teacher and student are the basic and core process in education. The research of the teacher-student interaction plays a prominent role to improve the effects of teaching and learning. With the development and use of new technologies in teaching and learning, the interaction made a dramatic change for teacher and student. Compared with the conventional education, computer is taken as a center of classroom education that manages interaction process and leads the quality of education.

It is a classical conclusion that there are three important interactions including student-content interaction, teacher-student interaction and student-student interaction [7]. The quality of teacher-student interaction would influence the interaction efficiency of the other two directly. At the same time, the effect of student-student interaction could act on the result of learning. Hence, the emotional elements in interaction processes should be taken into consideration seriously in classroom education. Figure 1 shows the interaction of teacher and student in classroom. In the figure solid arrows mean teacher–student interaction of classroom teaching and student-student interaction of classroom activities. Dashed arrows mean emotion interaction or influence among teacher and students in classroom.

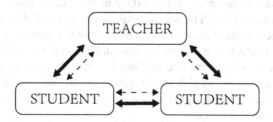

Fig. 1. The interaction of teacher and student in classroom.

Emotion is fundamental to human experience, cognition and activities such as learning, communication, and rational decision-making, which is proved by many researches. A research conducted by Daniel Goleman indicated that students who are anxious, angry, or depressed can't get knowledge well and take in information efficiently [8]. Some researches in neurosciences and psychology have found that emotions take massive influences widely with various behavioral and cognition processes such as attention, long-term memorizing and decision-making. Positive emotion influences cognitive organization and thought processes and takes a prominent role to improve creativity and efficiency in learning [9]. On the contrary negative emotion can block thought processes and decrease the results of learning significantly. Some researchers built a theory of emotion which takes the influence of emotion and behavior as a feedback system, and they found that emotion would influence behavior in both direct and indirect ways [10, 11].

It is important to make full use of new technology to help people understanding and exploring how teacher and student interact in classroom. Moreover people can improve the efficiency of education by influencing and managing emotions.

3   Educational Methods Influenced Students' Emotions

Nowadays a major challenge in classroom teaching is not only how to gain students' attention but also how to protect it against positive emotions such as disgust, boredom and self-abasement. New technologies in education can solve the problem and improve teaching and learning methods [12]. In general, educational methods prompt the efficiency of education and develop the skills of students in many ways such as slides, interactive multimedia, digital game and activities. Moreover, teacher can use different educational methods to influence and manage students' emotions and even enhance the learning process of students. For example, if the students lose interests on slides in classroom, the teacher could take another educational method to make them happy. The teacher also can use the group competition to stimulate the students' learning passion.

3.1 Interactive Multimedia

Interactive multimedia can stimulate students to study and help students to understand knowledge quickly. The interactive multimedia acts as a tool for cognitive, collaborative and communicative learning process. By making learning performances, simulating the real situations, learning through interactive multimedia and realizing real projects, will give sufficient effects to the students' understanding rate in a learning process. Thus, the application of the interactive multimedia helps making students relaxed and fostering the learning process. The interactive multimedia enables students to stimulate and engage in learning process by different experiences. In order to improve students' emotions, the teacher should design and develop the content of interactive multimedia for the courseware in classroom.

3.2 Digital Game

Digital game used for educational purposes can engage the students by fun interactive learning methods [13], and make students learning more breezily and not in a boring matter. It can not only enhance interactivity in teaching and learning process, but also influence students' emotions prominently. Game based education is a kind of tool which performances entertainment for educational purposes. The goal of game based education is to attract students' attention and raises students' motivation and interest. Meanwhile it is convenient for the teacher and provides an alternative and enjoyable educational method. The design of educational digital games not only should attract students and affect their emotions, but also is based on the content of courseware for classroom education.

3.3 Activities

Activities can make classroom teaching and learning rich and colorful, which integrate cooperative tasks and competitive elements to stimulate student's learning motivation. Activities employed in classroom include problem solution and task competition based on the content of the course. It turns out that choices of activities and the implementation affect students' emotions significantly. Adding elements of competitiveness plays a key role in the success of classroom activities especially while positive emotions need to be acted on students. It is the teacher's role and responsibility that when student is disin-teresting at learning in classroom, teacher could catch and influence student's emotion by fun activities.

4   The Architecture of Interaction System Based on Management of Students' Emotions

To improve the efficiency of teaching and learning in classroom, we proposed an inter-action system based on emotion management such as emotion recognition and influence, which is connected to cloud computing platform at the same time. The architecture of the proposed system is shown in Fig. 2. The architecture of the interaction system will be described and introduced as follow.

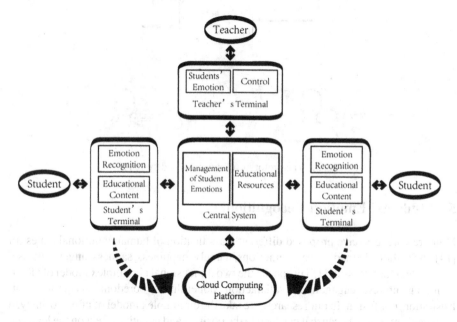

Fig. 2.   The architecture of interaction system based on management of students' emotions.

It includes three key parts: the central system, the teacher's terminal and the student's terminal. Central system is the core of the whole interaction system, which connects to both each terminal in classroom and cloud computing platform. The teacher's terminal displays the students' emotions transmitted by the central system, and accepts the teach-er's commands corresponding to the students' status. The student's terminal catches the data about emotions from common camera and infrared camera, processes facial data with emotion recognition, and transmits the information of emotions to the central system. Meanwhile it is also an interaction terminal on which students can experience interactive multimedia, play educational digital game and do activities of the course. Cloud computing platform collects every student's learning experience and information, and analyzes the habits and features of every student. It can help the central system to make perfect decision for the teacher. Figure 3 shows the design of system prototype in classroom. The central system is the core of the interaction system based on management of students' emotion. The classroom contents are not only managed in central system, but also controlled in teacher's terminal. The central system has three key technologies: decision-support system, emotion management and data store. It cooperates with cloud computing platform to compute and analyze emotion precisely.

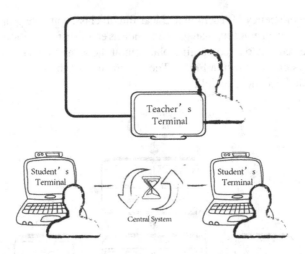

Fig. 3. The prototype of our proposed system.

5   Students' Emotion Recognition

Many researchers have proposed different classification of human emotional states. In [14], the authors defined six basic emotions, namely, happiness, sadness, anger, surprise, disgust, and fear. Russell [15] proposed the two dimensional circumplex model of affect, including interest, engagement, satisfaction, hopefulness, boredom, disappointment, frustration, confusion. In our research, we take the circumplex model of affect to analyze a student's emotion, because it can lead to the positive and negative effect on the learning of student.

We have lots of ways to observe students' emotions in classroom by their Behavioral and physiological changes, including facial expression, voices and actions. Facial expression is more easily detected than others. In our system, we use a method proposed in [16] for students' emotion recognition based on facial feature points detection with anthropometric model. For the evaluation of the method of emotion recognition, we select 20 students to do the experiment in the course. The result is listed in the Table 1 and shows the accuracy using the method of emotion recognition. Because some emotional states is difficult to appear in classroom, we select several states from the circumplex model of affect in our experiment, including interest, satisfaction, boredom, confusion and frustration.

Table 1. The results of emotion recognition in our experiment

	1	2	3	4	5
1	75 %	30 %	0 %	0 %	0 %
2	25 %	70 %	0 %	0 %	0 %
3	0 %	0 %	80 %	20 %	0 %
4	0 %	0 %	20 %	65 %	10 %
5	0 %	0 %	0 %	15 %	90 %

1: interest, 2: satisfaction, 3: boredom, 4: confusion, 5: frustration

6 Conclusion and Future Works

In this paper, we proposed architecture of interaction system based on management of students' emotion. It does not only help teacher manage teaching processes and understand students' emotion, but also improve the efficiency of student's learning in classroom education. Furthermore, we present several educational methods matched to our interaction system which can adopt students' emotion. In the future, through the development of computer technology and the improvement of education methods, it will become sustainable and intelligent, and promote the performance of classroom education. The school, teacher and student should create the innovation method and content in classroom teaching and learning.

References

1. Bannan-Ritland, B.: Computer-mediated communication, e-learning, and interactivity: a review of the research. J. Q. Rev. Distance Educ. **3**(2), 161–179 (2002)
2. Chris, E., Khaled, S.: Evaluation of the interactivity of web-based learning systems: principles and process. Innov. Educ. Teach. Int. **40**(1), 89–99 (2003)
3. Beard, C.: Student achievement: the role of emotions in motivation to learn - emotional maps. Pedagogic Research Project Report, Sheffield Hallam University (2005)
4. Suzuki, S., Shiraishi, A., Suzuki, H.: An emotional document investigation tool for academic writing. In: Proceedings of the Workshop on Research Goals and Strategies for Studying User Experience and Emotion, vol. 2(2), pp. 20–22 Lund, Sweden (2008)
5. Sylwester, R.: How emotions affect learning. Educ. Leaders. **52**(2), 60–65 (1994)
6. Jones, J.L., Esber, G.R., Mcdannald, M.A., et al.: Orbitofrontal cortex supports behavior and learning using inferred but not cached values. Science **338**(338), 953–956 (2012)
7. Moore, M.G.: Editorial: Three types of interaction. Am. J. Distance Educ. **3**(3), 1–7 (1989)
8. Goleman, D.: Emotional Intelligence: Why It Can Matter More Than IQ. An Academic Internet Publishers (AIPI) Publication (2007)
9. Isen, A.M.: Positive affect and decision making. In: Handbook of Emotions (2000)
10. Baumeister, R.F., Vohs, K.D., Dewall, C.N., et al.: How emotion shapes behavior: feedback, anticipation, and reflection, rather than direct causation. J. Pers. Soc. Psychol. Rev. **11**(2), 167–203 (1989)
11. Grichnik, D., Smeja, A., Welpe, I.: The importance of being emotional: how do emotions affect entrepreneurial opportunity evaluation and exploitation. J. Econ. Behav. Organ. **76**(1), 15–29 (1989)

12. Karich, A.C., Burns, M.K., Maki, K.E.: Updated meta-analysis of learner control within educational technology. Rev. Educ. Res. **84**(3), 392–410 (2014)
13. Zühal, O.: Edutainment: is learning at risk? Br. J. Educ. Technol. **34**(3), 255–264 (2003)
14. Ekman, P., Friesen, W.V., Ellsworth, P.: Emotion in the Human Face. Pergamon Press, New York (1972)
15. Russell, J.A.: A circumplex model of affect. J. Pers. Soc. Psychol. **39**, 1161–1178 (1980)
16. Abdat, F., Maaoui, C., Pruski, A.: Human-computer interaction using emotion recognition from facial expression. In: Uksim, European Symposium on Computer Modeling and Simulation, EMS 2011, vol. 47, pp. 196–201 (2011)

The Face-Tracking of Sichuan Golden Monkeys via S-TLD

Pengfei Xu[1(✉)], Yu Long[1], Dongmei Zheng[2], and Ruyi Liu[3]

[1] School of Information Science and Technology, Northwest University, Xi'an 710127, China
pfxu@nwu.edu.cn, 1198385502@qq.com
[2] Department of Finance and Economics, Shaanxi Youth Vocational College,
Xi'an 710000, China
470382743@qq.com
[3] School of Computer Science and Technology, Xidian University, Xi'an 710071, China
1051277391@qq.com

Abstract. Digital image technology has been widely used in wildlife monitoring, due to its advantages of non-obligatory, non-contact and non-invasive. However, the primary problem needing to be solved is how to detect and track the wild animals in these images and videos. This paper proposes a face-tracking algorithm for Sichuan golden monkeys by combing SVM and TLD, named as S-TLD. This algorithm is proposed based on the basic framework of TLD, and SVM is used as an alternate classifier to detect the face again, when the object appears in the video for the first time or TLD fails to tracking. Once SVM accomplishes the face detection, TLD completes the following tracking task. Experimental results demonstrate that S-TLD can be applied to the face detection and tracking of Sichuan golden monkeys in the videos, the location and facial information of the monkeys are very helpful for the study of their behavior habits.

Keywords: Color quantization · The golden monkey · Face-tracking · TLD · S-TLD

1 Introduction

It is an important part to study the behavior habits of the wild animals in the field of ecological, and the ecologists can analyze the animal behavior rules according to various types of data, which is obtained by some wildlife monitoring techniques [1]. With the advantages of non-obligatory, non-contact and non-invasive, digital image technology has been widely used in wildlife monitoring. While in these images and videos, to use the features of the animals to detect and track themselves accurately is a premise that ensures effective wildlife monitoring [2].

At present, there have been some works about the wildlife monitoring based on computer vision. For example, the system designed by Lahiri can identify zebras [3] based on the texture features of their fur. The group behavior of the birds are monitored based on the appearance features [4]. In addition, there are some behavior identification systems of wildlife. For example, Belongie has designed a visual system that can identify five basic behaviors of the murine [5]. And the system designed by Gonçalves can track the behavior of the snack [6].

T. Tan et al. (Eds.): IGTA 2016, CCIS 634, pp. 85–91, 2016.
DOI: 10.1007/978-981-10-2260-9_11

The golden monkeys are the first class protected animals in China, and they have great scientific and ornamental values. In the study of their behavior rules, the facial feature is one of the key factors for the individual recognition of the golden monkeys. At present, the facial features have been widely used in human face detection and recognition [7], and these features have also achieved lots of good results in animal identification [8, 9]. For example, Burghardt utilized the face detection method [10], which combines the Haar-like features and AdaBoost classifier, to track the lions' faces directly. There also are some methods for the extraction and location of the monkeys' faces. For example, Du and Zhang put forward an automatic location method based on the facial feature of rhesus monkey [11]. But the main solutions for the face detection and recognition of the golden monkeys are based on the methods by manually marking, artificial recognition according to the monkeys' photos or other methods, there is still no methods for the individual detection and tracking based on their facial features.

For the problem that the existing tracking methods are difficult to detect and track the wild animals when the videos are with the complicated background and the animals moves fast. This paper proposes an algorithm for the monkeys' face detection and tracking, which is named as S-TLD, to track the faces of Sichuan golden monkeys. This algorithm is put forward on the basic framework of TLD [12, 13], and SVM is introduced as an alternative classifier to resolve the problem that TLD fails to track when the objects move in a large range of motion or jump out of the videos.

2   The Face-Tracking of Sichuan Golden Monkey Based on S-TLD

The face-tracking algorithm proposed in this paper has two stages: 1. The image preprocessing stage. The color information of the fur in the monkeys' faces is used to detect the areas of their heads for each frame in the videos. 2. The face-tracking stage. The faces of the monkeys are detected and tracked by S-TLD on the basis of the locations of their heads. The framework of the proposed algorithm is shown in Fig. 1.

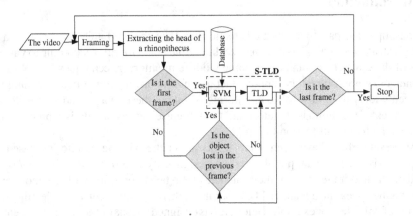

Fig. 1. The framework of the proposed algorithm

2.1 The Image Preprocessing Stage

In order to detect the faces of the monkeys with high efficiency, we need to remove the complicated background contained in each frame of the videos. Therefore, we use the color information of the fur in the monkeys' faces to detect the areas of their heads, then the face detection and tracking can be performed in the head areas, which will improve the efficiency of the algorithm.

Firstly, we make color quantization, the colors of the monkeys' facial fur are turn in to 72 colors. Due to the HSV color space is more suitable for human visual system, so we transform RGB to HSV. After color quantization, we make statistics and classification for these colors. The similarity of two kinds of colors in HSV, $m_i = (h_i, s_i, v_i)$ and $m_j = (h_j, s_j, v_j)$, can be described by the Eq. (1).

$$a_{i,j} = 1 - \frac{1}{\sqrt{5}}\sqrt{(v_i - v_j)^2 + (s_i\cos(h_i) - s_j\cos(h_j))^2 + (s_i\sin(h_i) - s_j\sin(h_j))^2} \tag{1}$$

Where the two colors have the most similarity when $a_{i,j} = 1$, and they have the biggest difference when $a_{i,j} = 0$. Finally, the maximum interval ranges in the color quantization results are selected respectively, and make a look-up table of the fur color. When we detect the monkeys' heads in the frames, we test each pixel, if the colors of the pixels are found in the look-up table, they are identified as the head pixels. To the end, we can obtain the head areas of the monkeys.

2.2 Face Detection and Tracking Based on S-TLD

2.2.1 The Training for the Alternative Classifier SVM

We select the face images of several golden monkeys with different ages and genders, and built a database with the face images $P = \{p^1, p^2, \cdots\cdots p^n\}$. Then the LBP features of these faces are extracted using the LBP operator. These training samples are used to train SVM to obtain a network model, which can detect the faces of the monkeys, and the Gaussian kernel function described as $K(x, x_i) = e^{\frac{\|x - x_i\|^2}{\sigma^2}}$ is used here. Furthermore, in order to improve the performance of SVM, we use more kinds of negative samples including leaves, soil, trees and sward etc., to enrich the diversity of the network model and optimize its parameters.

2.2.2 Face Tracking

There are two main kinds of common algorithms for object tracking. The first one is that the trackers are used to predict the positions of the objects according to their positions in the previous frame. But these methods will cause the error accumulation, and once the objects disappear in the videos, they would fail to track, even though the objects appear again. The second one is that the detectors are used to detect the objects in every frame. But these methods need offline training with plenty of the priori samples, and they are time-consuming, which has an adverse impact on the tracking efficiency. For these problems, this paper proposes a face-tracking algorithm of Sichuan golden monkey based on S-TLD. S-TLD is designed on the basic framework of the traditional TLD, which combines the tracker and detector, and an alternative classifier SVM is introduced to improve the performance. For each frame in the videos, the areas of the monkeys' heads can be obtained in the image processing stage. If the current frame is the first frame in the video, then the trained SVM network is used to detect the monkeys' faces. If the current frame is not the first frame and the objects do not lost, then TLD can detect and track the monkeys' faces. If the current frame is not the first frame, but the objects lost, then the trained SVM network is activated again to detect the faces. The framework of S-TLD is shown in Fig. 2.

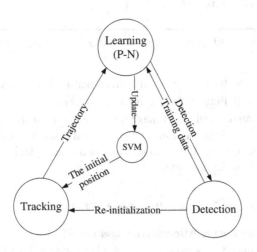

Fig. 2. The framework of S-TLD

At first, the initial positions of the monkeys' faces are detected by the alternative classifier SVM, and a sample database for the current video is established through multi-scale transformation. Besides, a cascading classifier in the detection module is used to classify the samples into the positive and negative samples.

Then, the tracker can estimate the new position of the faces. The tracking module is designed based on the Lucas-Kanade tracker and the forward-backward error. This module can create some tracking points around the object which is tracked in the frame t, and tracks these points forward to the frame $t + 1$ by Lucas-Kanade tracker. Furthermore, it tracks inversely to the frame t and calculates the forward-backward error. According to the changes of the coordinates and the distances of these points, the position and size of the object in the frame $t + 1$ can be obtained.

Finally, the learning module is started, this module is a semi-supervised learning algorithm named as P-N Learning. The expert P creates the new positive samples on the basis of the new positions of the objects. The expert N selects the most credible samples from those positive samples, and marks the rest ones as the negative samples. In addition, the positive samples are used to update the parameters of the detector.

In the process of the object tracking, if the object lose or the tracking fails for the reason that the golden monkeys move fast. S-TLD will activate the alternative classifier SVM again to track the initial position of the monkeys' faces, and amend the tracking results.

3   Experiments and Analysis

Figures 3 and 4 show the face-tracking results of the golden monkeys by S-TLD in the videos with different scenes. The faces with the red bounding box are tracked by S-TLD when the traditional TLD cannot work, and the faces with the yellow bounding box are tracked by TLD with the initial position provided by SVM in S-TLD. Here, 500 face images of the monkeys and 500 no-face images are used for the training of SVM before performing S-TLD, and then the samples detected by TLD are also used for the training of SVM in the tracking process of S-TLD.

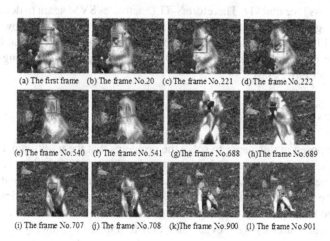

(a) The first frame   (b) The frame No.20   (c) The frame No.221   (d) The frame No.222

(e) The frame No.540   (f) The frame No.541   (g)The frame No.688   (h)The frame No.689

(i) The frame No.707   (j) The frame No.708   (k)The frame No.900   (l) The frame No.901

Fig. 3. The face-tracking results of the golden monkeys by S-TLD in the first video (Color figure online)

Figure 3(a) is the face-tracking result in the first frame, Fig. 3(a) is the tracking result by TLD in the frame No. 20, that means the monkey's face can be tracked successfully by TLD from the frame No. 2 to No. 20. But in the frame No. 221 (shown in Fig. 3(c)) and No. 540 (shown in Fig. 3(e)), TLD fails in the face-tracking when the monkey turns its face quickly. Then the face is detected again by SVM in S-TLD, and the current positions are used for the following tracking task. While TLD also cannot work when the monkey move fast, and S-TLD activates SVM to detect its face in the corresponding frames (as shown in Fig. 3(g, i, k)), which help TLD achieve the tracking task continually.

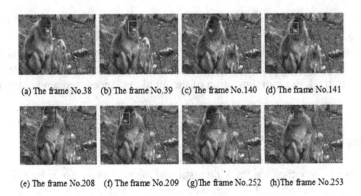

(a) The frame No.38   (b) The frame No.39   (c) The frame No.140   (d) The frame No.141

(e) The frame No.208   (f) The frame No.209   (g)The frame No.252   (h)The frame No.253

Fig. 4. The face-tracking results of the golden monkeys by S-TLD in the second video (Color figure online)

In the second video, the monkey turns its face frequently, so it is difficult to track the face accurately. The traditional TLD fails to track the face several times when the monkey turns its face quickly. Therefore S-TLD activates SVM again to detect the face, as shown in Fig. 4(a, c, e, g), then TLD continue to track the face in the following frames, as shown in Fig. 4(b, d, f, h). From these experiments, it can be seen that S-TLD has better performance than the traditional TLD; it can accomplish the tracking task better when the object moves fast.

4   Conclusion

S-TLD is proposed in this paper to solve the problems that the traditional TLD cannot work well when the object moves fast or out of the video. S-TLD is designed based on the basic framework of TLD, and SVM is used as an additional detector, and it can help TLD track the object continually when the object presents for the first time or jumps into the video again. Finally, the experimental results show that S-TLD can track the face of the golden monkey well, even when they turn their face quickly.

Acknowledgement.   The work was jointly supported by the National Natural Science Foundations of China under grant Nos. 61373177, 61502387, 61202198 and 61272195. The Science Research Project of the Education Department of Shanxi Province under grant Nos. 15JK1748 and 15JK1734. The Science Foundations of Northwest University under grant Nos. 14NW25, 14NW27, 14NW28. The Open Projects Program of National Laboratory of Pattern Recognition No. 201600031. Natural Science Foundation of Shaanxi Province, No. 2016JQ6029.

References

1. Nathan, R.: An emerging movement ecology paradigm. Proc. Natl. Acad. Sci. **105**(49), 19050–19051 (2008)

2. Wang, B., Wang, Z., Lu, H.: Facial similarity in Taihangshan macaques (Macaca mulatta tcheliensis) based on modular principal components analysis. Acta Theriologica Sinica **33**(3), 232–237 (2013)
3. Lahiri, M., Tantipathananandh, C., Warungu, R., et al.: Biometric animal databases from field photographs: identification of individual zebra in the wild. In: Proceedings of 1st ACM International Conference on Multimedia Retrieval, p. 6. ACM (2011)
4. Tweed, D., Calway, A.: Tracking multiple animals in wildlife footage. In: 2002 Proceedings of 16th International Conference on Pattern Recognition, vol. 2, pp. 24–27. IEEE (2002)
5. Belongie, S., Branson, K., Dollar, P., et al.: Monitoring animal behavior in the smart vivarium. In: Measuring Behavior, pp. 70–72. Wageningen, The Netherlands (2005)
6. Gonçalves, W.N., de Andrade Silva, J., Machado, B.B., Pistori, H., de Souza, A.S.: Hidden Markov models applied to snakes behavior identification. In: Mery, D., Rueda, L. (eds.) PSIVT 2007. LNCS, vol. 4872, pp. 777–787. Springer, Heidelberg (2007)
7. Zafeiriou, S., Zhang, C., Zhang, Z.: A survey on face detection in the wild: past, present and future. Comput. Vis. Image Underst. **138**, 1–24 (2015)
8. Sharma, S., Shah, D.J.: A brief overview on different animal detection methods. Sig. Image Process. **4**(3), 77–81 (2013)
9. Zhang, W., Sun, J., Tang, X.: From tiger to panda: animal head detection. IEEE Trans. Image Process. **20**(6), 1696–1708 (2011)
10. Burghardt, T., Calic, J.: Analysing animal behaviour in wildlife videos using face detection and tracking. IEE Proc. Vis. Image Sig. Process. (IET) **153**(3), 305–312 (2006)
11. Du, X., Zhang, H.: An automatic computer method for macaque facial localization. Lab. Anim. Comp. Med. **31**(3), 166–171 (2011)
12. Kalal, Z., Mikolajczyk, K., Matas, J.: Tracking-learning-detection. IEEE Trans. Pattern Anal. Mach. Intell. **34**(7), 1409–1422 (2012)
13. Kalal, Z., Mikolajczyk, K., Matas, J.: Face-TLD: Tracking-learning-detection applied to faces. In: 17th IEEE International Conference on Image Processing, pp. 3789–3792 (2010)

Random Selective Image Encryption Algorithm Based on Chaos Search

Hang Gao, Tiegang Gao[✉], and Renhong Cheng

College of Computer and Control Engineering, Nankai University,
Tianjin 300350, People's Republic of China
mailhunterg@qq.com,
{gaotiegang, chengrh}@nankai.edu.cn

Abstract. This paper presents a novel random selective image encryption scheme. In the scheme, image is firstly permutated by position and high four-bits of pixel; then the permutated image is diffused by adaptive random selective encryption based on hyper-chaos. The highlights of the scheme lie in that the high performance of the algorithm can be achieved through adaptive selection pixels for encryption through chaos search, and the chaos search can be accomplished in the whole image pixels or partial pixels. Large numbers of experiments and comparisons with the existing methods show the better performance of the proposed scheme.

Keywords: Chaos search · Hyper-chaos · Image encryption · Pixel permutation

1 Introduction

With the rapid developments in digital image processing and network communication, it becomes especially easy for dissemination of digital multimedia data over the Internet; this results in that the protection of digital information against illegal copying and distribution become a challenging problem. To cope with this problem, many image encryption schemes have been proposed [1–4]. Among them, chaos-based algorithms has suggested a new and efficient way to deal with the intractable problem of fast and highly secure image encryption, and it has been proved in many aspects chaotic maps have analogous but different characteristics as compared with conventional encryption algorithms [5–7].

The chaos-based encryption was first proposed in 1989 [8]. Since then, many researchers have proposed and analyzed a lot of chaos-based encryption algorithms [9–16]. The proposed algorithms not only use on one-dimensional and two-dimensional chaotic system [9, 10], they also use higher-dimensional chaotic systems or hyper-chaotic system [11, 12]. In the meantime, the chaos based image encryptions are achieved not only by chaos itself, they are also merged with DNA complementary rules and dynamic harmony search [13, 14]. As chaos has ergodicity, sensitive dependence on initial conditions and random-like behaviors, this makes it suitable for generation of random key stream and random permutation. For example, Fouda et al. proposed a one round encryption scheme for the fast generation of large permutation and diffusion keys

© Springer Science+Business Media Singapore 2016
T. Tan et al. (Eds.): IGTA 2016, CCIS 634, pp. 92–105, 2016.
DOI: 10.1007/978-981-10-2260-9_12

based on the sorting of the solutions of the Linear Diophantine Equation (LDE) whose coefficients are integers and dynamically generated from any type of chaotic systems [14]; Rehman proposed a image encryption based on whole set of DNA complementary rules and chaos, in the scheme, the image is permuted by Piecewise Linear Chaotic Map (PWLCM) while logistic sequence is used for the selection of encoding and decoding rules for each pixel of a block [15]; Recently, Zhang proposed an image encryption algorithm based on substitution and permutation, the encryption algorithm is composed of substitution in the DNA format and permutation in the hyper-image format, both of which have eliminated the relation between adjacent pixels in the image and adjacent bit planes in one pixel sufficiently [16].

In order to reduce the implementation time of encryption process, improve the robustness of the encrypted image, selective encryption algorithms are often used to guarantees the security while it needs less time through encrypting only carefully selected portions of the original image [17–19]. For example, a novel symmetric encryption technique for medical images is presented in [18]. It uses the genetic algorithm which makes it highly adaptive, in the scheme, the images are segmented into a number of regions and the sensitive regions are selected on the basis of pixel intensity and entropy measurements. But, this algorithm provides lower entropy and correlation measurements than the traditional AES, and recently, Ahmed proposed an effective selective encryption method, the algorithm selects the image block based on its entropy, and then uses the pseudo random number sequences, Arnold permutation, and the advanced encryption standard technique to achieve the goal of encryption [19].

In this paper, a novel random selective image encryption scheme based on chaos search is suggested. Different from traditional selective encryption, the proposed scheme select adaptively the image pixel for encryption by random, in order to achieve better performance of encryption, chaos search is used for finding the optimal selection of pixel. As far as I know, this is the first time that chaos search is used for image encryption. Large numbers of experiments show that the proposed scheme can achieve better performance, some comparison and analysis are presented to show the effectiveness of the proposed algorithm. The rest of this letter is organized as follows. Section 2 presents the proposed algorithm. Section 3 describes some simulation outcomes, some analysis and comparisons. Finally, Sect. 4 concludes the letter.

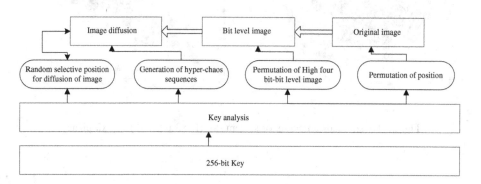

Fig. 1. Diagram of the proposed scheme

2   The Proposed Encryption Algorithm

The complete image encryption process consists of two parts, as shown in Fig. 1. In the stage of key analysis, 256-bit key is resolved into several different keys which will be used in the process of encryption. The processing of key analysis is described in the following section.

2.1   Generation of Key Stream Based on Hyper-Chaotic System

In the proposed encryption scheme, a hyper-chaotic system which is modeled by the following form will be used for generation of key stream.

$$\begin{cases} \dot{x}_1 = a(x_2 - x_1), \\ \dot{x}_2 = -x_1 x_3 + dx_1 + cx_2 - x_4, \\ \dot{x}_3 = x_1 x_2 - bx_3, \\ \dot{x}_4 = x_1 + k \end{cases} \tag{1}$$

where a, b, c, d and k are parameters, when $a = 36$, $b = 3$, $c = 28$, $d = -16$ and $-0.7 \leq k \leq 0.7$, the system is hyper-chaotic. The hyper-chaos attractors are shown in Fig. 2. with parameters $a = 36, b = 3, c = 28, d = -16$ and $k = 0.2$, its Lyapunov exponents are $\lambda_1 = 1.552$, $\lambda_2 = 0.023$, $\lambda_3 = 0$, $\lambda_4 = -12.573$. As the hyper-chaos has two positive Lyapunov exponents, so the prediction time of a hyper-chaotic system is shorter than that of a chaotic system. As a result, it is safer than chaos in security algorithm. For more detailed analysis of the complex dynamics of the system, please see relative reference [20].

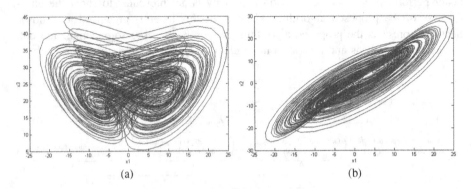

(a)   (b)

Fig. 2. Hyper-chaos attractors of system (a) x1−x3 plane (b) x1−x2 plane

2.2   Key Analysis

For a 256-bit key, without loss of generality, assume it is expressed by $b_1, b_2, \cdots, b_{256}$, then it is truncated into 64 bit by formula (2).

$$\begin{cases} b_i' = b_i \oplus b_{i+128}, i = 1, 2 \cdots, 128 \\ b_i'' = b_i' \oplus b_{i+64}', i = 1, 2 \cdots, 64 \end{cases} \tag{2}$$

For the produced 64 bit data, it is divided into 4 sections, every section includes 16 bits, apply formula (3) to turn the 16 bits data into a integer which belongs to [0, 65535]. Thus, we can get 4 integer numbers.

$$\begin{cases} x_1 = Bin2dec(b_1'' b_2'' \cdots b_{16}'') \\ x_2 = Bin2dec(b_{17}'' b_{18}'' \cdots b_{32}'') \\ x_3 = Bin2dec(b_{33}'' b_{34}'' \cdots b_{48}'') \\ x_4 = Bin2dec(b_{49}'' b_{50}'' \cdots b_{64}'') \end{cases} \tag{3}$$

Following that, multiply the above generated 4 number by 10^{-5}, and we will get four initial values $x_1(0), x_2(0), x_3(0), x_4(0)$ for use.

$$\begin{cases} x_1(0) = x_1 \times 10^{-5} \\ x_2(0) = x_2 \times 10^{-5} \\ x_3(0) = x_3 \times 10^{-5} \\ x_4(0) = x_4 \times 10^{-5} \end{cases} \tag{4}$$

2.3   Image Permutation of Position and Bit Level

Image data has strong correlations among adjacent pixels. In order to disturb the high correlation among pixels, an image total shuffling algorithm is used to shuffle the position of the plain-image. Assume that the dimension of the plain-image is $N \times M$, arrange the image pixels into a row vector is $P_i, i = 1, 2, \cdots MN$, where $P_i, i = 1, 2, \cdots MN$ stands for the grey value of the image. The arrange method of the pixels can be the simple 'from left to right and from top to bottom' method, the zigzag way, or the inverse S way as presented in Fig. 3.

The procedure of image position permutation is described as follows.

(1) For Logistic map $x_{n+1} = 4x_n(1 - x_n)$ and a given x_0, after doing some iterations, a new x_0 is derived.
(2) Continue to iterate Logistic map until we get $N \times M$ different data, $X_1, X_2, \cdots, X_{NM}$ data is got. Then rearrange these data in either ascending or descending order, and a new data sequences can be obtained which may be $G_1 < G_2, \cdots, < G_{NM}$.

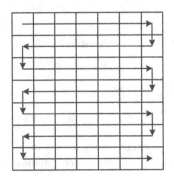 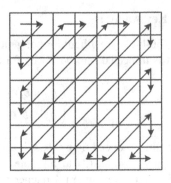

(a) Invers-S scanning   (b) Zigzag scanning

Fig. 3. Different ways of scanning

(3) Permute the pixel values according to the position of new sequences $G_i, i = 1, 2, \cdots NM$. That is to say, assume the position of $G_i, i = 1, 2, \cdots NM$ in the sequences of $X_1, X_2, \cdots, X_{NM}$ is L, $1 \leq L \leq NM$, then, pixel P_L which is in the position of L will be moved to the ith position of the vector P_i, $i = 1, 2, \cdots MN$. Then the image pixels row vector is P_i, $i = 1, 2, \cdots MN$ can be totally permutated. Figure 3 shows the results of 30 iterations of logistics map, the red number stands for the new position after sorting. It can be observed that the permutation is effective.

After the position shuffling is completed, the position of high 4 bit (5, 6, 7, 8) in new sequences of pixel will be permuted in the same way as that in the position permutation. Thus, the image permutation is finished (Fig. 4).

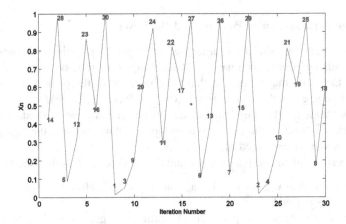

Fig. 4. Chaos based permutation for 30 positions

2.4 Image Diffusion

In this period, some random selective image pixels are encrypted, the total number of selective pixels may be adaptively adjusted by the demand. In general we may consider information entropy in encrypted image as a reference standard. The detailed method is given in the followings.

(1) For the permuted image I, some positions of pixel are selected for encryption. The selection method of pixel can be the same as permutation of image. In general, three-fourths or much more of the total pixel number are selected.

(2) Assume the selected pixels are $I_1, I_2, \cdots I_S$, S is the number of selected pixel numbers. Then iterate the hyper-chaotic system (1) for N_0 times by Runge-Kutta algorithm to avoid the harmful effect of transient procedure.

(3) The hyper-chaotic system is iterated for S times, and as a result, four decimal fractions x_1, x_2, x_3, x_4 will be generated for every iteration. These decimal values are preprocessed firstly as follows

$$x_i = \text{mod}((Abs(x_i) - Floor(abs(x_i)) \times 10^{14}, 256), \quad i = 1, 2, 3, 4 \quad (5)$$

where $Abs(x)$ returns the absolute value of x. $Floor(x)$ returns the value of x to the nearest integers less than or equal to x, $\text{mod}(x, y)$ returns the remainder after division.

(4) Generate $\bar{x}_1$ by using the following formula:

$$\bar{x}_4 = \text{mod}(x_4, 4) \quad (6)$$

(5) Fusion will be continued by employing Eq. (7) to encrypt selected pixels

$$I_i' = \begin{cases} swap(High - 4bit, Low - 4bit) & \bar{x}_4 = 0 \\ x_1 \oplus swap(High - 4bit, Low - 4bit) & \bar{x}_4 = 1 \\ x_1 \oplus x_2 \oplus swap(High - 4bit, Low - 4bit) & \bar{x}_4 = 2 \\ x_1 \oplus x_2 \oplus x_3 \oplus swap(High - 4bit, Low - 4bit) & \bar{x}_4 = 3 \end{cases} \quad (7)$$

2.5 Performance Optimization by Chaos Search

As the chaos has the property of ergodicity, we use it to search the space of encryption algorithm with high performance. Because the scheme includes two stages, the information entropy is used for chaos optimization, and the procedure of chaos search is presented in the following.

For a space of initial values of chaotic map, assume it is $[a, b] \subset [0, 1]$, and a definite step of progression h, the following steps is used to search some initial values, which can make the proposed algorithm achieve high performance.

(1) Let $x_0 = a$ as the initial of logistic map, and execute image permutation process.
(2) Calculate the information entropy H of permutated image.
(3) If the entropy is not satisfied with the demand, then let $x_0 = a + h$ and go to Step 1.

The iteration can be terminated by two ways. One is that, when the interval [a, b] is completely tested, the initial value x_0 that generate the max entropy of the permutated image will be selected; the other one is that for a expected entropy, if the entropy of permutated image is equal to or greater than it, the iteration will be terminated, the x_0 that generate the max entropy of the permutated image will be selected;

For optimization of the second stage, firstly the key stream is generated; the optimization is concerned about the selection of pixels that are used for diffusion. The details can be given in the following.

(1) For the permutated image, assume the expected pixel number for encryption is S, then for a given initial value x_0, generate NM random position, where NM is the total number of pixel of image.
(2) Select the S position pixel of rank ahead; use the image diffusion in the second stage to encryption the image.
(3) Calculate the entropy of encrypted image, if it is not equal to or greater than the predetermined, then, alter the initial value of chaos and generate a group of new position information for encryption.
(4) Repeat above process until a satisfactory entropy of encrypted image is achieved.

The second step optimization flowchart can be depicted by Fig. 5.

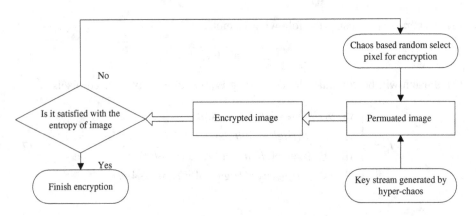

Fig. 5. Flowchart of chaos optimization

3   Experimental Analysis

3.1   Statistical Features for Performance Evaluation

In order to evaluate the performance of the encrypted image, some frequently used parameters can be used to measure the effects of the algorithm, some brief introduction are described in the following.

(1) Correlation of two adjacent pixels

Correlation of two adjacent pixels reflects the performance of the any encryption scheme, high correlation between adjacent pixels in the plain image must be reduced in cipher-image as much as possible. The correlations between two adjacent pixels are calculated by the following formulas:

$$E(x) = \frac{1}{N} \sum_{i=1}^{N} x_i \tag{8}$$

$$D(x) = \frac{1}{N} \sum_{i=1}^{N} (x_i - E(x_i))^2 \tag{9}$$

$$\text{cov}(x, y) = \frac{1}{N} \sum_{i=1}^{N} (x_i - E(x_i))(y_i - E(y_i)). \tag{10}$$

$$r_{xy} = \frac{\text{cov}(x, y)}{\sqrt{D(x)}\sqrt{D(y)}} \tag{11}$$

where x_i and y_i are grey values of two adjacent pixels in the image.

(2) NPCR and UACI

NPCR (number of pixels change rate) and the UACI (unified average changing intensity) are used to test the influence of one pixel change on the whole image encrypted by any encryption algorithm. The NPCR measures the percentage of different pixels between two encrypted images, while the UACI means the average difference between the pixels of two encrypted images:

$$C(i,j) = \begin{cases} 0, if\ C_1(i,\ j) = C_2(i,\ j) \\ 1, if\ C_1(i,\ j) \neq C_2(i,\ j) \end{cases} \tag{12}$$

$$\text{NPCR} = \frac{\sum_{i=1}^{M} \sum_{j=1}^{N} C(i,\ j)}{M \times N} \times 100\% \tag{13}$$

$$\text{UACI} = \frac{1}{M \times N} \sum_{i=1}^{M} \sum_{j=1}^{N} \frac{|C_1(i,\ j) - C_2(i,\ j)|}{255} \times 100\% \tag{14}$$

where, C1 and C2 are encrypted images by two plain images which have only one pixel difference, and $C_1(i,\ j)$ and $C_2(i,\ j)$ are the pixel values of C1 and C2, respectively.

(3) Information entropy

The well-known feature to recognize how much a sample image contains uncertainty information is entropy, for an ideal random image, the maximum value of information entropy is eight. It is given by formula (15).

$$H(s) = \sum_{i=0}^{2^M-1} P(s_i) \log_2 \frac{1}{P(s_i)} \qquad (15)$$

where M is the number of bits for a pixel's gray level, which is eight here, and $P(s_i)$ is the probability of occurrence of the i'th gray level in an image and could be obtained by Eq. (16)

$$P(s_i) = \frac{\textbf{number of pixels with gray levels i in image}}{\textbf{total number of pixels in image}} \qquad (16)$$

3.2   Experimental Results

In the experimental, the plain-image with the size of 512×512 shown in Fig. 3 are used, where Fig. 6(a–b) are 'Lena' and 'Mandrill' with the size of 512×512.

In experiments, for 25-bit key, the initial values $x_1(0)$, $x_2(0)$, $x_3(0)$, $x_4(0)$ of hyper-chaos can be got through key analysis. The initial value of logistic map for image permutation of position and bit level is $x_0 = x_1(0) \times x_2(0)$. The initial value of logistic map for image diffusion is $x_0 = x_1(0) \times x_4(0)$.

For image 'Lena' with the size of 512×512, when we set the entropy to be 7.9993 for our target, and select the 70 % of the total pixel number for encryption, the initial value of x_0 is set to 0.105328787600000, the round of diffusion is 6, and get the entropy of the encrypted image is 7.999358181373421; in the same condition, and select the 80 % of the total pixel number for encryption, then the round of diffusion is 5, the entropy is 7.999312643792280; in the same condition, and select the 90 % of the total pixel number for encryption, then the round of diffusion is 2, the entropy is 7.999335373676038.

(a). Lena   (b). Mandrill

Fig. 6. Image used for encryption

Especially, in the same condition, when we select the 100 % of the total pixel number for encryption, and set the entropy to be 7.9993 and round of encryption is 1, the search results is that when x_0 is set to be 0.105328587600000, the entropy of the encrypted image is 7.999309990712461, when the entropy is set to be 7.9994 and round of encryption is 1, the search results is that when x_0 is set to be 0.105330687600000, the entropy of the encrypted image is 7.999409316770808. The experimental results based on chaos search can be summarized in Table 1. The encrypted image of Lena and the corresponding histogram is shown in Fig. 7.

Table 1. Image encryption results based on chaos search

Image proportion of selection for encryption	Lena			Mandrill		
	100	90	80	100	90	80
Diffusion round	1	2	5	1	5	8
Entropy	**7.99941**	7.9993	7.9993	7.9994	7.9994	7.9994

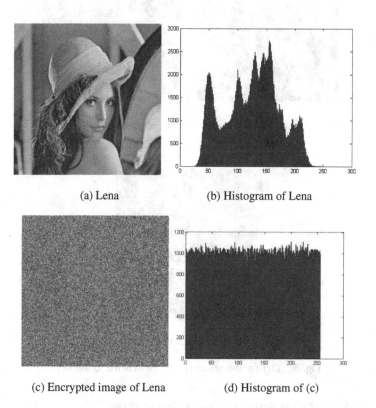

(a) Lena   (b) Histogram of Lena

(c) Encrypted image of Lena   (d) Histogram of (c)

Fig. 7. Encrypted image and histogram

3.3   Experimental Analysis

3.3.1   Key Space Analysis

A good encryption should have large key space to make brute-force attacks infeasible. In our algorithm, the key space size is 2^{256}. This is enough to resist all kinds of brute-force attacks.

3.3.2   Test for Sensitivity to the Key

High key sensitivity is generally required for preventing adaptive chosen-plaintext attacks and linear cryptanalysis. Figure 8 presents the test results, it can be seen, for the encrypted image, if we use different key from the key used for encryption, then the decrypted image will be totally different from the original one.

(a) Original image   (b) Encrypted image

(c) Decrypted image by wrong key.

Fig. 8. Test for the sensitivity of the scheme to the key

3.3.3   Analysis of Correlation of Two Adjacent Pixels

The test results of correlation between two adjacent pixels, the vertically, horizontally and diagonally adjacent pixels are shown in Table 2. It can be seen that the degree of correlation between adjacent pixels in encrypted image has been reduced greatly.

Table 2. Correlation coefficients of two adjacent pixels in two images

Coefficients	Plain-image			Cypher-image		
	Horizontal	Vertical	Diagonal	Horizontal	Vertical	Diagonal
Mandrill	0.7632	0.7937	0.7286	0.0002	0.0007	0.0003
Lena	0.9723	0.9835	0.9606	0.0002	0.0015	0.0035

3.3.4 Sensitivity Analysis

Here, the evaluation for sensitivity of an encryption scheme is used by the NPCR (number of pixels change rate) and the UACI (unified average changing intensity).

In the experiments, for image 'Lena', the pixel (value is 162) in the upper left corner is substituted by 160; for image 'Mandrill', the pixel (value is 116) in the upper left corner is substituted by 110. The NPCR and UACI are given in Table 3. It can be seen, the NPCR and UACI are very close to the ideal value, which means the encryption is hardly decrypted by differential attack.

Table 3. UACI and NPCR of images 'Lena' and 'Mandrill' after encryption

Images	Baboon	Lena
UACI	0.33592	0.33499
NPCR	0.9963	0.9961

3.3.5 Comparisons with Existing Schemes

Compared with some existing image encryption schemes, the proposed scheme is effective and achieves better performance. Because our goal of search is information entropy, some comparisons on the information entropy are summarized in Table 4.

Table 4. Comparison of information entropy between some existing schemes

Information entropy	Ours	Ref. [14]	Ref. [15]	Ref. [16]	Ref. [19]
Lena	**7.99941**	7.9992	7.99914	7.99934	7.9993
Mandrill	**7.99943**	7.9991	N/A	7.99933	N/A

The comparisons of correlation coefficients between plain images and ciphered images are presented in Table 5. Better results are achieved compared with most of the existing schemes mentioned in this paper.

Table 5. Comparison of correlation coefficients of image 'Lena' and 'Mandrill'

Coefficients	Plain-image			Cypher-image		
	Horizontal	Vertical	Diagonal	Horizontal	Vertical	Diagonal
Ours	0.9418	0.9762	0.9217	0.0002	0.0015	0.0035
Ref. [14]	0.9690	0.9637	0.9492	0.0026	0.0034	0.0019
Ref. [15]	0.9811	0.9896	0.9770	−0.0007	0.0006	0.0031
Ref. [16]	0.9722	0.9881	0.9596	−0.0033	0.0094	0.0021

The comparison of NPCR and UACI are summarized in Table 6. As can be seen in the table, these two values are higher when image 'Lena' is encrypted with the proposed scheme, which means more sensitivity has been achieved.

Table 6. UACI and NPCR of image 'Lena' with size 256×256

Schemes	Ours	Ref. [14]	Ref. [15]	Ref. [16]
UACI	0.33499	0.3340	0.3334	0.3295
NPCR	0.9961	0.9962	0.9368	9961

4 Conclusions

This paper presents a novel random selective image encryption scheme. In the scheme, image is firstly permutated by position and high four-bits of pixel; then, the permutated image is diffused by adaptive random selective encryption based on hyper-chaos. The highlights of the scheme lie in that the high performance of the algorithm can be achieved through chaos search, and the chaos search can be accomplished in the whole image pixels or partial pixels. Large numbers of experiments show the better performance of the proposed scheme, some security analysis are also given to demonstrate that the key space of the proposed algorithm is large enough to make brute-force attacks infeasible, many evaluation parameters comparison between the proposed algorithm and some existing scheme have been given to demonstrate the high performance of the new image encryption scheme, which may has some potential application in image encryption and information transmission based on Internet.

Acknowledgments. The authors would like to thank the support from the Program of Natural Science Fund of Tianjin (Grant #16JCYBJC15700).

References

1. Chang, C.C., Hwang, M.S., Chen, T.S.: A new encryption algorithm for image cryptosystems. J. Syst. Softw. **58**, 83–91 (2001)
2. Fridrich, J.: Symmetric ciphers based on two-dimensional chaotic maps. Int. J. Bifurcat. Chaos 8(6), 1259–1284 (1998)
3. Zhang, L.H., Liao, X.F., Wang, X.B.: An image encryption approach based on chaotic maps. Chaos, Solitons Fractals **24**, 759–765 (2005)
4. Kocarev, L.: Chaos-based cryptography: a brief overview. IEEE Circ. Syst. Mag. **1**(3), 6–21 (2001)
5. Wang, X., Liu, L.: Cryptanalysis of a parallel sub-image encryption method with high-dimensional chaos. Nonlinear Dyn. **73**, 795–800 (2013)
6. Caragata, D., Tutanescu, I.: On the security of a new image encryption scheme based on a chaotic function. Signal, Image Video Process. **8**, 641–646 (2014)
7. Eslami, Z., Bakhshandeh, A.: An improvement over an image encryption method based on total shuffling. Opt. Commun. **286**, 51–55 (2013)

8. Matthews, R.: One the derivation of a chaotic encryption algorithm. Cryptologia **8**(1), 29–42 (1989)
9. Pareek, N.K., Patidar, V., Sud, K.K.: Image encryption using chaotic logistic map. Image Vis. Comput. **24**, 926–934 (2006)
10. Kanso, A., Ghebleh, M.: A novel image encryption algorithm based on a 3D chaotic map. Commun. Nonlinear Sci. Numer. Simul. **17**(7), 2943–2959 (2012)
11. Gao, T., Chen, Z.: A new image encryption algorithm based on hyper-chaos. Phys. Lett. A **372**(4), 394–400 (2008)
12. Wei, X., Guo, L., Zhang, Q., Zhang, J., Lian, S.: A novel color image encryption algorithm based on DNA sequence operation and hyper-chaotic system. J. Syst. Softw. **85**(2), 290–299 (2012)
13. Zhang, Q., Guo, L., Wei, X.: A novel image fusion encryption algorithm based on DNA sequence operation and hyper-chaotic system. Optik-Int. J. Light Electron Opt. **124**(18), 3596–3600 (2013)
14. Armand Eyebe Fouda, J.S., Yves Effa, J., Sabat, S.L., et al.: A fast chaotic block cipher for image encryption. Commun. Nonlinear Sci. Numer. Simulat. **19**, 578–588 (2014)
15. ur Rehman, A., Liao, X., Kulsoom, A.: Selective encryption for gray images based on chaos and DNA complementary rules. Multimed. Tools Appl. **74**, 4655–4677 (2015)
16. Zhang, S., Gao, T.: An image encryption scheme based on DNA coding and permutation of hyper-image. Multimed. Tools Appl. doi:10.1007/s11042-015-2982-x
17. Moumen, A., Bouye, M., Sissaoui, H.: New secure partial encryption method for medical images using graph coloring problem. Nonlinear Dyn. **82**, 1475–1482 (2015)
18. Mahmood, A., Dony, R., Areibi, S.: An adaptive encryption based genetic algorithms for medical images. In: 2013 IEEE International Workshop on Machine Learning for Signal Processing (MLSP), pp. 1–6
19. Ayoup, A.M., Hussein, A.H., Attia, M.A.A.: Efficient selective image encryption. Multimed. Tools Appl. doi:10.1007/s11042-015-2985-7
20. Tiegang, G., Zhuzhi, C.Z.Y., Guanrong, C.: A hyper-chaos generated from chaotic Chen's system via linear controller. Inter. J. Modern Phys. C **17**(4), 471–478 (2006)

The Recognition of Cirrhotic Liver Ultrasonic Images of Multi-feature Fusion Based on BP_Adaboost Neural Network

Shourun Wang$^{(\boxtimes)}$, Zhenkuan Pan, Weibo Wei, Ximei Zhao,
and Guodong Wang

College of Computer Science and Technology,
Qingdao University, Qingdao, China
{wangrun365,qduwwb,xmzhao_qdu,15806532260}@163.com,
zkpan@126.com

Abstract. Due to the recognition rate of single character is low, the method of multi-feature fusion was proposed. BP_Adaboost neural network (BP_ANN) was first used to recognize the B-scan ultrasonic image of cirrhotic liver. Gray level co-occurrence matrix (GLCM) and gray level difference statistics (GLDS) were introduced in this paper. In order to improve the objectivity of the experimental results, uniform local binary pattern (U_LBP) was also applied. The texture features were extracted by any combination of these three methods. Then the feature which was extracted by above combination was input to BP_ANN. It was shown that the combination of GLCM and GLDS was better than any others in this experiment, and the recognition rate was 97 %. The design of BP_Adaboost network and the determination of neurons in hidden layer were also discussed.

Keywords: Neural network · Texture feature · Pattern recognition · Cirrhotic liver · Multi-feature fusion

1 Introduction

Medical imaging is a non-invasive diagnostic method [1], the area that can not be directly observed in human body is shown with this technology. So, ultrasonic imaging technology is widely applied to diagnose cirrhotic in the clinical nowadays.

B-scan is mainly used to the ultrasonic diagnose of liver. Amplitude characteristic of ultrasound echo signal is reflected in the two-dimensional B-scan image. The brightness of the image represents the amplitude of the returned ultrasonic signal [2]. According to the pathology knowledge, the symptoms of cirrhosis usually shows liver to deform (enlargement in early stage, obvious reduction in later period), liver parenchyma to harden, weight to lighten, edge to sharpen, and capsule to thicken. Besides the appearance is brown or taupe and the surface diffuses varying sizes of nodules and collapse region [3]. Therefore, the fibrotic liver in the B-scan image is generally expressed as the surface echo appears uneven, stepped and jagged, brightened dot increased and unevenly distributed [4]. Two types of B-scan image are shown in Fig. 1.

© Springer Science+Business Media Singapore 2016
T. Tan et al. (Eds.): IGTA 2016, CCIS 634, pp. 106–114, 2016.
DOI: 10.1007/978-981-10-2260-9_13

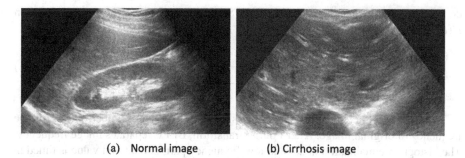

(a) Normal image   (b) Cirrhosis image

Fig. 1. Two types of ultrasonic image

Doctors can determine normal or lesions by observing the changes of patients' liver tissue components. However, doctors diagnose live diseases with eyes, which is in general confusing and highly subjective. This mainly depends on the doctor's experience. Some diseases are highly similar in their diagnostic criteria, which tend to confuse the judgement of doctors. Diagnostic accuracy only using visual interpretation is currently estimated to be around 72 % [5, 6].

To solve these problems in diagnosis, researchers have developed more quantitative criteria using computer aided diagnosis system [7]. In this paper this system was improved. Due to single feature is sensitive to noise interference and recognition rate is low, the method of multi-feature fusion was proposed. And BP_Adaboost network was applied to classify the liver ultrasonic images. The discussion was emphasized on different combinations of features and the problem of the design of BP_ANN.

2   Image Preprocessing

Image preprocessing mainly includes format conversion, denoising and enhancement etc. At first, the obtained ultrasonic images are transformed into gray level images. Next, an important job is to denoise and enhance. Its purpose is to improve the quality of medical images, and reduce the effect of noise as far as possible. Medical ultrasound images are populated by speckle noise generally [8, 9], but some detail characteristics, such as the edge is the important feature analyzing and diagnosing pathological changes of organs. Therefore, this is vital for restraining the noise as well as preserving the original characteristics of the image as much as possible.

In this paper, the traditional median filtering method is employed to denoise. Then the method of Butterworth low pass filter (BLPF) [10] is used to enhance images. Because energy mainly concentrate in the low-frequency, the noise and details are mostly in high-frequency. So handling two component separately can reduce the loss of details and prevent noise amplification. First of all, the Fourier transform is made, and filter is used to separate the high and low frequency part. Comparing with several common filters such as Chebyshev type I and Chebyshev type II filter, the ripple in passband and stopband acquired by Butterworth filter are all equal. The filtering result do not have significant ringing effect [10]. So BLPF is chosen. The transfer function $H(u, v)$ is as follows:

$$H(u, v) = \frac{1}{1 + \left[\frac{D(u,v)}{D_0}\right]^{2n}} \quad (1)$$

Where, D_0 is the cut-off frequency, n is BLPF's exponent number, $D(u, v)$ is the frequency of original image. After Fourier transform, BLPF separates image frequency. The histogram equalization is done in low-frequency part, and a fixed value is timed in high-frequency part, then combine the two parts again, and do an inverse Fourier transform. Some original pictures (a, b, c) and processed images (d, e, f) are shown in Fig. 2.

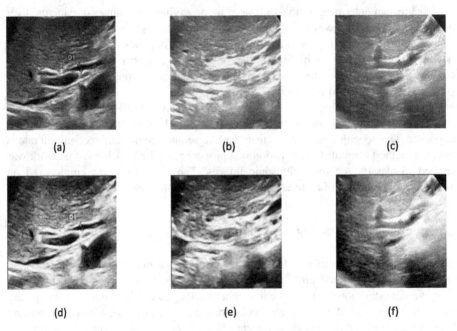

(a)   (b)   (c)

(d)   (e)   (f)

Fig. 2. Original and processed images

3   Feature Extraction

This process helps us to obtain useful image information and achieves the purpose of image recognition. Firstly, doctors guide us to choose large effective regions. Then, Small regions of interest (ROIs) are selected within those large regions. It is worth mentioning that we should pay attention to avoiding the great vessels when choose ROI. In this paper, the size of ROI was set to 50*50 pixels. Then features of ROI are extracted with gray level co-occurrence matrix [11], gray level difference statistics [12] and uniform local binary pattern [13]. Because these three kinds of features can be obtained easily and calculated conveniently. Besides, they can describe the local texture characteristics very well.

3.1   Gray Level Co-occurrence Matrix (GLCM)

The definition of GLCM is as follows. It is supposed that an image to be analyzed is rectangular and has N_x columns and N_y rows, the gray level appearing at each pixel is quantized to N_g levels. Let $L_x = \{1, 2, \ldots, N_x\}$ be the columns, $L_y = \{1, 2, \ldots, N_y\}$ be the rows, and $G_x = \{0, 1, \ldots, N_g - 1\}$ be the set of N_g quantized gray levels. The image I can be represented as a function that assigns some gray level in G to each pixel or pair of coordinates in $L_y \times L_x$; $I : L_y \times L_x \rightarrow G$. The texture-context information is specified by the matrix of relative frequencies $p(i, j, d, \theta)$ with two neighboring pixels separated by distance d occur on the image, i is a pixel value and j is the other [14]. Such matrices of gray-level co-occurrence frequencies are a function of the angular relationship and distance between the neighboring pixels.

In this experiment, four textural features are used. These features are defined as follows:

(i)   Energy: It is also called Angular Second Moment, which is a texture homogeneity measure of an image. It is defined as:

$$f_1 = \sum_i \sum_j p(i, j, d, \theta)^2 \tag{2}$$

(ii)   Contrast: It describes local variations in an image. It is defined as:

$$f_2 = \sum_i \sum_j (i - j)^2 p(i, j, d, \theta) \tag{3}$$

(iii)   Correlation: It expresses the similarity of co-occurrence matrix elements in row or column direction. It is defined as:

$$f_3 = -\frac{\sum_i \sum_j (i - \mu_x)(j - \mu_y) p(i, j, d, \theta)}{\sqrt{\sigma_x \sigma_y}} \tag{4}$$

$$\sigma_x = \sum_i (i - \mu_x)^2 \sum_j p(i, j, d, \theta) \tag{5}$$

$$\sigma_y = \sum_j (j - \mu_y)^2 \sum_i p(i, j, d, \theta) \tag{6}$$

Where μ_x, μ_y are mean.

(iv)   Entropy: It describes the information content of image, which measures the complexity of texture.

$$f_4 = -\sum_i \sum_j p(i, j, d, \theta) \log(p(i, j, d, \theta)) \tag{7}$$

we set $d = 1$, $\theta = 0^0, 45^0, 90^0, 135^0$. Through the above calculation, each feature index will get four values, and then calculate the mean and standard deviation of the four values as characteristic of the image. At last 8 features were got.

3.2   Gray Level Difference Statistics (GLDS)

GLDS is assumed $g(x,y)$ is a pixel value of image, the gray difference between this pixel and its neighborhood pixel $g(x + \Delta x, y + \Delta y)$ is as below:

$$g_\Delta(x,y) = g(x,y) - g(x+\Delta x, y+\Delta y) \qquad (8)$$

$g_\Delta(x,y)$ in (8) is defined as gray difference. Suppose gray difference level is m, the number of each $g_\Delta(x,y)$ is counted up, and histogram of $g_\Delta(x,y)$ is drawn. Finally occurred probability $p_\Delta(i)$ of each $g_\Delta(x,y)$ is calculated based on histogram.

In this study, texture features including contrast, angular second moment, mean and entropy were extracted from the graylevel difference statistics [15]. Their mathematical expressions are as below:

$$\text{Contrast: } CON = \sum_i i^2 p_\Delta(i) \qquad (9)$$

$$\text{Angular second moment: } ASM = \sum_i (p_\Delta(i))^2 \qquad (10)$$

$$\text{Mean : } MEAN = \frac{1}{m} \sum_i i p_\Delta(i) \qquad (11)$$

$$\text{Entropy : } ENT = - \sum_i p_\Delta(i) \log p_\Delta(i) \qquad (12)$$

Where, i is the value of gray difference. Based on different direction of pixel difference, four gray difference histograms are drawn. Each histogram got four different characteristics. Thus 16 texture features were calculated at last.

4   BP_Adaboost Neural Network

The BP neural network (BP_NN) is a multilayer feedforward neural network that contains a vast number of neuron nodes. Its output is decided by the network connection, weight and activation function. The Adaboost algorithm is an iterative algorithm. It is capable of increasing the classification accuracy of randomly assigned weak classifiers [16]. As BP_NNs possess a simple structure, generalise sufficiently, and are fault-tolerant, self-learning, and self-adapting. Therefore, BP_NNs are used as the weak classifiers of BP_Adaboost neural network model (BP_ANN).

In this method, the network adjusts the data weight based on correct or incorrect classification, and output is decided by comprehensive performance of multiple neural network. The implementation process is shown in Fig. 3.

Fig. 3. The implementation procedure of Adaboost strong classifier

1. M training samples were selected randomly from the sample space, the weight distribution of each sample is initialized with $D_t(i) = 1/m$. Then the weights and thresholds of neural network are initialized.
2. The number of weak classifier is K, and they are trained individually. Each weak classifier is a traditional BP neural network. When weak classifier t is trained, training data is used to train the neural network and forecast the output. The classification error sum e_t of sequence $g(t)$ is calculated as follows:

$$e_t = \sum_i D_t(i) \quad i = 1, 2, \ldots, m \quad (g_t(t_i) \neq y_i) \tag{13}$$

   Where, $g_t(t_i)$ is predictive classification results, m is the number of training sample, y_i is the desired classification results.
3. On the basis of the classification error e_t of sequence $g(t)$, weighs a_t can be calculated as follows:

$$a_t = \frac{1}{2} \ln\left(\frac{1 - e_t}{e_t}\right) \tag{14}$$

4. According to weight a_t, the weight of training sample is adjusted in the next round. For the samples of correct classification, its weight is reduced in the next training; For the samples of incorrect classification, its weight is increased. The formula is shown as follows:

$$D_{t+1}(i) = \frac{D_t(i)}{B_t} * \exp[-a_t y_i g_t(x_i)] \quad i = 1, 2, \ldots, m \tag{15}$$

   Where, B_t, normalizing factor, makes the sum of weight distribution is one under the condition of weight ratio unchanged. The definition of y_i and $g_t(x_i)$ is as same as formula (13).
5. Assume that get T groups of weak classification function $f(g_t, a_t)$ after training T rounds. Combining function $f(g_t, a_t)$ and weight a_t to get a strong classifier $h(x)$:

$$h(x) = sign\left[\sum_{t=1}^{T} a_t \cdot f(g_t, a_t)\right] \tag{16}$$

Where, *sign* is called signum function, and

$$sign(x) = \begin{cases} -1, & x < 0 \\ 0, & x = 0 \\ 1, & x > 0 \end{cases} \tag{17}$$

5   Experiment and Results

For the present work, large numbers of liver ultrasonic images were collected by doctors who are from the Affiliated Hospital of Medical College of Qingdao University using an ultrasound machine. We got 80 normal and 80 cirrhosis images, preprocess the images with the proposed method.

For the experimental study, large hepatic regions were delineated by doctors. Then, small ROIs (50*50) were manually selected within those large regions. We extracted 200 normal samples and 200 cirrhosis samples separately. We choose top 100 samples from two types of samples as the training set respectively, the rest of the 200 samples were used to test. Features were extracted for each sample based on the above method and two characteristic matrices (training matrix and testing matrix) were formed. The feature values were normalized by subtracting minimum value and dividing by maximum value minus minimum value [17].

The BP_ANN structure includes one input layer, one or more hidden layers, and one output layer. The number of input neuron is determined by the number of feature. The output layer has one neuron to indicate the input pattern is a normal or cirrhosis liver. The desired output of normal liver is 1, and hepatic cirrhosis is −1.

The number of weak classifier K = 10. The learning rate for input and hidden layer are 0.1, the allowed error is 0.005, training circle is 100. The hidden layer employs log-sigmoid function, and the output layer employs Purelin. The Levenberg-Marquardt algorithm is used for training function. Different features were extracted with above method, then input them to BP_ANN. Performance measures for 200 samples (100 normal liver and 100 cirrhotic liver) are shown in Table 1.

In the next experiment, a BP_ANN with two hidden layers was designed. The combination of GLCM and GLDS was applied to extract texture feature. The experiments were shown in Table 2.

It is shown that the combination of GLCM and GLDS is best from Table 1 apparently. Compared with Table 2, the number of hidden layer of BP_ANN was set to 1 and the quantity of neuron was set to 7, the accuracy is 97 %. This showed that it was significative introducing the BP_ANN into cirrhosis identification.

During the experiment, GLCM shows stronger adaptability and robustness. If the image is small, GLCM is a good choice. However, four matrixes are needed to be

Table 1. The result of BP_ANN with one hidden layer

Method	The number of hidden layer neurons							
	5	7	10	12	15	20	22	25
GLCM	no convergence	no convergence	89 %	89 %	88 %	88 %	86 %	84 %
GLDS	no conver-gence	76 %	88 %	83 %	85 %	79 %	78 %	71 %
U_LBP	no convergence	93 %	92 %	89 %	84 %	86 %	86 %	85 %
GLCM and U_LBP	no convergence	89 %	90 %	87 %	85 %	85 %	85 %	82 %
GLDS and U_LBP	no convergence	91 %	88 %	84 %	87 %	86 %	83 %	83 %
GLCM and GLDS	no convergence	97 %	96 %	96 %	95 %	92 %	85 %	81 %

Table 2. Accuracy of BP_ANN with two hidden layers

The number of hidden layer neurons	5, 7	8, 7	10, 14	7, 11	12, 14	18, 16	17, 19	20, 22
Accuracy	no convergence	94 %	92 %	96 %	90 %	88 %	91 %	82 %

calculated, and four different features are extracted for each GLCM. It is indispensible to considerate the cost of time. U_LBP can describe local texture feature well. The recognition rate of single U_LBP feature can achieve to 93 %. But this method need to extract 59 dimensional feature vector, which increases the computation time. GLDS is weaker for texture description ability. Because GLDS is easily influenced by outside factors such as noise, light etc. But the combination of GLDS and GLCM can express the texture characteristics very well.

BP_ANN with two hidden layers also has a good performance. But it has some drawbacks, such as slow training speed, and it is uneasy to determine the number of neurons.

6   Conclusion

The combination of GLCM and GLDS was first proposed and used to recognize cirrhotic liver ultrasonic images. BP_ANN was first introduced into the cirrhosis identification of ultrasound images. In this paper, eight texture features were extracted with GLCM and sixteen features with GLDS, then a eigenvector matrix was constructed. The experiment showed the combination of GLCM and GLDS was superior to other methods, and the recognition rate with strong classifier was higher than the average correct rate of weak classifiers. In order to further improve the recognition rate, more advanced fusion methods for classifying can be studied, and the Adaboost algorithm can be introduced into other types of neural network in the future work.

References

1. Tromberg, B.J., Shah, N., Lanning, R., Cerussi, A., Espinoza, J., Pham, T., Svaasand, L., Butler, J.: Non-invasive in vivo characterization of breast tumors using photon migration spectroscopy. Neoplasia **2**, 26–40 (2000)
2. Nicholas, D., Nassiri, D., Garbutt, P., Hill, C.: Tissue characterization from ultrasound B-scan data. Ultrasound Med. Biol. **12**, 135–143 (1986)
3. Chunyan, Han: The value of ultrasound in the diagnosis of liver cirrhosis and sonographic findings. J. ChiN. Rural Physician MeD. Specialty **12**, 159 (2010)
4. Schwenzer, N.F., Springer, F., Schraml, C., Stefan, N., Machann, J., Schick, F.: Non-invasive assessment and quantification of liver steatosis by ultrasound, computed tomography and magnetic resonance. J. Hepatol. **51**, 433–445 (2009)
5. Kadah, Y.M., Farag, A.A., Zurada, J.M., Badawi, A.M., Youssef, A.-B.M.: Classification algorithms for quantitative tissue characterization of diffuse liver disease from ultrasound images. IEEE Trans. Med. Imaging **15**, 466–478 (1996)
6. Gosink, B., Lemon, S., Scheible, W., Leopold, G.: Accuracy of ultrasonography in diagnosis of hepatocellular disease. Am. J. Roentgenol. **133**, 19–23 (1979)
7. İçer, S., Coşkun, A., İkizceli, T.: Quantitative grading using grey relational analysis on ultrasonographic images of a fatty liver. J. Med. Syst. **36**, 2521–2528 (2012)
8. Dong, Y., Zhang, H., Sun, Y.: Study of Motion Blurred Image Restoration Method (2015)
9. Tianjing, W., Baoyu, Z., Zhen, Y.: Compression perception signal acquisition scheme based on filtering. Chin. J. Sci. Instrum. 573–581 (2013)
10. Lizhi, W.: Computer Assistant Diagnosis based on Texture Features of Ultrasonic Liver Images. Central South University, Changsha (2013)
11. Haralick, R.M., Shanmugam, K., Dinstein, I.H.: Textural features for image classification. IEEE Trans. SMC Syst. Man Cybern. **3**, 610–621 (1973)
12. Weszka, J.S., Dyer, C.R., Rosenfeld, A.: A comparative study of texture measures for terrain classification. IEEE Trans. Syst. Man Cybern. **6**, 269–285 (1976)
13. Ahonen, T., Hadid, A., Pietikainen, M.: Face description with local binary patterns: application to face recognition. IEEE Trans. Pattern Anal. Mach. Intell. **28**, 2037–2041 (2006)
14. Madzarov, G., Gjorgjevikj, D.: Multi-class classification using support vector machines in decision tree architecture. In: EUROCON 2009, IEEE, pp. 288–295. IEEE (2009)
15. Soh, L.-K., Tsatsoulis, C.: Texture analysis of SAR sea ice imagery using gray level co-occurrence matrices. IEEE Trans. Geosci. Remote Sens. **37**, 780–795 (1999)
16. Zhang, H., Huo, Q., Ding, W.: The application of adaBoost-neural network in storedproduct insect classification. In: IEEE International Symposium on IT in Medicine and Education, 2008, ITME 2008, pp. 973–976. IEEE (2008)
17. Mala, K., Sadasivam, V., Alagappan, S.: Neural network based texture analysis of CT images for fatty and cirrhosis liver classification. Appl. Soft Comput. **32**, 80–86 (2015)

The Improved Canny Edge Detection Algorithm Based on an Anisotropic and Genetic Algorithm

Mingjie Wang[1], Jesse S. Jin[1,2(✉)], Yifei Jing[1], Xianfeng Han[1],
Lei Gao[2], and Liping Xiao[2]

[1] School of Computer Software, Tianjin University, Tianjin 300000, China
{wang_major,hanxianf}@163.com, jinsheng@tju.edu.cn,
lovejing0306@foxmail.com
[2] Beijing Aerospace Institute of Automatic Control, Beijing 100085, China
{thrstone,xlp027}@sina.com

Abstract. Edge detection plays a crucial role in image processing. This paper proposes an improved Canny edge detection algorithm to deal with existing problems in traditional algorithms. Firstly, we use the anisotropic filter to denoise original grayscale images. This method can effectively suppress noise and preserve the edge feature. Secondly, the paper searches optimizing high and low thresholds used in Canny operator utilizing genetic algorithm based on the Otsu evaluative function to avoid human factors. In our experiment, we got the optimizing value (227, 84), and the interclass variance (3833) for image Lena. Compared with the traditional operator, this improved algorithm can reduce the false positive rate and improve the accuracy of detection. Meanwhile, the experiment shows that the algorithm is also robust in pedestrian detection.

Keywords: Canny · Anisotropic filter · Genetic algorithm · OTSU · Adaptation

1 Introduction

In the area of image processing and computer vision research, the edge information plays a critical role in the process of image information analysis. Therefore, how to obtain important edge information effectively has become one of key researches among experts.

Image edge is where of step type or roof type of changes on pixel values occur in the image. Some of the more commonly used edge detecting operators are Sobel operator, Prewitt operator, Laplacian operator, LogLaplacian operator and so forth. Although these operators have advantages of simple algorithm and small amount of calculation, there are certain limitations of their application. Sobel operator and Prewitt operator can utilize convolution to work out first-order differential of each pixel dot. If the convolution kernel is too large, the edge will be coarsening, but if the kernel is too small, a lot of false edges will be generated; Laplace operator detects image edges by calculating second-order differential partial zero-value points, so the noise points in

© Springer Science+Business Media Singapore 2016
T. Tan et al. (Eds.): IGTA 2016, CCIS 634, pp. 115–124, 2016.
DOI: 10.1007/978-981-10-2260-9_14

image will influence accuracy of detection greatly; Log operator first uses Gaussian filter to do data smoothing, then carries out Laplace non-directional operation, and makes the zero crossing points the edge points of image. This method can detect many false edges in local area where there are only slight changes of gray scale. Meantime, the interference immunity of operators is relatively weak [1].

In order to improve deficiencies of the above detection operators, in 1986, Canny [3] put forward Canny edge detection operator. Concurrently, he offered three strictest measurements of edge detection performance. Canny operator are widely used in pragmatic application in recent years. However, the operator itself still needs to be improved. First, since Canny detection operator uses Gaussian filter, when smoothing noise points, undoubtedly some edge information will get lost. Besides, during the process of using Canny operators, the high and low thresholds which can determine accuracy of edge detection need to be preset manually according to transcendental knowledge, which makes the result of detection highly subjective.

This article aims to improve the two disadvantages mentioned above, as a result, an improved self-adaptive Canny edge detection algorithm with high precision can be acquired. This algorithm is characterized by no human intervention, high edge detection accuracy, self-adaption and so forth. Consequently, it has better effect in practical application areas, such as pedestrian detection and vehicle detection.

2   Traditional Canny Edge Detection Principle

2.1   Canny Operator Detection Procedure

Gaussian Filter. Affected by factors such as image acquisition equipment, compression and decompression operation, the image inevitably will have random noises. Therefore, in order to eliminate noise points' disturbance to edge information and negative influence to subsequent image processing, filtering operation at this step is considered very important. Filter function used by Canny operation is:

$$G(x, y, \sigma) = \frac{1}{2\pi\sigma} e^{(-\frac{x^2+y^2}{\sigma^2})} \tag{1}$$

Calculating Gradient Magnitude and Direction. Using Sobel operator to calculate first order differential G_x in the x direction of each pixel point and first order differential G_y in the y direction of each pixel point, and then using formulas (2) and (3) to calculate gradient value $M(x, y)$ and gradient direction $\theta(x, y)$ of each pixel point.

$$M(x, y) = [G_x^2 + G_y^2]^{0.5} \tag{2}$$

$$\theta(x, y) = \arctan(G_y/G_x) \tag{3}$$

Non-maximum Suppression. In detection of Canny operator, the purpose of this step is to satisfy single-pixel edge response measurement, and guarantee the single-pixel character of outline. It can determine whether a point is edge point by seeking the maximum in the θ direction in 3×3, 8-direction area at (x, y). If $M(x, y)$ is the local maximum value in the θ direction, then this point is edge point.

Double Threshold Selection. Canny operator presets high and low threshold T_{high} and T_{low} and traverses gradient image processed by non-maximum suppression. The point with a gradient value larger than T_{high} will be regarded as strong edge point. It contains very few of false edge points, but will cause edge discontinuities. Therefore, searching rest local maximum points to fill spaces between strong edge points is needed, which will make the outline of image more consistent. We can see that the selection of high and low threshold can impose great impact on results of detection. If the setting of T_{high} is too big, many edge points will be missed; but if the setting is too small, lots of useless false edges will be detected. Consequently, the manual setting of high and low thresholds greatly reduces flexibility and robustness of Canny operator.

3 The Canny Edge Detection Based on Anisotropic Filtering

Traditional Canny operator uses binary Gaussian function as filter. This filtering method has good smoothing and suppressing effect on random noises following Gaussian distribution, but also has smoothing effect on image edges, which causes partial losses of outline information, thereby interfering the judgment of subsequent edge points. In addition, Gaussian filter will make the gradient value of the whole picture more centralized compared to the original picture. Gradient values of each pixel point will be reduced, making the differentiation between edge points and non edge points decrease, which brings certain difficulties to selection of high and low thresholds. In order to suppress noise points and at the same time preserve image edge information as much as possible, this article carries out filter operation by treating image edge zone and smoothing zone differently.

3.1 Edge Zone

Edge zone is the area where gradient values change greatly and edges are included. For this zone, this article adopts anisotropic filtering. So-called anisotropic means using different Gaussian filtering scales in x and y direction. The formula is as follow

$$G(x, y, \sigma_x, \sigma_y) = \frac{1}{2\pi\sigma_x\sigma_y} e^{\left(-\frac{x^2+y^2}{\sigma_x\sigma_y}\right)} \tag{4}$$

In it, σ_x, σ_y are standard deviations of Gaussian distribution in x and y direction respectively.

In order to conduct weak smoothing in the edge gradient direction, strong smoothing should be conducted in the edge tangential direction. This method rotates binary Gaussian body θ degrees (in the pixel point gradient direction) along the z axis, which makes oval short axis direction of Gaussian function's projection on xy surface equal to gradient direction of this pixel point, thus we can work out filter operator function:

$$G(d_1, d_2, \sigma_x, \sigma_y) = \frac{1}{2\pi\sigma_x\sigma_y}e^{(-\frac{d_1^2+d_2^2}{\sigma_x\sigma_y})} \tag{5}$$

In which, d_1 and d_2 are the distance between points and u axis and distance between points and v axis after rotation respectively.

In xy coordinate system, function of straight line u is $y = x \tan\theta$, function of straight line v is $y = -\frac{1}{\tan\theta}x$. According to the distance formula between points and lines, we can know:

$$d_1 = \frac{|x \tan\theta - y|}{\sqrt{(\tan\theta)^2 + 1}} \tag{6}$$

$$d_2 = \frac{|-x\frac{1}{\tan\theta} - y|}{\sqrt{(\frac{1}{\tan\theta})^2 + 1}} \tag{7}$$

According to formulas (6) and (7), we can know $d_1^2 = (x \sin\theta - y \cos\theta)^2$, $d_2^2 = (x \cos\theta + y \sin\theta)^2$, then we substitute formula (5) and get anisotropic filtering operator expression:

$$G(d_1, d_2, \sigma_x, \sigma_y) = \frac{1}{2\pi\sigma_x\sigma_y}e^{(-\frac{(x \sin\theta - y \cos\theta)^2 + (x \cos\theta + y \sin\theta)^2}{\sigma_x\sigma_y})} \tag{8}$$

Figure 1 shows images of original Gaussian operator and anisotropic Gaussian operator:

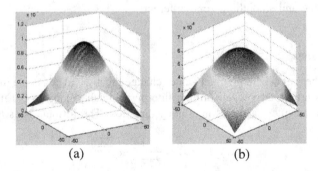

(a)   (b)

Fig. 1. Anisotropic Gaussian function projection. (a) Anisotropic Gaussian function. (b) Original Gaussian function

When it comes to determining smoothing scale σ_u and σ_v in two directions, one simple method is to use IDS model [4] proposed by Cornsweet and other experts according to Human Visual System. Its scale is identified as $\sigma^2 = \frac{1}{I(x,y)}$ ($I(x,y)$ is the normalized pixel value). Then we obtain short scale axis according to a certain proportion relationship between short scale axis and long scale axis, and use convolution kernel generated on this basis to conduct convolution operation on the image.

4 Canny High and Low Thresholds Self-adaptive Confirmation Based on Genetic Algorithm and OTSU

4.1 Gradient Magnitude Maximum Between-Cluster Variance Based on High and Low Thresholds

The self-adaptive confirmation process of Canny operator high and low thresholds aims to seek best high and low threshold combination. This article will adopt Otsu method to evaluate the rationality and the degree of excellence of high and low thresholds selected.

In Canny operator, high and low thresholds divide gradient value sets after images have been sequenced into three subsets T_1, T_2, and T_3, and they respectively consist of gradient values satisfying $x_i > T_{high}$, $T_{low} < y_i < T_{high}$ and $z_i < T_{low}$. The Otsu method uses variance yields obtained according to these three subsets to describe classification degree of this high and low threshold.

Specific procedures are as follows:

(1) Utilizing Sobel operator to calculate image gradient value T'.

(2) Sequencing T' in descending order, deleting repeated gradient values, only keeping different gradient values, and at the same time counting the frequency of each value occurring in T', to get gradient set T and frequency set *num*.

(3) Calculating frequency $\frac{num[i]}{sum}$ of each gradient value (*sum* is the total number of pixel points).

(4) According to high and low thresholds to divide set T and obtaining subsets T_1, T_2 and T_3.

(5) Calculating average value $e_1 = \dfrac{\sum\limits_{i=1}^{M_1} x_i p_i}{\sum\limits_{i=1}^{M_1} p_i}$, $e_2 = \dfrac{\sum\limits_{i=1}^{M_2} y_i q_i}{\sum\limits_{i=1}^{M_2} q_i}$ and $e_3 = \dfrac{\sum\limits_{i=1}^{M_3} z_i f_i}{\sum\limits_{i=1}^{M_3} f_i}$ of each subset.

In which, M_1, M_2 and M_3 are respectively numbers of elements contained in corresponding subset; p_i, q_i and f_i are frequencies of each gradient value in corresponding subset.

(6) Calculating expected value of set $T e = \sum\limits_{i=1}^{sum} \dfrac{num[i]}{sum} T[i]$.

(7) Calculating between-cluster variance $\sigma = (e_1 - e)^2 \sum\limits_{i=1}^{M_1} p_i + (e_2 - e)^2 \sum\limits_{i=1}^{M_2} q_i + (e_3 - e)^2 \sum\limits_{i=1}^{M_3} f_i$.

4.2   Genetic Algorithm Based on Between-Cluster Variance Evaluation Function

Genetic algorithm is a simulation of biological evolution process. Basically, it is a global optimization search algorithm and has advantages of global optimization, simple algorithm train of thought, high efficiency and so on. Therefore, this article uses genetic algorithm to determine self-adaptive high and low threshold of Canny operator.

Main steps are as follows:

(1) Initial population production. Initial population consists of a certain number of chromosome coding. This article adopts real coding method, and randomly generates the high and low threshold combination within the scope between the maximum gradient value and the minimum gradient value in the image.
(2) Fitness value calculation. This article uses between-cluster variance Otsu as fitness function to calculate fitness value of each individual.
(3) Selection operator. Calculating fitness probability of each individual and cumulative probability according to fitness value; making use of Russian roulette to conduct selection operation on initial population. The higher the individual fitness value, the higher the probability of being selected to be inherited to the next generation.
(4) Genetic recombination. Conducting gene exchange on individuals of population according to fixed crossover probability P_c to guarantee diversity of population. This article adopts single point crossover method.
(5) Genetic mutation. Conducting gene mutation on individuals of population according to fixed mutation probability P_m and the positions of mutation are generated randomly.

Repeating the above steps until the termination conditions are satisfied and sequencing the terminated population in descending order according to fitness value.

5   Experiment Results and Analysis

5.1   Influence of Anisotropic on Canny Edge Detection

This article uses genetic algorithm based on Otsu evaluation function to conduct high and low threshold combination search on Lena image, in which the parameters used by genetic algorithm are: number of initial population 100, number of iterations 50, crossover rate $P_c = 0.25$, mutation rate $P_m = 0.15$. The best combination eventually got is $T_{high} = 227$, $T_{low} = 84$, and the maximum between-cluster variance is $\sigma = 3833.1335$.

Substituting the above high and low thresholds into Canny operator and traditional operator in this article, and then respectively conducting edge detection on the image of Lena. The detection results are shown in Fig. 2.

As can be seen from detection results, although traditional Canny operator adopts the same high and low thresholds (227, 84) as improved Canny operator utilizing anisotropic filtering does, the detection results obtained are obviously different from

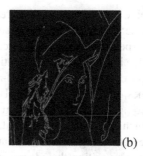

(a) Canny detection without anisotropic filtering   (b) Algorithm in this article

Fig. 2. Influence of anisotropic filtering on Canny operator

each other. The edge detection results in Fig. 2(a) involve more false edges and noise points, and the outline is jagged, for example we can see from the detection effects in the eye and hair region, there is much impure substance, which does harm to the future processing of outline characteristics.

5.2 Influence of Self-adaptive Thresholds on Canny Edge Detection

Respectively using traditional Canny operator involving anisotropic smoothing (anisotropic filtering, and high and low thresholds are set to 200, 40), reference [5] operator (anisotropic filtering, and high and low thresholds are set to 227, 113) and the improved Canny operator in this article (anisotropic filtering, and high and low thresholds are set to 227, 84) to conduct edge detection on the image of Lena in Fig. 3, and the results are shown in Fig. 3.

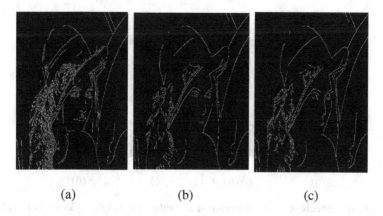

(a)   (b)   (c)

Fig. 3. Canny edge detection under different settings of high and low thresholds. (a) Traditional algorithm involving anisotropic smoothing. (b) Reference [5] algorithm. (c) Algorithm in this article.

Traditional Canny algorithm requires setting high and low thresholds manually. However, the setting is often not suitable for the current environment if it is made according to experience. Under this circumstance, it is easy to increase false edges or miss lots of edge information and the anti-interference ability is weak. The reference [5] algorithm requires high thresholds self-adaptive confirmation, and the low threshold will be 0.5 times of the high threshold. The detection results evidently miss lots of edge information compared to the algorithm in this article, which leads to loss of edge information such as folding on the hat, hence hindering the post-processing of the image. As a result, the algorithm in this article has better anti-interference ability, and at the same time can position the edges accurately without losing any edge information. Furthermore, it is responded by single pixels, which contributes to stronger detail expression. The overall detection performance and effects are better than traditional Canny operator involving anisotropic smoothing and the improved algorithm in reference [5].

5.3   The Detection Effects of Improved Canny Operator in Pedestrian Detection Image

According to the above experiment procedure with regard to the image of Lena, conducting edge detection on the image of pedestrian (Fig. 4(a)) used in pedestrian detection application, we will get the best high and low thresholds 313, 122, and the maximum between-cluster variance is 10935. The comparison of detection effects is in Fig. 4.

We can see from Fig. 4 that the detection results of traditional Canny operator include many false edges, and the outline includes many noise points, which would lay a negative influence on next step processing of pedestrian detection. However, the detection result of reference [5] operator loses part of the outline. This loss in detection is not good for further processing. The algorithm in this article has a high retention of outline information and a relatively better edge extraction effect.

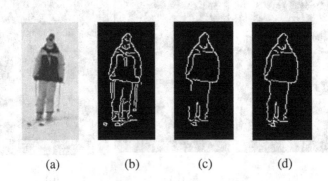

(a)   (b)   (c)   (d)

Fig. 4. Detection effects of different detection algorithm. (a) Original picture. (b) Traditional operator. (c) Reference [5] operator. (d) Operator in this article

6 Conclusion

In order to improve accuracy and self-adaptability of Canny operator edge detection, this article first uses Anisotropic filtering to improve Canny operator original Gaussian filters, trying to keep edge information as much as possible while smoothing noises. Then for defects brought about by setting high and low thresholds manually, this article uses genetic algorithm based on Otsu evaluation function to search for the best high and low threshold combination, which can avoid inaccuracy of manually-set thresholds in traditional Canny operator and improve the gradient classification ability of high and low thresholds. Experiment results show that, the detection results of this method have advantages of smooth and dedicate edge character, high precision, self-adaption and so on. Number of false edges has been reduced, and simultaneously the missing detection of real edges is also decreased. Therefore, the algorithm in this article has certain robustness and is worthy of being promoted. It can be applied in areas like pedestrian detection and so forth. Although this article enhances the performance of edge detection greatly, there are still places that need further improvement. The parameters used in the experiment which utilizes genetic algorithm to conduct search for best combination are set according to transcendental knowledge, and at a later stage we can determine more suitable parameters of genetic algorithm in edge detection through experiments.

References

1. Wang, Z., Wu, F.: Inertial product energy and edge detection. Chin. J. Comput. **32**(11), 2212–2219 (2009)
2. Feng, K., Zhu, M., Zhong, Y., Fan, L.: An improved Canny edge detection AGT algorithm. Comput. Appl. Softw. **29**(3), 265–266 (2012)
3. Canny, J.: A computational approach to edge detection. IEEE Trans. Pattern Anal. Mach. Intell. **8**(6), 679 (1986)
4. Wang, H., Zhang, K., Li, Y.: Anisotropic Gaussian filtering for infrared image. J. Infrared Millim. Waves **24**(2), 110–111 (2005)
5. Zhang, Z., Xi, J., Liu, Y.: Canny operator study based on GCV criteria and Otsu. Comput. Sci. **40**(6), 279–282 (2013)
6. Huang, J., Chen, B.: An optimal algorithm of edge detection based on Canny. Comput. Simul. **27**(4), 252–255 (2010)
7. Li, M., Yan, J., Li, G., Zhao, J.: Self-adaptive Canny operator edge detection technique. J. Harbin Eng. Univ. **28**(9), 1002–1007 (2007)
8. Lian, R., Wang, W.: Anisotropic diffusion and adaptive smoothing algorithm. Comput. Eng. Appl. **49**(20), 141–144 (2013)
9. Wang, N., Zhao, H., Ju, S., Du, H.: An improved Canny edge detection self-adaptive algorithm. J. Sichuan Univ. (Nat. Sci. Ed.) **51**(3), 479–482 (2014)
10. Health, D.M., Sarkar, S., Sanocki, T.: A robust visual method for assessing the relative performance of edge-detection algorithms. IEEE Trans. Pattern Anal. Mach. Intell. **19**(12), 1338–1358 (1997)

11. Chen, Y., Zhu, C.: Improved edge detection algorithm based on Canny operator. Comput. Appl. Softw. **25**(8), 51–53 (2008)
12. Geng, H., Luo, M., Hu, F.: Improved self-adaptive edge detection method based on Canny. In: 2013 Fifth International Conference on Intelligent Human-Machine Systems and Cybernetics, Hangzhou, China (2003)

An Algorithm of Detecting Moving Foreground Based on an Improved Gaussian Mixture Model

Mingjie Wang[1], Jesse S. Jin[1,2(✉)], Xianfeng Han[1], Wei Jiang[1],
Yifei Jing[1], Lei Gao[2], and Liping Xiao[2]

[1] School of Computer Software, Tianjin University, Tianjin 300000, China
{wang_major, hanxianf, jiangweitju}@163.com,
jinsheng@tju.edu.cn, lovejing0306@foxmail.com
[2] Beijing Aerospace Institute of Automatic Control, Beijing 100085, China
{thrstone, xlp027}@sina.com

Abstract. Objective: The technique of detecting moving regions has been playing an important role in computer vision and intelligent surveillance. Gaussian mixture models provide an advanced modeling approach for us. Although this method is very effective, it is not robust when there are some lighting changes and shadows in the scenes. This paper proposes a mixture model based on gradient images. **Method:** We firstly calculate gradient images of a video stream using the Scharr operator. We then mix RGB and gradient, and use a morphological approach to remove noise and connect moving regions. To further reduce false detection, we make an AND operation between two modeling results and result in final moving regions. **Result**: Finally, we use three video streams for analysis and comparison. Experiments show that this method has effectively avoided false detection regions resulting from lighting change and shadow, and improves the accuracy of detection. **Conclusion**: The approach demonstrates its promising characteristics and is more applicable in real-time detection.

Keywords: GMM (Gaussian mixture Model) · Gradient image · Scharr operator · Sobel · Morphological · AND operation

1 Foreword

In area of computer vision, the moving foreground detection is the foundation of intelligent surveillance, and its accuracy will influence the subsequent processes [1] including target tracking, object classification, etc. Moving foreground detection is about detecting the moving area in a video stream according to certain characteristics of video sequences. Only on this can the feature extraction of target and pattern recognition be conducted, which makes advanced image analysis and interpretation possible. Therefore, the study on foreground detection algorithms has significant importance [2].

The advanced background modeling methods mainly include average background model, nuclear density model, Gaussian mixture model (GMM) and so on. Nowadays, the GMM brought forward by Grimson and Stauffer in 1999 should be the most widely

© Springer Science+Business Media Singapore 2016
T. Tan et al. (Eds.): IGTA 2016, CCIS 634, pp. 125–136, 2016.
DOI: 10.1007/978-981-10-2260-9_15

used and most effective one. In the Gaussian mixture model, every state is demonstrated by a Gaussian process function [4] and is an expansion of single Gauss distribution. The single Gauss model regards each individual pixel in video sequences as an independent random variable and assumes they all follow Gauss distribution. The single Gauss model to a certain degree improves the deficits of traditional background modeling method like background subtraction method. However, in actual scene, pixels are usually in the form of multi-modal. Consequently, Grimson and other experts present that each pixel should follow a mixed Gauss distribution. The part with high weight in the Gauss distribution represents background area, while the part with low weight represents the moving area.

The GMM effectively improves deficits of low-level modeling methods and is robust with respect to repetitively moving background area, detection of slowly moving target, etc. However, under the influence of sudden change of illumination and shadows formed because objects are shaded, standard mixture model will mistake the background detection for foreground. In order to solve this problem, this article raises the Gaussian Mixture Model based on gradient images (G-GMM) which integrates with traditional Gaussian Mixture Model based on RGB (GMM) to form a new background model. This combines advantages of both by keeping the complete moving areas at the same time effectively eliminating disturbance of changes of illumination as well as shadows, which greatly enhances accuracy and stability of moving foreground detection.

2 Traditional GMM

Traditional GMM regards each pixel of video sequence as a random variable and assumes they all follow the mixed distribution consisting of K single Gauss distribution. Five fixed example pixels are taken from the experimental video LabText.avi, and the RGB value is sampled in the first 400 frames. Then the weighted sum of R, G, B for all samples is drawn in a coordinate graph, as in Fig. 1.

A typical mixed model assumes pixels are independent of each other and the whole video is a stable randomized procedure. The probability density function is as follows:

$$P(X_t) = \sum_{i=1}^{K} w_i^t \eta(X_t, \mu_i^t, \Sigma_i^t) \tag{1}$$

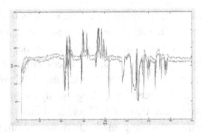

Fig. 1. The weighted sum of RGB for five example pixels in the video sequence (0.299R + 0.587G + 0.114B)

In which X_t is the pixel value of the corresponding pixel at time of t; K is the number of single Gaussian distribution in the mixture model, and the bigger K's value the better the classification effect; the amount of calculation will follow up and increase. Normally the value will be $3 \sim 5$. w_i^t is the weight estimation of ith Gaussian distribution at the time of t in the mixture model; μ_i^t is the mean value of ith Gaussian distribution at the time of t in the mixture model; Σ_i^t is the co-variance matrix of ith Gaussian distribution at the time of t in the mixture model; limited by the complication of calculation, the co-variance matrix usually is approximated to $\sigma_i^t I$ (that is, imagine three channels of pixels are independent of each other, and in which I is unit matrix), η is probability density function of single Gaussian distribution [5]

$$\eta(X_t, \mu, \Sigma) = \frac{1}{\sqrt{(2\pi)^n} \sqrt{|\Sigma|}} e^{-\frac{(X_t-\mu)^T \Sigma^{-1}(X_t-\mu)}{2}} \tag{2}$$

Based on Fig. 1 and formulas above, we can know the probability density function of mixture model is determined by weight, mean value and variance. Suppose the parameter vector of the model is $\theta(w_1, \mu_1, \sigma_1, w_2, \mu_2, \sigma_2 \ldots w_K, \mu_K, \sigma_K)$. The process of Gaussian mixture background modeling is actually the process of constantly estimating and updating parameter vector θ.

In multivariate statistics, the common method used for parameter estimation is the Maximum Likelihood Estimation Method; however during the background modeling, pixel value X is the only observation data that can be used. The classification number of this pixel value cannot be observed, and the incomplete data when looking for the maximum value of Likelihood function will lead to a transcendental equation with plural roots. It is caused by the fuzziness between the observation data X and its matching distribution sequence number. As a result, after introducing the hidden data Y to make up a complete data pair (X, Y), we use EM method of calculation to conduct parameter estimation and can get the updating formula of weight w_k^t

$$w_k^t = (1 - \alpha)w_k^{t-1} + \alpha L_k^t \tag{3}$$

In which α is the learning rate of the mixture model and determines the speed of background modeling. If it is set too big, the iteration will get over the optimal value making the algorithm fail to converge. If it is set too small, the convergence rate will be slowed down resulting in higher detection error rate. When new pixel values match with the Kth distribution $L_k^t = 1$, or $L_k^t = 0$; the weight of K distribution is adjusted in the process of iteration by using formula (3) and new pixel values. When new pixel values match with the Kth distribution of the mixture model, the mean value and variance of this distribution will be updated according to formulas (4) and (5)

$$\mu_t = (1 - \rho)\mu_{t-1} + \rho X_t \tag{4}$$

$$\sigma_t = (1 - \rho)\sigma_{t-1} + \rho(X_t - \mu_t)^T(X_t - \mu_t) \tag{5}$$

In which, ρ is another learning rate, $\rho = \alpha\eta(X_t|\mu_k, \sigma_k)$ [5]. If there is no distribution matching with X_t in the present mixture model, the Gaussian distribution with the minimum weight will be replaced by new Gaussian distribution with an mean of X_t and at the same time one larger variance and smaller weight of its will be initialized. The rest mean value and variance of Gaussian distribution remain and only the weight is attenuated. Then each weight will go through normalization processing [6], and each Gaussian distribution will be sequenced from high to low according to priority $\left(p_k^t = \frac{w_k^t}{\sigma_k^t}\right)$, then a judgment threshold λ will be set. The weight of the sorted Gaussian distribution will be accumulated from the maximum value and when $\sum_{i=1}^{N} w_i^t \geq \lambda$, the accumulation stops. At that time, we believe the first N distributions feature background pixels, thereby constructing new background model [7].

The above process is the traditional Gaussian Mixture Model based on RGB. Compared to low-level modeling method such as background subtraction method, it has better performance in terms of foreground detection. This model can not only update background adaptively, but also allow repetitive moving areas to be existed in the background. Although the moving background will be identified as foreground when it enters the scene, staying for a longer time, it will be absorbed and turned into background pixel. Unfortunately, in practical application, there is always sudden illumination change and shading. The Grimson's GMM under this circumstance will result in wrong foreground detection, as illustrated in Fig. 2.

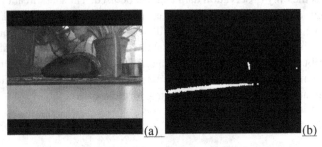

(a) original picture of video sequence 1

(b) false foreground detection caused by illumination changes

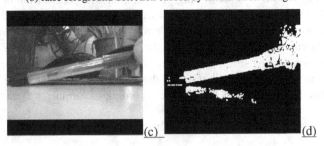

(c) original picture of video sequence 2

(d) false detection caused by shadows

Fig. 2. False detection of the traditional GMM resulted from illumination changes and shadows

Figure 2 illustrates the deficiency of traditional GMM in practical application. In applications with strict requirements of detection accuracy, false detection caused by such as fire and smoke detection alarm system, illumination changes and shadows will lead to false alarm, and further unnecessary expenses.

3   Gradient Image

Gradient is a kind of feature descriptor which is identified as local discontinuity of pixels and is mainly used to feature sudden change of pixels, texture structure and so on. The gradient value of a pixel point in the image is the first-order differential of pixel function regarding coordinate of this point and is used to describe the speed of pixel value change. Now we only consider the special gradient in X and Y directions; the formula is in (6)

$$|\nabla I(x,y)| = \sqrt{\left[\frac{\partial I(x,y)}{\partial x}\right]^2 + \left[\frac{\partial I(x,y)}{\partial y}\right]^2} \tag{6}$$

In the image, the pixel function $I(x,y)$ is a discrete non-differentiable function, so we can only use approximation methods to approach its first-order differential in the X and Y directions. Common first-order differential operators mainly include Roberts operators, Prewitt operators, Sobel operators, Scharr operators and so forth, among which, Sobel operators are the most popular. Its essence is convolution operation. It is easy to calculate this kind of operators and the speed of processing is fast; besides, the cost of time and internal storage is low. A regular Sobel operator (the size of its core is 3×3) is defined as follows [9]:

$$\frac{\partial I(x,y)}{\partial x} = \left| \begin{array}{l} I(x+1,y+1) + 2I(x+1,y) + I(x+1,y-1) \\ -I(x-1,y+1) - 2I(x-1,y) - I(x-1,y-1) \end{array} \right| \tag{7}$$

$$\frac{\partial I(x,y)}{\partial y} = \left| \begin{array}{l} I(x-1,y-1) + 2I(x,y-1) + I(x+1,y-1) \\ -I(x-1,y+1) - 2I(x,y+1) - I(x+1,y+1) \end{array} \right| \tag{8}$$

According to the calculation of formulas (6), (7) and (8), we can get gradient values of each point in the image (single channel/three-channel). The size of the convolution kernel in a Sobel operator determines the accuracy of gradient calculation. Big kernels can better approach derivatives but the cost is high; small kernels are sensitive to noises [10]. In this article, we will analyze operators and how to choose the size of cores in the next section.

Creating image T with a similar size of original picture I and the same number of channels and making $T = |\nabla I(x,y)|$. T is called the gradient image of I, as illustrated in Fig. 3.

(a) original picture (b) gradient image based on Sobel operators (the size of core is 5*5)

Fig. 3. Gradient image

Compared to colored images, gradient images have the feature of not being easily influenced by illumination change, quantization noises, shadows, mild distortion of images and affine transformation etc. [11]. For example, when the weather in the video scene changes from sunny to cloudy, the pixel values of colored images will also change greatly. On the contrary, pixel values of corresponding gradient images will not be changed. The reasons are as follows.

Suppose the pixel changing amplitude caused by illumination change or shadows in the convolution area is ΔI. Here we assume the light evenly changes, then the pixel value in the areas changes to $I(x, y) + \Delta I$; introducing it into formulas (7) and (8), we can know

$$\frac{\partial[I(x,y) + \Delta I]}{\partial x} = \left| \begin{array}{c} I(x+1,y+1) + \Delta I + 2I(x+1,y) + 2\Delta I + I(x+1,y-1) + \Delta I \\ -I(x-1,y+1) - \Delta I - 2I(x-1,y) - 2\Delta I - I(x-1,y-1) - \Delta I \end{array} \right|$$

$$= \frac{\partial I(x,y)}{\partial x}$$

In the same way, $\frac{\partial[I(x,y) + \Delta I]}{\partial y} = \frac{\partial I(x,y)}{\partial y}$. As a result, theoretically the gradient value in the image influenced by balanced illumination will not change.

4   G-GMM Background Modeling

GMM Based on Sobel Gradient Images. The essence of Sobel operators is to conduct convolution operation at each pixel point. The common 3×3 convolution core is $\begin{bmatrix} -1 & 0 & 1 \\ -2 & 0 & 2 \\ -1 & 0 & 1 \end{bmatrix}, \begin{bmatrix} 1 & 2 & 1 \\ 0 & 0 & 0 \\ -1 & -2 & -1 \end{bmatrix}$. The size of a convolution core determines the accuracy of gradient calculation. The sizes Sobel operators support are $3 \times 3, 5 \times 5$ and 7×7. We can separately use these three convolution operations to get gradient image sequence and conduct GMM and foreground detection on this basis. The result is shown in Fig. 4.

GMM Based on Scharr Gradient Images. In Sobel operators, the weights of convolution cores are small, which makes the gradient calculation is easy to be influenced by noises and leads to unsatisfying accuracy. Therefore, we use Scharr filter to sole the inaccuracy caused by approximation of 3×3 Sobel operator gradients. The Scharr filter is as fast as Sobel filter, but the accuracy is higher [12]. The convolution cores of

(a1) original pictures; (a2) GMM based on 7×7 core gradients; (a3) GMM based on RGB

(b1) original pictures; (b2) GMM based on 5×5 core gradients; (b3) GMM based on RGB

(c1) original pictures; (c2) GMM based on 3×3 core gradients; (c3) GMM based on RGB

Fig. 4. Three GMMs based on Sobel operators having different core sizes

Scharr operators are $\begin{bmatrix} -3 & 0 & 3 \\ -10 & 0 & 10 \\ -3 & 0 & 3 \end{bmatrix}$, $\begin{bmatrix} 3 & 10 & 3 \\ 0 & 0 & 0 \\ -3 & -10 & -3 \end{bmatrix}$. The gradient images in video sequences can be calculated by using Scharr operators, see formula (9), which can also be used to conduct GMM and detect moving foreground. The result is shown in Fig. 5.

$$|\nabla I(x,y)| = 0.5 \times \left[\frac{\partial I(x,y)}{\partial x}\right] + 0.5 \times \left[\frac{\partial I(x,y)}{\partial y}\right] \tag{9}$$

From Fig. 5, we can know, the foreground detection algorithm based on Scharr gradient images has the benefits of being resistant to illumination changes, shadows and so forth just like the foreground detection algorithm based on 5 × 5 Sobel gradient images. In addition, the former has better noise-resistance than the latter, which leads to less false detection points. Therefore, in this experiment, we will use Scharr operators to calculate gradient image sequence.

Morphological Filter AND Operation. This article first carries out two conductive erosion calculation on foreground detection results based on gradient images, eliminates most isolated false detection points, and then uses one dilation calculation to connect moving areas making the internal part of targets more substantial and well connected, which also facilitates further AND operation. The results of morphological filtering are shown in Fig. 6, after morphological filtering, foreground detection

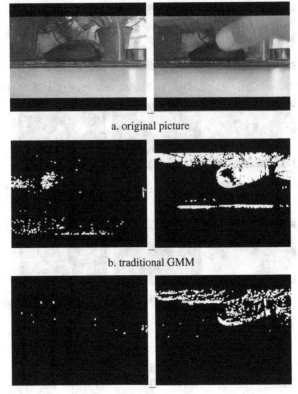

a. original picture

b. traditional GMM

c. G-GMM based on Scharr operators

Fig. 5. G-GMM

algorithm based on G-GMM can eliminate most isolated false detection points, meantime keep the moving connected region and enhance the accuracy of foreground detection.

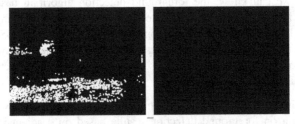

a traditional GMM foreground detection

b GMM foreground detection based on gradient images (including morphology filter)

Fig. 6. The effect of morphology filter

The morphology filter eliminates most noises in G-GMM detection results. When the video scene is relatively simple, it has good detection effect and nearly no false detection points. When the scene is complicated, some noises still exist due to limitation of gradient calculation accuracy, but it still has strong robustness to influence of illumination and shadows. In order to further eliminate false detection points, we combine the detection result of traditional GMM and G-GMM, keeping the high accuracy of foreground detection and eliminating shadow detection. Assume the foreground detection result of traditional GMM is $T(x, y)$, and the result of G-GMM is $G(x, y)$. The final result is $F(x, y)$. Combining two results in AND operation: $F(x, y) = T(x, y) \cap G(x, y)$, then we can get the final detection result.

Improved GMM Flow Chart. The improved Gaussian Mixture foreground detection flow is shown in Fig. 7 [14].

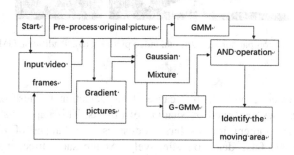

Fig. 7. The process of improved Gaussian Mixture Models

5 Experiment and Analysis

In this experiment, the initial value of learning speed in GMM is preset as 0.01 and Scharr operators are used in gradient image calculation. Three videos are compared in the following pictures and the video information can be found in Table 1.

Table 1. Information of experimental videos

Name of video	Source	Format	Resolution	Type
original_view_40	Documents [15]	avi	180*144	Outdoors
LabFire	VisiFire	avi	320*240	Indoors
LabText	Self-collected	avi	320*240	Indoors

Carrying out moving foreground detection on three videos in Table 1 by using traditional GMM and models in this article respectively. The results are shown in Fig. 8.

Figure 8b shows results of foreground detection of GMM based on RGB. There are lots of false detection points in both video 1 and video 3. The results of video 1 prove the algorithm in this article has higher stability because in a stable background video, the learning speed of gradient background is faster than RGB [16]. The traditional

Fig. 8. Experimental comparison (a). Original video pictures; (b). Traditional GMM; (c). Method in this article

GMM used in video 2 and video 3 causes false detection because of illumination changes and shadows generated by shading of objects. This paper makes use of the characteristic that gradient images have robustness to changes of illumination to eliminate the above false detection effectively. At the same time, it makes use of morphological operation AND operation to guarantee the accuracy of foreground detection effectively, and has certain robustness indoors and outdoors. In order to explain the false detection rate of this algorithm more accurately, we run statistics on the first 100 frames in the above three videos and calculate relative detection rate and get the following result.

From the comparison in Fig, 9, we can see the method of this article represented by dotted lines all show excellent performance in foreground detection in three videos used in the experiment. It can both overcome the detection deficiency of traditional Gaussian Mixture Model and obtain high accuracy. Besides, it also has fast convergence rate [17].

Although the method in this article solves the problems of traditional GMM when illumination changes and shadows occur and effectively reduces false detection rate of moving foreground, it has some disadvantages. First, the algorithm adopts gradient approximation Scharr operators when doing the gradient image calculation. When facing complicated scenes, noises still exist. Next, the time this algorithm cost is three times more than that of traditional algorithm. When the video pixels are high, the real-time is what we need to consider [18]; however, the real-time in the video used in the experiment can be guaranteed. In this day and age when hardware resources are relatively rich, the requirement of practical application for accuracy of foreground detection is higher in order to avoid huge waste caused by poor detection. To sum up, the detection model proposed by this paper is more suitable for real-time detection of moving foreground.

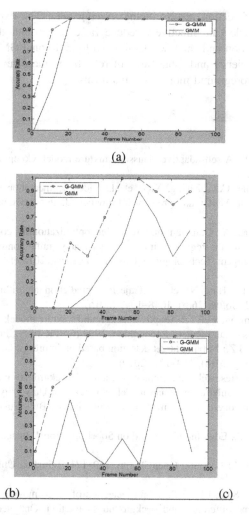

Fig. 9. The comparison of detecting accuracy rate (a). Video 1 (original_view_40); (b). Video 2 (LabFire); (c). Video 3(LabText)

6 Conclusion

Compared to some low-level foreground detection methods like background subtraction method, traditional Gaussian mixture model has higher detection efficiency; however, it still cannot solve the problems generated by illumination changes and shadows. In order to solve this problem, this article proposes a G-GMM based on gradient images. First we use Scharr filter operators to calculate gradient image sequences, then conduct Gaussian mixture modeling according to sequences of original pictures and sequences of gradient images and also use morphology filter to carry out filtering and connecting operation on the initial results. In order to maintain accuracy of detection and eliminate shadows, we compare detection results of two models and finally obtain the detection results in the moving area. The experiment shows the method in this article can effectively reduce false foreground detection caused by changes of illumination and shadows. Compared to traditional GMM, this method has better detection efficiency and robustness, thereby being more suitable for application on actual moving foreground monitoring platforms.

References

1. Chen, Z., Ellis, T.: A self-adaptive Gaussian mixture model. Comput. Vis. Image Underst. **122**, 35–46 (2014)
2. Yuan, C.F., Wang, C.X., Zhang, X.G., et al.: Video segmentation of illumination abrupt variation based On MOGs and gradient information. J. Image Graph. **12**(11), 2068–2070 (2007)
3. Basri, I., Achamad, A.: Gaussian mixture models optimization for counting the numbers of vehicle by adjusting the region of interest under heavy traffic condition. In: International Seminar on Intelligent Technology and Its Applications, 2015 (ISITIA 2015), Surabaya (2015)
4. Qiao, S.J., Jin, K., Han, N., et al.: Trajectory prediction algorithm based on Gaussian mixture model. J. Softw. **26**(5), 1048–1049 (2015)
5. Stauffer, C., Grimson, W.E.L.: Adaptive background mixture models for real-time tracking. In: Computer Vision and Pattern Recognition, 1999 (CVPR 1999), Fort Collins, CO (1999)
6. Cui, W.P., Shen, J.Z.: Moving target detection based on improved Gaussian mixture model. Opto-Electron. Eng. **37**(4), 119–121 (2010)
7. Chen, X.Y.: The research and implementation of background modeling and updating algorithm based on mixture gaussian model. Northeastern University, Shenyang (2009)
8. Lei, L.Z.: On the edge detection method of digital image. Bull. Surv. Mapp. **40**(3), 40–41 (2006)
9. Lu, Z.Q., Liang, C.: Edge thinning based on Sobel operator. J. Image Graph. **5**(6), 516–518 (2000)
10. Yu, S.Q., Liu, R.Z.: Learning OpenCV, pp. 169–171. Tsinghua University Press, BeiJing (2009)
11. Pan, X.H., Zhao, S.G., Liu, Z.P., et al.: Detection of video moving objects by combining grads-based frame difference and background subtraction. Optoelectron. Technol. **29**(1), 34–36 (2009)
12. Meng, Y.F., OuYang, N., Mo, J.W., et al.: A shadow removal algorithm with Gaussian mixture model. Comput. Simul. **27**(1), 210–212 (2010)
13. Ma, Y.D., Zhu, W.F., An, S.X., et al.: Improved moving objects detection method based on Gaussian mixture model. Comput. Appl. **27**(10), 2544–2546 (2007)
14. He, K., Ju, S.G., Lin, T., et al.: Image denoising on TV numerical computation. J. Univ. Electron. Sci. Technol. China **42**(3), 459–461 (2013)
15. Gorelick, L., Blank, M., Shechtman, E., et al.: Actions as space-time shapes. IEEE Trans. Pattern Anal. Mach. Intell. **29**(12), 2247–2248 (2007)
16. Fan, W.C., Li, X.Y., Wei, K., et al.: Moving target detection based on improved Gaussian mixture model. Comput. Sci. **42**(5), 286–288 (2015)
17. Feng, W.H., Gong, S.R., Liu, C.P.: Foreground detection based on improved Gaussian mixture model. Comput. Eng. **37**(19), 179–182 (2011)
18. Sun, D., Liu, J.F., Tang, X.L.: Edge detection based on density gradient. Chin. J. Comput. **32**(2), 299–302 (2009)

Structured Sparsity via Half-Quadratic Minimization

Jinghuan Wei[1], Zhihang Li[2], Dong Cao[2], Man Zhang[2($\boxtimes$)], and Cheng Zeng[1]

[1] Hebei University of Technology, Tianjin, China
{weijinghuan1991,zeng_ch}@126.com
[2] CaZ, Cas, Beijing, China
{lizhihang2016,dong.cao,zhangman}@nlpr.ia.ac.cn

Abstract. This paper proposes a general framework for the problem of structured sparsity via half-quadratic (HQ) minimization. Based on the theory of convex conjugacy, we firstly define an $l_{2,1}^{\varepsilon}$-norm and induce a family of penalty functions for structured sparsity. Then we build and discuss some important properties of these functions. By introducing the multiplicative auxiliary variable in HQ, we further reformulate the structured sparsity problem as an augmented half-quadratic optimization problem, and propose a general iteratively reweighted framework to alternately minimize the cost function. The proposed framework can be used in sparse representation, group sparse representation and multi-task joint sparse representation. Finally, in terms of the task of multi-biometric information fusion, we apply our proposed methods to obtain a novel fusion strategy, named structured fusion. Experimental results on the multi-biometric problems corroborate our claims and validate the proposed methods.

Keywords: Structured sparsity · Half-quadratic · Biometric

1 Introduction

The problem of sparse estimation has recently received much interest and become increasingly important in signal processing, computer vision and statistics. Based on the compressive sensing theory that a sparse signal can be represented by a small number of linear bases, robust sparse representation [18], group sparse representation [1], multi-task joint sparse representation [17,24], and structured sparse representation [12,13,19], have been proposed from different application scenarios in recent literature.

Over the past few years, a large family of algorithms have been developed to solve the sparse estimation problem, among which the iteratively reweighted least squares (IRLS) technique is commonly used. IRLS is first introduced in compressive sensing to find a sparse solution [3,4,20]. In [8,22], the iteratively reweighted strategy is further used to detect outliers for robust sparse representation. The authors in [6,7] harness a similar IRLS technique in low-rank matrix

© Springer Science+Business Media Singapore 2016
T. Tan et al. (Eds.): IGTA 2016, CCIS 634, pp. 137–148, 2016.
DOI: 10.1007/978-981-10-2260-9_16

recovery. Although these methods are developed based on various motivations, they can be almost summarized into a two-step alternate minimization: one step is to calculate weights via a minimizer function; the other is to solve a weighted sub-problem. In addition, since the weighting function of absolute function $|.|$ in l_1 and $l_{2,1}$ norms is unpredictable near the origin, a descending item ε is often used in sparse estimation [5]. To the best of our knowledge, there is still no a unified scheme to analyze and discuss the relationship between these different methods.

This paper aims to address the above problem from the theory of convex conjugacy [2,15], and build an iteratively reweighted optimization framework to solve the problem of structured sparsity via half-quadratic (HQ) optimization [15]. First, we harness the convex conjugacy theory to study structured sparsity induced norm. We define an $l_{2,1}^{\varepsilon}$ norm and induce a family of penalty functions for sparse estimation, which unifies previously used norms into a convex conjugacy framework. Second, based on the multiplicative form of HQ, we recast the problem of complicated structured sparsity as an augmented half-quadratic optimization problem. Third, we specify the proposed framework to solve the task of multi biometric information fusion, leading to a new fusion strategy, called structured fusion here. Moreover, considering that there are often occlusion and corruption in biometrics, we introduce an additional error item to control noise in structured fusion. Experimental results on several multi-biometric problems demonstrate our framework's effectiveness.

The main contributions of this work are two-fold:

(1) A family of penalty functions and a general optimization framework are proposed for structured sparsity, which are important in both theory and practice. This HQ framework not only unifies previous related studies within a common framework but also provides a general platform to develop new methods for sparse representation, group sparse representation and multi-task joint sparse representation.
(2) A new fusion strategy is proposed for multi-biometric information fusion. Different from feature-level or score-level fusion, our method can efficiently combine structure information during multi-biometric fusion. Experimental results show that structured fusion is useful in face synthesis, and multi-biometric recognition.

The remainder of this work is organized as follows. We begin with the study of structured sparsity inducing norms from convex conjugacy in Sect. 2. In Sect. 3, we propose a general optimization framework for structured sparse representation using HQ optimization, based on which a structure fusion method for multi-biometrics is proposed in Sect. 4. Section 5 validates our methods in terms of two different biometric applications. Finally, we summarize this paper and discuss future work in Sect. 6.

2 Structured Sparsity Inducing Norms

In this section, we first briefly review $l_{2,1}$-norm based structured sparsity. Then we specifically discuss the multiplicative forms of $l_{2,1}^\varepsilon$- and l_α-norm and their corresponding minimizer functions in HQ optimization, which induces a family of loss functions for structured sparsity.

2.1 $l_{2,1}$ Norm for Structured Sparsity

Suppose that there is a training set with K different tasks, each of which is indexed by $k \in \{1,\dots,K\}$ and defined on a training subset $X^k = [X_1^k,\dots,X_C^k] \in R^{d^k \times n^k}$ with C classes and an input query data $y^k \in R^{d^k}$. Here n^k and d^k are the number of training samples and the dimensionality of the k-th task respectively. And $N = \sum_{k=1}^K n^k$ is the total number of training samples.

In structured sparsity, $\mathcal{G}$ is assumed to be a subset of the power set of $\{1,\dots,N\}$ and satisfies $\bigcup_{G\in\mathcal{G}} G = \{1,\dots,N\}$. $\mathcal{G}$ is possible to be any structure because it is not necessarily a partition of $\{1,\dots,N\}$ [9]. The following $l_{2,1}$-norm is usually considered for structured sparsity,

$$\Omega(\omega) \doteq \sum_{G\in\mathcal{G}} (\sum_{j\in G} (\mathbf{p}_j^G)^2 \omega_j^2)^{\frac{1}{2}} = \sum_{G\in\mathcal{G}} \|\mathbf{p}_j^G \otimes \omega\|_2 \tag{1}$$

where $(\mathbf{p}^G)_{G\in\mathcal{G}}$ is a N-dimensional vectors such that $\mathbf{p}_j^G > 0$ if $j \in G$ and $\mathbf{p}_j^G = 0$ otherwise. If β^k is a linear representation w.r.t. the k-th task, $\omega \doteq [\beta^1;\dots;\beta^K] \in R^N$. Given a different setting of $\mathcal{G}$, we can obtain l_1 norm, group l_1 norm, hierarchical norms, and so on [9].

Considering that (1) mainly involves an $l_{2,1}$-norm and many methods in compressed sensing and sparse representation [3–5,20] often harness a parameter ε, we define a new $l_{2,1}^\varepsilon$-norm as an approximation to $l_{2,1}$-norm as follows,

$$l_{2,1}^\varepsilon \doteq \phi_\varepsilon(\|\beta\|_2) = \sqrt{\varepsilon + \|\beta\|_2^2} \tag{2}$$

2.2 A Family of Functions for Structured Sparsity

Before discussing $l_{2,1}^\varepsilon$-norm in (2), we first introduce the multiplicative form of HQ optimization. Based on the theory of convex conjugacy, one has the following lemma in HQ optimization,

Lemma 1. *Let $\phi(.)$ be a function satisfying six conditions in [15], there exists a dual potential function $\varphi(.)$ (or named conjugate function in [2]), such that*

$$\phi(x) = \inf_{q\in R} \{qx^2 + \varphi(q)\} \tag{3}$$

where q is determined by a minimizer function $\delta(.)$ with respect to $\phi(.)$ [15].

According to Lemma 1, we can reformulate a loss function $\phi(.)$ as a half-quadratic augmented form. In the following, we make use of Lemma 1 to derive different loss functions which are commonly used in structured sparsity. First, let $\Omega(\omega|\Lambda) \doteq \sum_{i=1}^{N} \phi_\varepsilon(\omega_i)$ and $\varepsilon \geq 0$, we have the following proposition.

Proposition 1. *For a fixed vector ω, we have the following multiplicative form of $\Omega(\omega|\Lambda)$,*

$$\Omega(\omega|\Lambda) = \min_q \sum_{i=1}^{n} (q_i \omega_i^2 + \varphi_\varepsilon(q_i)) \tag{4}$$

where q_i is an auxiliary variable in HQ and $\varphi_\varepsilon(.)$ is the dual potential function of $\phi_\varepsilon(.)$. The minimum of (4) is uniquely determined by $q_i = 1/\sqrt{\varepsilon + \|\omega_i\|_2^2}$.

Proof. For each ω_i, we have $\phi_\varepsilon(\omega_i) = \min_q \{q\omega_i^2 + \varphi_\varepsilon(q)\}$ according to (3). To sum all $\phi_\varepsilon(\omega_i)$ over i, we have (4). Since $\varepsilon \geq 0$ and $\sqrt{\varepsilon + \omega_i^2} \geq |\omega_i|$, we directly have $\|\omega\|_1 \leq \Omega(\omega|\Lambda)$. $\qquad\square$

Proposition 1 establishes a new proof and general analysis for $\Omega(\omega|\Lambda)$. The conjugated formulation in Proposition 1 has been widely used in compressed sensing from different viewpoints.

Considering $l_{2,1}^\varepsilon$-norm in (2) based on Lemma 1, we have the following proposition.

Proposition 2. *For a fixed vector β, we have the following multiplicative form of $l_{2,1}^\varepsilon$ norm,*

$$\sqrt{\varepsilon + \|\beta\|_2^2} = \min_q \left\{ q\|\beta\|_2^2 + \varphi_\varepsilon(q) \right\} \tag{5}$$

where q is an auxiliary variable in HQ. The minimum of (5) is uniquely determined by $q = 1/\sqrt{\varepsilon + \|\beta\|_2^2}$.

Proof. Substituting $\phi(.)$ and x in (3) by $\phi_\varepsilon(.)$ and $\|\beta\|_2$ respectively, we have (5). $\qquad\square$

Proposition 2 presents a novel and simple proof of conjugated formulation of $l_{2,1}^\varepsilon$-norm, which has been recently applied in robust feature selection [14] and subspace learning [10]. Proposition 2 provides a simple and general analysis, and builds a HQ relationship between different methods.

Third, considering l_α-norm, $\|\beta\|_\alpha = (\sum_{i=1}^{n} |\beta_i|^\alpha)^{1/\alpha}$, we have the the following HQ formulation.

Proposition 3. *For a fixed vector β, we have the following multiplicative form of l_α norm,*

$$\|\beta\|_\alpha = \min_z \left\{ \sum_{i=1}^{n} z_i \beta_i^2 + \sum_{i=1}^{n} z_i \varphi_\alpha(q_i)/q_i \right\} \tag{6}$$

where z_i and q_i are auxiliary variables in HQ, and $\varphi_\alpha(.)$ is the dual potential function of $\phi_\alpha(.)$. The minimum of (6) is uniquely determined by $z_i = \alpha |\beta_i|^{\alpha-2} \|\beta\|_\alpha^{1-\alpha}$.

Proof. The proof of this proposition based on ϕ_α is given in supplementary material.   □

In [10], Proposition 3 has been partly used to reformulate structured sparsity inducing norms to a half-quadratic form. Different from the lemma in [10], here Proposition 3 gives a half-quadratic reformulation of l_α norm from the viewpoint of the convex conjugacy [2].

The above three new propositions unify previous norms used in IRLS based compressive sensing algorithms into a common HQ framework. Based on both the theory of convex conjugacy and multiplicative form of HQ optimization, we can derive a family of penalty functions for structured sparsity.

3   Structured Sparse Representation

In this section, we first make a HQ analysis for the IRLS based sparse representation algorithm. Then we develop an efficient algorithm for structured sparse representation.

3.1   HQ Minimization for Sparse Representation

In compressed sensing, one often solves the following l_1 minimization problem to find the sparsest solution of an underdetermined linear system. Let $\phi(.)$ be a loss function which has a multiplicative form of HQ, we get the following minimization problem,

$$\min_\beta \sum_{i=1}^n \phi(\beta_i) \quad \text{s.t.} \quad X\beta = y \tag{7}$$

Based on Lemma 1, we have the augmented objective of (7)

$$\mathcal{J}(\beta, q) \doteq \sum_{i=1}^n q_i \beta_i^2 + \sum_{i=1}^n \varphi(q_i) \quad \text{s.t.} \quad X\beta = y \tag{8}$$

where $q = [q_1, \ldots, q_n]$ is an auxiliary vector in HQ and determined by the minimizer function $\delta(.)$ of $\phi(.)$. Then the optimization problem in (7) can be solved in an alternate minimization way,

$$q_i^t = \delta(\beta_i) \tag{9}$$

$$\beta^t = \arg\min_\beta \sum_i q_i^t \beta_i^2 \quad \text{s.t.} \quad X\beta = yeq : SF_a os \tag{10}$$

where t is the iteration number. To solve the constrained optimization problem in (10), we introduce Lagrange multipliers Λ and obtain the following Lagrangian function,

$$\mathcal{L}(\beta, q) = \beta^T Q\beta - \Lambda^T(X\beta - y) \tag{11}$$

where Q is an $n \times n$ diagonal matrix whose i-th diagonal entry is q_i. Setting the derivative of $\mathcal{L}(\beta, q, \varepsilon)$ with respect to β to zero, we obtain

$$\partial \mathcal{L}(\beta, q)/\partial \beta = 2Q\beta - X^T \Lambda = 0 \qquad (12)$$

Left multiplying both sides of (12) by XQ^{-1}, and using the equality constraint $X\beta = y$, we have:

$$2X\beta - XQ^{-1}X^T \Lambda = 0 \Rightarrow \Lambda = 2(XQ^{-1}X^T)^{-1}y \qquad (13)$$

Substitute (13) back into (12), we have analytic solution of (10): $\beta^* = Q^{-1}X^T(XQ^{-1}X^T)^{-1}y$. To reduce computational cost of matrix inverse, we can compute β^* by solving $Q^{-1}X^T((XQ^{-1}X^T)\backslash y)$.

In each iteration, it is easy to prove that β^* is always a feasible solution to the linear system $X\beta = y$ regardless of the value of Q. Minimizer function $\delta(.)$ punishes each coefficient in β until the algorithm converges. If the problem is analyzed to be sparse, the alternate minimization method in (9) and (10) will find the sparsest solution. Give a specific function $\phi(.)$, the minimization method becomes IRLS methods used in [4,5].

3.2 HQ Minimization for Structured Sparse Representation

Give a structured sparsity $\Omega(\omega) = \sum_G \phi_\varepsilon(\|\mathbf{p}^G \otimes \omega\|_2)$ in (1), one has the following multi-task objective,

$$\min_\omega \Omega(\omega) \quad \text{s.t. } X^k \beta^k = y^k \ (k \in \{1, \dots, K\}) \qquad (14)$$

Based on Proposition 2, we obtain the augmented minimization problem of (14),

$$\min_{\omega, q} \sum_G \{q^G \|\mathbf{p}^G \otimes \omega\|_2^2 + \varphi_\varepsilon(q^G)\} \qquad (15)$$
$$\text{s.t.} \quad X^k \beta^k = y^k, \quad k \in \{1, \dots, K\}$$

where $q = [q^G]_{G \in \mathcal{G}}$ is an auxiliary vector in HQ optimization and $\varphi_\varepsilon(.)$ is the dual potential function of $\phi_\varepsilon(.)$. We can distribute $[q^G]$ into each task, and rewrite (15) as follows,

$$\min_{[\beta^1, \dots, \beta^k]} \sum_k (\beta^k)^T Q_k \beta^k \qquad (16)$$
$$\text{s.t.} X^k \beta^k = y^k, \quad k \in \{1, \dots, K\}$$

where Q_k is an $n^k \times n^k$ diagonal matrix whose i-th diagonal entry is determined by q^G. According to (11), (12) and (13), we can derive the optimal solution of each task k,

$$\beta^{k*} = Q_k^{-1}(X^k)^T(X^k Q_k^{-1}(X^k)^T)^{-1}y^k \qquad (17)$$

Accordingly, we have a general minimization algorithm for structured sparsity. In each iteration, we determine the weights via the minimizer function of HQ, and then compute a sparse solution for each task according to (17). Algorithm 1 summarizes the alternate minimization procedure. We can also substitute $\phi_\varepsilon(.)$ in (14) with $\phi_\alpha(.)$ or other functions.

Algorithm 1. Half-quadratic structured sparsity

Input: X^k, y^k ($k \in \{1, \ldots, K\}$), and a structure G.
Output: $\beta^1, \ldots, \beta^K$

1: **repeat**
2:    **Weighted least squares step:**
      For each task k, compute
      $\beta^{k*} = Q_k^{-1}(X^k)^T(X^kQ_k^{-1}(X^k)^T)^{-1}y^k$
3:    **Half-quadratic step:**
      For each G, compute auxiliary variable,
      $q^G = \delta_\varepsilon(\|\mathbf{p}^G \otimes \omega\|_2)$ ($\omega = [\beta^{1*}; \ldots; \beta^{K*}]$)
4:    **Weighting step:**
      For each task k, compute Q_k according to all q^G.
5: **until** Converges

Given a special setting of $\Omega(\omega)$, we can obtain l_1-norm, l_{21}-norm and other norms for sparse estimation [13]. Based on the HQ analysis, we can build a relationship between different algorithms, and develop new iteratively reweighted methods based on different loss functions. In particular, experimental results and analysis in [14,15] show that HQ based methods are often substantially faster than gradient based ones.

4 Structured Fusion

In multi-biometric problems, one often needs to combine several biometrics to identify a person. In this section, we apply the general framework in Algorithm 1 to multi-biometric problems, resulting in a new fusion strategy, named structured fusion. Different from both feature-level and score-level fusion, our method can combine structure information during fusion of multi-biometrics. Due to occlusion and corruption in biometrics, we further introduce an error item to detect outliers, and accordingly have the following objective for structured fusion,

$$\min_{\beta, e} \ \Omega_\beta\left([\beta^1; \ldots; \beta^K]\right) + \Omega_e\left([e^1; \ldots; e^K]\right) \tag{18}$$

$$\text{s.t.} \ \ X^k\beta^k + e^k = y^k, \quad k \in \{1, \ldots, K\}$$

where $e^k \in R^{d^k}$, and $\beta^k = [\beta_1^k; \ldots; \beta_C^k]$ contains the representation coefficients in the k-th task. Note that there is no sparsity assumption on each e^k. If there are outliers that are significantly different from those data represented by $X^k\beta^k$, $\Omega_e(.)$ plays a role of robust M-estimators [8,25] and can naturally detect outliers. If outliers are sparse, e^k is also naturally sparse due to M-estimators.

For multi-biometric fusion, we consider a simple case of (18), i.e., structure $\Omega_\beta(.)$ is defined by class information and the noise item is independent. That is coefficients of all tasks belong to the same class are treated as a group (or structure). Then we have,

$$\min_{\beta,e} \sum_{c=1}^{C} \phi_\varepsilon(\|\beta_c\|_2) + \sum_{k=1}^{K} \|e^k\|_1 \tag{19}$$
$$\text{s.t.} X^k\beta^k + e^k = y^k, \quad k \in \{1,\ldots,K\}$$

where $\beta_c = [\beta_c^1;\ldots;\beta_c^K]$ contains the representation coefficients from the c-th class across different tasks. Instead of using the absolute function $|.|$, we harness $\phi_\varepsilon(.)$ in the l_1 norm in (19). Based on the HQ optimization, we have the following augmented cost function of (19),

$$\min_{\beta,e,p,q} \sum_{c=1}^{C} (q_c \|\beta_c\|_2^2 + \varphi_\varepsilon(q_c)) + \sum_{k=1}^{K} \sum_{j=1}^{d^k} (p_j^k(e_j^k)^2 + \varphi_\varepsilon(p_j^k))$$

$$\text{s.t.} \quad X^k\beta^k + e^k = y^k, \quad k \in \{1,\ldots,K\} \tag{20}$$

Let $\omega^k = [\beta^k;e^k] \in R^{(n^k+d^k)}$ and $A^k = [X^k\ I^k] \in R^{d^k \times (n^k+d^k)}$ where I^k is an identity matrix. We can rewrite (20) for each task k as,

$$\min_{\omega^k}(\omega^k)^T Q_k \omega^k \quad \text{s.t.} \quad A^k\omega^k = y^k \tag{21}$$

where Q_k is an $(n^k + d^k) \times (n^k + d^k)$ diagonal matrix whose diagonal entry is determined by p or q. The analytic solution of (21) is,

$$\omega^{k*} = Q_k^{-1}(A^k)^T(A^k Q_k^{-1}(A^k)^T)^{-1}y^k \tag{22}$$

It is easy to prove that $\omega^{k*} = [\beta^{k*};e^{k*}]$ always satisfies that $X^k\beta^{k*} + e^{k*} = y^k$. Algorithm 2 gives the alternate minimization method to solve (19).

The computational complexity of Algorithm 2 mainly lies in solving K linear system problems in (22). Fortunately, we observe that the K linear systems are independent such that we can easily extend Algorithm 2 to be parallel. As a result, the computational cost of Algorithm 2 is the same as that of solving a single sparse task.

Algorithm 2. Robust structured fusion via half-quadratic optimization

---

Input: X^k and y^k ($k \in \{1,\ldots,K\}$).
Output: $\beta^1,\ldots,\beta^K$ and $e^1,\ldots,e^K$
  1: **repeat**
  2:   **Weighted least squares step:**
       For each task k, computing
       $\omega^{k*} = Q_k^{-1}(A^k)^T(A^k Q_k^{-1}(A^k)^T)^{-1}y^k$
  3:   **Half-quadratic step:**
       For each auxiliary variable,
       $q^c = \delta_\varepsilon(\|\beta_c\|_2)$ and $p_j^k = \delta_\varepsilon(e_j^k)$
  4:   **Weighting step:**
       For each task k, computing Q_k according to all q^c and p_j^k.
  5: **until** Converges

---

5   Applications

In this section, we give two application examples of our structured fusion in Algorithm 2 and validate its sparsity and effectiveness.

5.1   Algorithms

By specifying different settings of Algorithm 2, we obtain three new robust methods for sparse estimation, namely,

Robust sparse coding (RSC-IRLS): If β_c has one item and $K = 1$, we will have a robust sparse coding method for robust sparse representation. Theoretically speaking, if there is a sparse solution, RSC-IRLS finds the same solution as [21].

Group sparsity (GS-IRLS): If we only specify that $K=1$ in Algorithm 2 (i.e., there is only one task), then we obtain a robust group sparse representation method.

Structured fusion (SF-IRLS): We directly use Algorithm 2 to solve multiple biometric tasks.

To make a distinction between our methods and previous ones, we use '-IRLS' to denote that the methods are based on an iteratively reweighted strategy. To make an approach be tractable and practical, we simplify the parameter setting and in particular make use of a hard value (i.e., $\varepsilon = 1e - 7$). The number of iterations is set to 20. As in [21,23], we use reconstruction error of each class (i.e., $\left\| X_c^k \beta_c^k - y^k \right\|_2$) to perform classification. Each data vector is normalized to have unit norm.

5.2   Face Synthesis for Biometric Forensics

In biometric forensics, one often needs to synthesize a face image from multiple clues. In our life, we also say that one person's eyes like another's meanwhile his/her nose likes other different person's. To simulate this scenario, we make use of different components of face images to synthesize a new face as in [11]. We have four tasks in this experiment. For the first three tasks, the input images are eyes, nose and jaw components from three different persons respectively. For the fourth task, the input image is a synthesis from the three components. The dimensions of image features for four tasks are 1058, 552, 966 and 2,576 respectively. For the first three tasks, the training set of each task contains 8 frontal face images without illumination variation from two sessions. The training set of the fourth task is composed of 4 frontal face images without illumination variation from the first session. Hence the training set of each task is different.

Figure 2(a) shows three different face images from a man and two women and their mean face image, facial component images and their synthesis face image. Figure 2(b) shows reconstructed face image by FS-IRLS and its corresponding sparse representation in the fourth task. We observe that the mean face of the three images seems to be from a man whereas the reconstructed face by FS-IRLS seems to be from a smiling woman. The two largest coefficients belong to the two

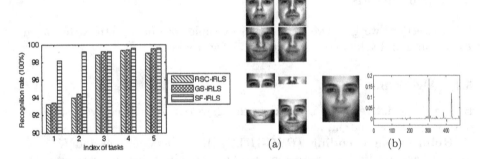

Fig. 1. Recognition rates of three sparse representation methods on fusion of multiple biometrics. The numbers 1, 2 and 3 on the x axis indicate three tasks. The numbers 4 and 5 indicate the mean and min operators of these three tasks respectively.

Fig. 2. (a) First row: three different face images and their mean face images. Second row: facial component images and their synthesis face images. (b) Reconstructed face image and its corresponding sparse representation learned by FS-IRLS.

women respectively. This may be due to that in this dataset areas around eyes and jaw are more informative than those around the nose. Figure 2 demonstrates that FS-IRLS can efficiently combine different information for biometric forensics and is useful in face synthesis.

5.3   Fusion of Multiple Biometrics

A key ability for a biometric system is to provide multi-biometric solutions, including face, palm, iris, and so on. How to efficiently fuse these solutions becomes more and more important. Recently, sparse representation has shown that it will be informative and discriminative for both face recognition [21] and iris recognition [16]. In this subsection, we apply our structured fusion algorithm (FS-IRLS) to solve the multi-biometric fusion problem.

The experimental data is collected from a long-distance and near-infrared system. When a person walks through the system, his/her left and right iris images, and face images are captured. The whole data set consists of 2400 images from 100 persons. Each person has 8 left iris images, 8 right iris images and 8 face images. Accordingly we have three different tasks, each of which has 800 images. For each task, we use the first three images per person as the testing set and the remaining five images per person as the training set. Hence, for each task, the sample numbers of the testing set and the training set are 300 and 500 respectively. Each iris image is preprocessed and normalized to an 1,122-dimension vector and each face image is resized to an 1,024-dimension vector.

Figure 1 shows recognition rates of three robust sparse representation methods. We see that recognition rates of RSC-IRLS and GS-IRLS are low for two iris tasks. This may be due to iris image blurring incurred by movement. For each task, both GS-IRLS and FS-IRLS can improve recognition rates as compared with RSC-IRLS. As expected, FS-IRLS achieves the highest recognition rate. Since FS-IRLS can harness structure information across different tasks, it outperforms other sparse methods.

6 Conclusion

This paper has studied structured sparsity from a new HQ perspective. Based on the multiplicative form of HQ optimization, we have proposed a family of penalty functions and a general HQ optimization framework for structured sparsity, which are of theoretical and practical importance. Then we applied the proposed framework to solve the fusion of multi-biometric information and obtained a new structured fusion strategy. Experimental results in terms of face synthesis and multi-biometric recognition have corroborated our claims and validated the effectiveness of the proposed methods.

References

1. Bach, F.R.: Consistency of the group lasso and multiple kernel learning. J. Mach. Learn. Res. **9**, 1179–1225 (2008)
2. Boyd, S., Vandenberghe, L.: Convex Optimization. Cambridge University Press, Cambridge (2004)
3. Chartrand, R., Yin, W.: Iteratively reweighted algorithms for compressive sensing. In: Proceedings of the IEEE Conference on Acoustics, Speech and Signal Processing, pp. 3869–3872 (2008)
4. Daubechies, I., Devore, R., Fornasier, M., Gunturk, C.S.: Iteratively reweighted least squares minimization for sparse recovery. Commun. Pure Appl. Math. **63**(1), 1–38 (2010)
5. Fornasier, M.: Theoretical Foundations and Numerical Methods for Sparse Recovery. Walter de Gruyter, Berlin (2010)
6. Fornasier, M., Rauhut, H., Ward, R.: Low-rank matrix recovery via iteratively reweighted least squares minimization. SIAM J. Optim. **21**(4), 1614–1640 (2011)
7. He, R., Sun, Z., Tan, T., Zheng, W.-S.: Recovery of corrupted low-rank matrices via half-quadratic based nonconvex minimization. In: Proceedings of the IEEE Conference on Computer Vision and Pattern Recognition, pp. 2889–2896 (2011)
8. He, R., Zheng, W.S., Hu, B.G.: Maximum correntropy criterion for robust face recognition. IEEE Trans. Pattern Anal. Mach. Intell. **33**(8), 1561–1576 (2011)
9. Jenatton, R., Audibert, J.-Y., Bach, F.: Structured variable selection with sparsity-inducing norms. J. Mach. Learn. Res. **12**, 2777–2824 (2011)
10. Jenatton, R., Obozinski, G., Bach, F.: Structured sparse principal component analysis. In: Proceedings of the International Conference on Artificial Intelligence and Statistics (2009)
11. Li, A., Shan, S., Chen, X., Gao, W.: Face recognition based on non-corresponding region matching. In: Proceedings of the IEEE International Conference on Computer Vision, pp. 1060–1067 (2011)

12. Moayedi, F., Azimifar, Z., Boostani, R.: Structured sparse representation for human action recognition. Neurocomputing **161**, 38–46 (2015)
13. Morales, J., Micchelli, C.A., Pontil, M.: A family of penalty functions for structured sparsity. In: Advances in Neural Information Processing Systems, pp. 1612–1623 (2010)
14. Nie, F., Huang, H., Cai, X., Ding, C.: Efficient and robust feature selection via joint $l_{2,1}$-norms minimization. In: Advances in Neural Information Processing Systems, pp. 1813–1821 (2010)
15. Nikolova, M., Ng, M.K.: Analysis of half-quadratic minimization methods for signal and image recovery. SIAM J. Sci. Comput. **27**(3), 937–966 (2005)
16. Pillai, J.K., Patel, V.M., Chellappa, R., Ratha, N.K.: Secure and robust iris recognition using random projections and sparse representations. IEEE Trans. Pattern Anal. Mach. Intell. **33**(9), 1877–1893 (2011)
17. Suk, H.-I., Wee, C.-Y., Lee, S.-W., Shen, D.: Supervised discriminative group sparse representation for mild cognitive impairment diagnosis. Neuroinformatics **13**(3), 277–295 (2015)
18. Sun, Y., Wang, X., Tang, X.: Deeply learned face representations are sparse, selective, and robust. In: Proceedings of the IEEE Conference on Computer Vision and Pattern Recognition, pp. 2892–2900 (2015)
19. Wang, L., Pan, C.: Visual tracking via manifold regularized local structured sparse representation model. In: IEEE International Conference on Image Processing, pp. 1150–1154 (2015)
20. Wipf, D., Nagarajan, S.: Iterative reweighted l_1 and l_2 methods for finding sparse solutions. IEEE J. Sel. Top. Signal Process. **4**(2), 317–329 (2010)
21. Wright, J., Ma, Y., Mairal, J., Sapiro, G., Huang, T.S., Yan, S.: Sparse representation for computer vision and pattern recognition. Proc. IEEE **98**(6), 1031–1044 (2010)
22. Yang, M., Zhang, L., Yang, J., Zhang, D.: Robust sparse coding for face recognition. In: Proceedings of the IEEE Conference on Computer Vision and Pattern Recognition, pp. 625–632 (2011)
23. Yuan, X., Liu, X., Yan, S.: Visual classification with multitask joint sparse representation. IEEE Trans. Image Process. **21**, 4349–4360 (2012)
24. Zhang, H., Nasrabadi, N.M., Zhang, Y., Huang, T.S.: Joint dynamic sparse representation for multi-view face recognition. Pattern Recogn. **45**(4), 1290–1298 (2012)
25. Zhang, Z.: Parameter estimation techniques: a tutorial with application to conic fitting. Image Vis. Comput. **15**(1), 59–76 (1997)

Deformable Part Model Based Hand Detection against Complex Backgrounds

Chunyu Zou, Yue Liu[✉], Jiabin Wang, and Huaqi Si

Beijing Engineering Research Center of Mixed Reality and Advanced Display,
School of Optoelectronics, Beijing Institute of Technology,
Beijing 100081, China
zoucy@hotmail.com, liuyue@bit.edu.cn,
wangjiabin315@163.com, 1601296077@qq.com

Abstract. Hand detection is a challenging task in hand gesture recognition system and the detection results can be easily affected by changes in hand shapes, viewpoints, lightings or complex backgrounds. In order to detect and localize the human hands in static images against complex backgrounds, a hand detection method based on a mixture of multi-scale deformable part models is proposed in this paper, which is trained discriminatively using latent SVM and consists of three components each defined by a root filter and three part filters. The hands are detected in a feature pyramid in which the features are variants of HOG descriptors. The experimental results show that the proposed method is invariant to small deformations of hand gestures and the mixture model has a good performance on NUS hand gesture dataset - II.

Keywords: Hand detection · Deformable part model · Latent SVM · HOG features · Complex backgrounds

1   Introduction

Hand gestures are important body languages in human daily communication. Traditional HCI (Human Computer Interaction) devices such as keyboard and mouse are subject to the limitations of operational distance and convenience, so it's a natural way for us to interact with the computer using hand gestures. Hand gesture recognition has various applications such as sign language recognition, remote video conference, games and VR (Virtual Reality). Glove based and vision based methods are usually used in hand gesture recognition system, in which glove based method requires user to wear special gloves which can deliver the movements of hands and fingers to the computer [1]. Such an approach can accurately recognize various hand gestures in real time, but it is an unnatural and expensive way to interact with the computer because of the adoption of the complex glove equipment. Vision based hand gesture recognition has become popular in recent years, it doesn't require the user to wear gloves and only a camera is used to capture images of hands, which is a natural and friendly way for us to interact with the computer [2]. Figure 1 shows the process of vision based hand gesture recognition.

© Springer Science+Business Media Singapore 2016
T. Tan et al. (Eds.): IGTA 2016, CCIS 634, pp. 149–159, 2016.
DOI: 10.1007/978-981-10-2260-9_17

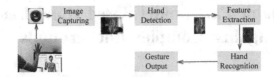

Fig. 1. Process of vision based hand gesture recognition

There are two types of hand gesture used in HCI system, i.e. static gesture and dynamic gesture, in which static gesture positions remain unchanged during a period of time and dynamic hand gesture positions are temporal and change with respect to time [3]. Static hand gesture recognition becomes popular in recent years because dynamic hand gestures can be considered as actions composed of a series of static hand gestures. The most difficult problem of vision based static hand gesture recognition is to detect hands against complex backgrounds, although depth cameras such as Kinect, Leap-Motion and RealSense are robust and precise to detect hands according the depth and image information, they are not available in most existing systems. So it's important to study the hand detection approach in RGB images against complex backgrounds.

Skin color, motion information, shape or combination of these visual features are usually used to detect hands in RGB images. Hand detection in static RGB images is a challenging task for various hand shapes, viewpoints, changes in illumination, or complex backgrounds. In this paper, a hand detection method based on a mixture of multi-scale deformable part models is proposed and the mixture model is trained using latent SVM with positive examples from images which are labeled with bounding boxes around the entire hand gestures and "hard negative" examples. The mixture model is tested on NUS hand gesture dataset - II [16] and the experimental results show that the mixture model has a person independent performance.

2 Related Work

There are plenty of existing literatures about hand detection, which can be summarized into the skin color, motion information, shape, and machine learning based methods.

Moving skin pixels were detected in video streaming and Mean-shift algorithm was adopted to detect hand in [5]. The method performed well as long as non-skin objects appeared in the scene. The derived motion, skin color and morphological information were combined to detect hands in [9]. Morphological features were used to estimate the probability of a pixel belonging to the hand region in the current frame. The method can detect hands indoors in real time and the similar method was adopted in [10]. Dardas et al. first subtracted the face region using Viola and Jones method [8] and detected the remained region using a skin detector and hand gesture contour comparison algorithm [6, 7]. The algorithm detected only four simply defined hand gestures in real time.

The performance of skin color or motion information based methods are restricted by strong assumptions and isn't robust in actual applications. Some methods combined the skin color with machine learning were proposed. Eng-Jon and Richard presented an unsupervised approach and detected the locations of the hands using a boosted cascade of classifiers in grey scale images, in which provided good detection accuracy [11]. Wu and Huang proposed an approach called Discriminant-EM (D-EM) [12] to help supervised learning reduce the number of labeled training samples, but the method can't address the issues of complex backgrounds. Zondag et al. constructed a real-time hand detector using HOG features [4] in combination with two variations of the AdaBoost algorithm [13]. Liew and Yairi focused on an appearance approach and proposed a feature extraction method based on sparse pixel-pairwise intensity comparisons for hand detection [14]. The method was robust against image noises, cluttered backgrounds, and partial occlusion. Mittal et al. first detected possible hand gesture using a hand shape detector, a context based detector, and a skin based detector respectively. A second stage classifier was learnt to compute a final confidence score for hand detection [15]. The method was time consuming although it can achieve very good recall and precision. Pisharady et al. utilized a biologically inspired approach based on the computational model of visual cortex and a Bayesian model of visual attention to generate the saliency map by calculating the posterior probabilities of pixel locations to be part of a hand gesture. The hand gesture was extracted by segmenting input image after setting threshold value of the saliency map. The method provided a good hand detection accuracy in spite of complex backgrounds. The disadvantages were slow processing speed and high computational complexity.

Some researchers introduced general object recognition methods to detect hands. The most commonly used detection methods include rigid templates [4] or bag of features [17], which performs poorly on hand detection owing to hand's variable appearance and the wide range of hand gestures. It's obvious that an "elastic" or "deformable" model to detect hands is necessary. Felzenszwalb and Huttenlocher developed a multi-scale deformable part model in [18] and the mixture of the deformable part models in [19]. The mixture of the deformable part models can capture significant variations in appearance and was often expressive enough to represent a rich object category.

In consideration of the success of the mixture of deformable part models on human detection, we develop a hand detection method based on the mixture model. A mixture model including three components each defined by a root filter and several part filters is trained. A meaningful gesture consists of a palm, some fingers and the joint of palm and fingers, so we define three part filters corresponding to each root filter in hand detection task.

3   Overview of the Proposed Method

We propose a hand detection method based on a mixture of multi-scale deformable part models. The mixture model is trained using a discriminative procedure that only requires bounding box labels for the positive examples.

3.1   HOG Features

Skin features [5–8, 15], shape context features [6, 7], Haar-like features [8, 10, 13], SIFT features [6, 7], morphological features [9], biologically inspired features (C2 features) [3], HOG features [4] or the combinations of these features [13, 15] have been used for hand detection in recent years. HOG features are originally proposed by Dalal and Triggs in [4] for human detection. We describe a variation of HOG features of an image at a particular resolution following the construction in [4].

We compute gradients using finite difference filters, $[-1, 0, +1]$ and its transpose. The image is first divided into 8×8 non-overlapping pixel regions called cells. For each cell, we accumulate a 1-dimensional HOG feature set over pixels in that cell. However, the feature set of a cell is a little different from that in [4, 18]. In this paper, in order to capture information of hand gestures as much as possible, a 31-dimensional feature set is constructed which includes 18-dimensional contrast sensitive features, 9-dimensional contrast insensitive features and 4-dimensional magnitude features from the reconstruction of 36-dimensional features in [18].

For each cell in an image, the gradient orientation of each pixel is firstly discretized into eighteen orientation bins. The contribution of each pixel to gradient orientation depends on the gradient magnitude. Then the cell is normalized at four 2×2 neighborhood cells called a block with respect to the total energy of each block (see Fig. 2). We sum over different normalizations and get an 18-dimensional contrast sensitive feature set F_1. Then the same method is used but each pixel is discretized into nine orientation bins which leads to a vector of length 9×4 representing the local gradient information inside a cell. Not only the sum over different normalizations but also the sum over nine contrast insensitive orientations are computed, which reduce the 9×4 vector into a 13-dimensional feature set F_2. The final HOG feature set is $\{F_1, F_2\}$.

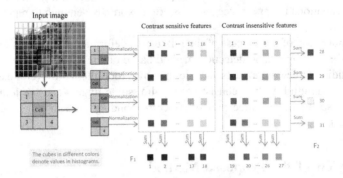

Fig. 2. Representations of 31-dimensional HOG features of a cell

The new features are low-dimensional and can capture local appearance which are invariant to small deformations. For a color image, the gradient of each color channel is computed and the highest gradient magnitude is picked as the final value.

A standard HOG feature pyramid is built for multi-scale hand detection. The feature pyramid consists of several couple levels, the resolution of each bottom level is twice the corresponding top resolution as shown in Fig. 3. The top level HOG features represent coarse information such as hand contour while the corresponding bottom level HOG features represent finer information such as fingers or the palm in different states.

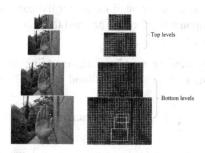

Fig. 3. HOG feature pyramid for and hand gesture hypothesis

3.2 Hand Model

The mixture model involves three components each defined by a coarse root filter covering an entire hand gesture and three finer part filters covering smaller parts such as fingers or the palm. The filters in the mixture model are applied to the HOG feature pyramid to calculate the responses of an input image. We require the level of each part is such that the feature map at that level is computed at twice the resolution of the root level (see Fig. 3).

The score of F at a position (x, y) in a feature map M from the HOG feature pyramid is the "dot product" of the filter and a sub-window of the feature map with top-left corner at (x, y), while the filter F is a matrix with $w \times h \times 31$ weights.

$$score(x, y) = F[w, h, 31] \cdot M[x+w, y+h]. \qquad (1)$$

We denote the filter $F[w, h, 31]$ as F'. The score of F at $p(x, y, l)$ in a feature pyramid H is $F' \cdot \phi(H, p, w, h)$, written as $F' \cdot \phi(H, p)$ later for convenience, where $\phi(H, p, w, h)$ denotes the HOG features in the $w \times h$ sub-window.

The goal is to get the best placement of root filter and part filters $z = (p_0, p_1, \ldots p_n)$ in a component, where $p_i = (x_i, y_i, l_i)$ specifies the position for lth filter in the feature pyramid. The score of a placement is given by the scores of each filter minus a deformation cost that depends on the relative position of each part filter with respect to the root filter, plus the bias,

$$score(p_0, p_1, \ldots p_n) = \sum_{i=0}^{n} F'_i \cdot \phi(H, p_i) - \sum_{i=1}^{n} d_i \cdot \phi_d(dx_i, dy_i) + b. \qquad (2)$$

Where the deformation cost and b are defined by [19]. The formula (2) can be written as dot product, $\beta \cdot \psi(H, z)$, where z specifies latent information of hand's parts.

$$\beta = (F_0' \dots, F_n', d_1, \dots, d_n, b). \tag{3}$$

$$\psi(H, z) = (\phi(H, p_0), \dots, \phi(H, p_n), -\phi_d(dx_1, dy_1), \dots, -\phi_d(dx_n, dy_n), 1). \tag{4}$$

This illustrates the connection between the model and linear classifiers. Latent SVM [19] is used to train our hand model for the partially labeled data. For the mixture model, three components are combined and the mixture model with the similar expression as the component is trained.

Learning. The process of learning model parameters using latent SVM is described in the following parts and more details can be found in [19]. The objective function is:

$$L_D(\beta) = \frac{1}{2}\|\beta\|^2 + C\sum_{i=1}^{n} max(0, 1 - y_i f_\beta(x_i)). \tag{5}$$

β is trained from labeled examples $D(x_1, y_1, \dots, x_n, y_n)$, where x_i is an example with a binary label $y_i \in \{-1, 1\}$. Generally $L_D(\beta)$ is not convex for a positive example and is convex for a negative example. However, $L_D(\beta)$ becomes convex for each example if there is a single possible latent value Z_p for each positive example. Note that,

$$L_D(\beta) = min_{Z_p} L_D(\beta, Z_p). \tag{6}$$

Which means $L_D(\beta) \leq L_D(\beta, Z_p)$ and we can minimize $L_D(\beta, Z_p)$ using coordinate descent algorithm: Optimize $L_D(\beta, Z_p)$ over Z_p by selecting the highest scoring latent value for each positive example and over β using stochastic gradient descent algorithm. However, the stochastic descent algorithm is so sensitive to local minima that the mixture model is initialized as in [19].

There are very large numbers of negative examples in an image. It's reasonable to construct training data consisting of the labeled positive examples and "hard negative" examples. The hard negative examples are those that are incorrectly classified or inside the margin of the classifier defined by in the previous training.

Detection. An overall score is computed for each root location according to the best possible placement of the parts for hand detection,

$$score(p_0) = max_{p_1, \dots, p_n} score(p_0, p_1, \dots p_n). \tag{7}$$

The root locations with high score define detections, and part locations with respect to root locations define a full hand hypothesis. Dynamic programming and generalized distance transforms methods [20] are used to compute the best root location. The response of each filter to the feature pyramid is first computed as follows,

$$R_{i,l}(x, y) = F_i' \cdot \phi(H, (x, y, l)). \tag{8}$$

Then the responses of part filters are transformed using generalized distance transform algorithm.

$$D_{i,l}(x,y) = \max_{dx,dy}(R_{i,l}(x+dx, y+dy) - d_i \cdot \phi_d(dx, dy)). \qquad (9)$$

The final root scores at each level can be expressed by the sum of the root filter response at that level with transformed responses at such level that the resolution of the level is twice the root detection level.

$$\text{score}(x_0, y_0, l_0) = R_{0,l_0}(x_0, y_0) + \sum_{i=1}^{n} D_{i,l_i}(2(x_0, y_0) + v_i) + b. \qquad (10)$$

The hands are detected in a feature pyramid of an input image. There is a hand in an image if the score is higher than a threshold. The desired output is to predict the bounding boxes of a hand gesture. We eliminate the repeated detections by non-maximum suppression (NMS). The final root scores of labeled positive examples are used to learn four linear functions for predicting the bounding box by least-squares regression (LSR). Figure 4 illustrates the detection process using a component of the mixture model.

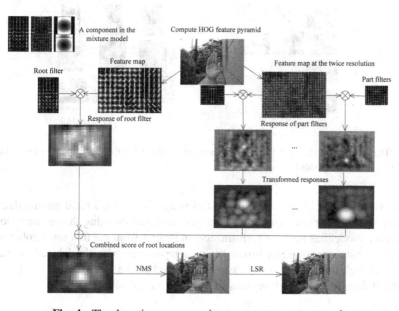

Fig. 4. The detection process using a component at one scale

4   Experimental Results

The mixture model of hand gesture is trained and evaluated on NUS hand gesture dataset - II [16], (see Table 1).

In practice, all positive examples from subsets A and B are labeled with bounding boxes covering the entire hand gestures. The part locations are treated as latent variables during the training process using latent SVM. The positive example set is

Table 1. NUS hand gesture dataset - II

Subsets	Descriptions
A	2000 hand gesture color images
B	750 hand gesture color images with human noises
C	2000 background images without the hand gestures

composed of half original positive examples from subset A and the corresponding flipped positive examples. Margin sensitive method [19] is used to mine hard negative examples from subset C. The positive example set is split into three groups according to the orientations of hand gestures (see Fig. 5(a)) which lead to a mixture model with three components (see Fig. 5(b)). The operation is different from [19] whose positive examples are split according the aspect ratio of the bounding boxes. The detection accuracy is improved by performing the operation. The proposed mixture model is symmetric along the vertical axis, so it can detect gestures of either hand.

(a)   (b)

Fig. 5. The mixture model. (a) The split positive examples with three groups. (b) The mixture model with three components.

The mixture model is tested on the rest of images from NUS hand gesture dataset-II. Figure 6 shows some examples of hand gesture detection using the mixture model. The mixture model has the best performance on images from the first three columns in which the prediction bounding boxes has a large overlap with the labeled bounding boxes. Although the mixture model can detect hand in the images from the last two columns, it fails to capture all regions of the hand gestures.

Fig. 6. Hand detection results. The first row shows some results from subset A while the second row from subset B. The prediction bounding boxes are in red while the ground-truth bounding boxes are in blue. (Color figure online)

The subsets A and C are used to test the capability of the mixture model as in [3]. The presence of hand is detected if the score of the best placement is above the threshold. Figure 7(a) shows the ROC of the hand detection task. The effects of overlaps on detection performance are also studied as shown in Fig. 7(a). The overlap between the prediction bounding box and a ground-truth bounding box is an important index in hand detection. The proposed hand detection model is also tested on a harder subset B with human noise and subset C (see Fig. 7(b)).

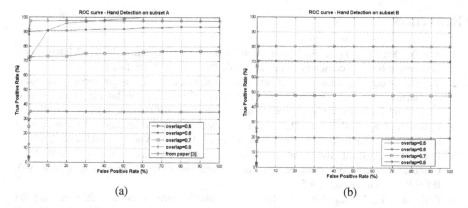

(a)   (b)

Fig. 7. ROC curve of hand detection. (a) ROC curve of subset A without human noises (b) ROC curve of subset B with human noises.

It can be seen from the experimental results that the proposed mixture model performs better on subset A when the overlap is 0.5 compared to [3] and can detect hand correctly at a low false positive rate. In general, the mixture model is better than the method from [3]. Since the performance is regarded to be better if the overlap is higher in the hand detection system, the performance decreases with the increase of overlaps. However, it's sufficient for the capture of all the information of a hand gesture when the overlap is 0.6. The presence of human may reduce the detection performance as shown in Fig. 7(b). The mixture model's detection time is about 0.5 s, which is less compared to the biologically inspired approach in [3].

5   Conclusions

A hand detection method based on the mixture of deformable part models is proposed in this paper. More components and part filters in the mixture model will improve the performance, but may lead to time consumption and expensive detection task. The mixture model is robust to hand shapes, viewpoints, lights or complex backgrounds and invariant to the small deformations of hand gestures to an extent. The performance of the mixture model on the harder dataset including influence of human needs to be improved. The richer mixture model combining skin color or building connections among parts is helpful to improve the detection accuracy. The higher detection accuracy will produce the better recognition results in hand gesture recognition system. A well-defined hand gesture set for interaction should be designed and a robust hand gesture recognition system should be studied in the future work.

Acknowledgements. This research was supported by the National Natural Science Foundation of China under grant No. 61370134, the National High Technology Research and Development Program of China (863 Program) under grant No. 2013AA013904.

References

1. Zhu, Y., Yang, Z., Yuan, B.: Vision based hand gesture recognition. In: 2013 International Conference on Service Sciences, pp. 260–265. IEEE Press, Shenzhen (2013)
2. Yu, C., Wang, X., Huang, H., Shen, J.: Vision-based hand gesture recognition using combinational features. In: 2010 6th International Conference on Intelligent Information Hiding and Multimedia Signal Processing, pp. 543–546. IEEE Press, Darmstadt (2010)
3. Pisharady, P.K., Vadakkepat, P., Loh, A.P.: Attention based detection and recognition of hand postures against complex backgrounds. Int. J. Comput. Vis. **101**, 403–419 (2013)
4. Dalal, N., Triggs, B.: Histograms of oriented gradients for human detection. In: 2005 IEEE Computer Society Conference on Computer Vision and Pattern Recognition, pp. 886–893. IEEE Press, San Diego (2005)
5. Dadgostar, F., Sarrafzadeh, A., Messom, C.: Multi-layered hand and face tracking for real-time gesture recognition. In: Köppen, M., Kasabov, N., Coghill, G. (eds.) ICONIP 2008, Part I. LNCS, vol. 5506, pp. 587–594. Springer, Heidelberg (2009)
6. Dardas, N.H., Georganas, N.D.: Real-time hand gesture detection and recognition using bag-of-features and support vector machine techniques. IEEE Trans. Instrum. Meas. **60**(11), 3592–3607 (2011)
7. Dardas, N.H., Petriu, E.M.: Hand Gesture detection and recognition using principal component analysis. In: 2011 IEEE International Conference on Computational Intelligence for Measurement Systems and Applications, pp. 1–6. IEEE Press, Ottawa (2011)
8. Viola, P., Jones, M.J.: Robust real-time object detection. Int. J. Comput. Vis. **2**(57), 137–154 (2004)
9. Stergiopoulou, E., Sgouropoulos, K., Nikolaou, N., Papamarkos, N.: Real time hand detection in a complex background. Eng. Appl. Artif. Intell. **35**, 54–70 (2014)
10. Fang, Y., Wang k., Cheng J., Lu, H., C.: A real-time hand gesture recognition method. In: 2007 IEEE International Conference on Multimedia and Expo, pp. 995–998. IEEE Press, Beijing (2007)
11. Ong, E.J., Bowden, R.: A boosted classifier tree for hand shape detection. In: 6th IEEE International Conference on Automatic Face and Gesture Recognition, pp. 889–894. IEEE Press, Jeju Island (2006)
12. Wu, Y., Huang, T.S.: View-independent recognition of hand postures. In: IEEE Conference on Computer Vision and Pattern Recognition, pp. 88–94. IEEE Press, Hilton Head Island (2000)
13. Zondag, J.A., Gritti, T., Jeanne, V.: Practical study on real-time hand detection. In: 2009 3rd International Conference on Affective Computing and Intelligent Interaction and Workshops, pp. 1–8. IEEE Press, Amsterdam (2009)

14. Liew, C.F., Yairi, T.: Generalized BRIEF: a novel fast feature extraction method for robust hand detection. In: 2014 22nd International Conference on Pattern Recognition, pp. 3014–3019. IEEE Press, Stockholm (2014)
15. Mittal, A., Zisserman, A., Torr, P.H.S.: Hand detection using multiple proposals. In: 2011 British Machine Vision Conference, pp. 75.1–75.11. BMVA Press, Scotland (2011)
16. NUS Hand Posture Datasets. https://www.ece.nus.edu.sg/stfpage/elepv/NUS-HandSet
17. Zhang, J.G., Marszalek, M., Lazebnik, S., Schmid, C.: Local features and kernels for classification of texture and object categories: a comprehensive study. Int. J. Comput. Vis. **73**(2), 213–238 (2007)
18. Felzenszwalb, P.F., McAllester, D., Ramanan, D.: A discriminatively trained, multiscale, deformable part model. In: 2008 IEEE Conference on Computer Vision and Pattern Recognition, pp. 1–8. IEEE Press, Anchorage (2008)
19. Felzenszwalb, P.F., Girshick, R.B., McAllester, D., Ramanan, D.: Object detection with discriminatively trained part-based models. IEEE Trans. Pattern Anal. Mach. Intell. **32**(9), 1627–1645 (2010)
20. Felzenszwalb, P.F., Huttenlocher D.: Distance transforms of sampled functions. Technical report 2004-1963, CIS, Cornell University (2004)

A Construction Algorithm of Measurement Matrix with Low Coherence for Compressed Sensing

Shengqin Bian$^{(\boxtimes)}$, Zhengguang Xu, and Shuang Zhang

School of Automation and Electrical Engineering,
University of Science and Technology Beijing, Beijing, China
{xiaobian, zhangshuang}@ustb.edu.cn, xzg_1@263.net

Abstract. In order to improve the accuracy and range for application of signal reconstruction, a new measurement matrix optimization method is proposed based on the Gram matrix. The new method can reduce the mutual coherence between the measurement matrix and the sparse transform matrix. Numerical experiments verify the success of the optimized method. Compared with the original Gaussian random matrix and other optimized measurement matrices, the performance and stability of our proposed have a slight increase.

Keywords: Compressive sensing (CS) · Signal reconstruction · Gram matrix · Mutual coherence · Measurement matrix

1 Introduction

Sparse signal recovery problem has been widely studied within signal and image processing fields in recent years [1–5]. A signal or image with an underlying sparse structure can be compressed, stored or transmitted more efficiently than general signals. Compressed sensing (CS) is an innovative idea, stating that signals which have a sparse representation on suitable basis can be reconstructed from a number of random linear projections with dimension considerably lower than that required by the Shannon-Nyquist theorem.

Consider a signal $x \in \mathbb{R}^N$ which can be sparsely expressed over a fixed basis $\Psi = [\Psi_1, \Psi_2, \cdots, \Psi_L]$. Such signal x can be described by

$$x = \sum_{i=1}^{L} \alpha_i \Psi_i \quad \text{or} \quad x = \Psi\alpha \tag{1}$$

with $\|\alpha\|_0 \leq K \ll N$. The l_0-norm ($\|\bullet\|_0$) simply counts the number of non-zeros and is a measure of sparse degree. When most of the coefficients of α are zero or they can be discarded without much loss of information, signal x can be reconstructed exactly through the CS system. In most cases sparse representation can always be found through orthogonal basis such as FFT, DWT or DCT according to the characteristic of the signals.

© Springer Science+Business Media Singapore 2016
T. Tan et al. (Eds.): IGTA 2016, CCIS 634, pp. 160–166, 2016.
DOI: 10.1007/978-981-10-2260-9_18

Given a measurement matrix $\Phi \in \mathbb{R}^{M \times N}$ which maps signal from $\mathbb{R}^N$ into $\mathbb{R}^M$, we can get the compressed measurements $y \in \mathbb{R}^M (M \ll N)$ through

$$y = \Phi x \tag{2}$$

By the above formula (1), observation process can be expressed as

$$y = \Phi x = \Phi \Psi \alpha = A\alpha \tag{3}$$

Matrix A is referred as equivalent dictionary of the CS system. As inequality $M \leq N \ll L$ established, equivalent dictionary A is over complete. Thus, given measurement vector y and the equivalent dictionary A, the coefficients vector α calculated with formula (3) tends to be not unique, but we can seek the sparest. The main challenge is to solve the following inverse question:

$$\min_{\alpha} \|\alpha\|_0 \text{ s.t.} y = A\alpha \tag{4}$$

The main difficulty in solving (4) is its non-convexity that requires a combinatorial search through all possible sparse solutions. Under the assumption of sparse, several estimation approaches can be used. These include greedy algorithms, such as Orthogonal matching pursuit(OMP) and thresholding matching pursuit, and Basis pursuit(BP) algorithm which relaxes l_0 norm to l_1 norm to solve the problem by linear program.

In CS theory, Measurement matrix Φ is drawn at random with Gaussian or Bernoulli distributions, which simplifies its theoretical analysis, and also facilitates a simple implementation. In order to be able to attain a small M and yet have a stable reconstruction, measurement matrix Φ should be incoherent with sparse transform matrix Ψ. In other words, the mutual coherence between projection matrix Φ and sparse transform matrix Ψ should be reasonably small. Thus the correlation between any distinct pair of columns in equivalent matrix A should be very small. Some recent researchers attempt to find an optimal structure for Φ with the aim of increasing the reconstruction quality and to take fewer measurements [6–9]. Elad [7] proposed an iteratively method to minimize the t-averaged mutual coherence using a shrinkage operation followed by a singular value decomposition (SVD) step. Duarte-Carvajalino [9] et al. addressed the problem by making any subset columns of A as orthogonal as possible, or equivalently, making the Gram matrix $\tilde{G} = \tilde{A}^T \tilde{A}$ as closely as possible to identity matrix. Zhao [8] et al. adopted the advantage of an eigenvalue decomposition to minimize the square sum of the non-diagonal elements of Gram matrix. The results of all previous methods reveal the improved performance which is an evidence of the benefits that optimal sampling leading to higher reconstruction quality.

In this paper, a method to optimize the projection matrix is proposed based on the coherence bound of the Gram matrix. The object is to find an exact solution to decrease the mutual coherence with a given sparse transform matrix. Method in paper [7] needs many iterative steps to achieve good performance, while the proposed method in this paper takes less iterative steps than the others.

The remainder of the paper is organized as follows. In Sect. 2, we provide the criteria that can be used for measuring the coherence of a matrix. In Sect. 3, the proposed approach for optimization of the measurement matrix is described. In Sect. 4, experimental results are presented and the performance obtained compared with optimization methods in paper [7, 8]. Finally, the discussion and conclusion are presented in Sect. 5.

2 Basic Principles

Definition 1: For a matrix A, the mutual coherence is defined as the largest absolute and normalized inner product between different columns in A. Formally, described as

$$\mu\{A\} = \max_{1 \leq i,\, j \leq N,\, i \neq j} \left\{ \frac{|a_i a_j|}{\|a_i\|_2 \bullet \|a_j\|_2} \right\} \tag{5}$$

A desired measurement matrix Φ should have small mutual coherence with respect to sparse transform matrix Ψ. There is an alternative description for $\mu\{A\}$ by referring to the corresponding Gram matrix $\tilde{G} = \tilde{A}^T \tilde{A}$, in which $\tilde{A}$ is column-normalized version of A. The off-diagonal elements of $\tilde{G}$ are the inner products that appear in (5). Mutual coherence is the off-diagonal entry with largest magnitude. In the success of reconstruction algorithms mutual coherence plays an important role. It has been demonstrated that if the sparse level of the signal following inequality (6) in a noiseless setting then BP and OMP both guaranteed to successfully reconstruct the signal.

$$\|\alpha\|_0 \leq \frac{1}{2} \left(1 + \frac{1}{\mu(A)} \right) \tag{6}$$

Usually we set two coherence measures to study the performance of various optimized methods, one is maximum mutual coherence and the other is average mutual coherence. In particular, they can be drawn from off-diagonal entries of $\tilde{G}$ which correspond to inner product between any two distinct vectors.

$$\mu_{max} = \max_{i \neq j, 1 \leq i,\, j \leq N} |\tilde{g}_{ij}| \tag{7}$$

$$\mu_{ave} = \frac{\sum_{j \neq i} \sum_{i \neq j} |\tilde{g}_{ij}|}{N(N-1)} \tag{8}$$

It is important to note that minimum possible absolute off-diagonal entries of $\tilde{G}$ are zero and occurred only when $\tilde{A}$ is orthogonal matrix with $M = N$; but in CS system we only deal with $M \ll N$, so that we have $0 \leq \mu_{max}(\tilde{G}) \leq 1$. The diagonal entries in matrix $\tilde{G}$ always equal to one because columns have been normalized.

3 The Proposed Method

Starting with a measurement matrix $\Phi \in \mathbb{R}^{M \times N}$ which constructed from random i.i.d. (independent and identically distributed) columns, and sparse transform matrix $\Psi \in \mathbb{R}^{N \times L}$, we aim at minimizing $\mu_{max}(\Phi\Psi)$ with respect to Φ.

Input: Sparse representation matrix $\Psi \in \mathbb{R}^{N \times L}$, an arbitrary measurement matrix $\Phi \in \mathbb{R}^{M \times N}$, Iteration counter $t = 0$, we set $\mu_{max(0)} = 0, \mu_{ave(0)} = 0$, number of iterations is Iter;

Output: Optimized measurement matrix $\Phi \in \mathbb{R}^{M \times N}$;
  Loop:

(1) Normalize:Normalize the columns in the matrix $\Phi\Psi$ and obtain the effective dictionary $\hat{A}_t$;

(2) Compute Gram Matrix: $G_t = \hat{A}_t^T \hat{A}_t$;

(3) Compute coherence low bound: $W(A) = \sqrt{\frac{L-M}{M(L-1)}}$;

(4) Shrink: Update off-diagonal of the Gram matrix and obtain $\hat{G}_t$ by

$$\hat{g}_{ij} = \begin{cases} \frac{1}{2}g_{ij} & |g_{ij}| > 2 \bullet W(A) \\ g_{ij} & |g_{ij}| \leq 2 \bullet W(A) \end{cases}$$

When there are no elements greater than $2 \bullet W(A)$, we update the off-diagonal of $\hat{G}_t$ by

$$\hat{g}_{ij} = \begin{cases} 0.9g_{ij} & |g_{ij}| > \max_{i \neq j}(|g|_{ij}) \\ g_{ij} & |g_{ij}| \leq \max_{i \neq j}(|g|_{ij}) \end{cases}$$

(5) Reduce Rank: Apply SVD and force the rank of $\hat{G}_t$ to be equal to M, we get $\hat{G}_t = U \bullet S \bullet V^T$, the maximum M singular value of matrix S is reserved.

(6) Update Φ by: $\hat{\Phi}_t = \sqrt{S(1:M, 1:M)} * U^T(:, 1:L)$;

(7) Advance: Set $t = t + 1$;
    Result: The output of the above algorithm is $\hat{\Phi}_{Iter}$

4 Results

For a matrix of size 50*120, the minimal possible coherence is 0.1085. Figure 1 shows the result of the optimized method. Figure 1(a) is the initial Gram matrix, Fig. 1(b) is Gram matrix after 30 iterations, Fig. 1(c) is absolute of the final Gram matrix after 30 iterations. As can be seen, the iterative procedure succeeds well in shrink the off-diagonal entries of Gram matrix. The off-diagonal elements tend to have same value after 30 iterations.

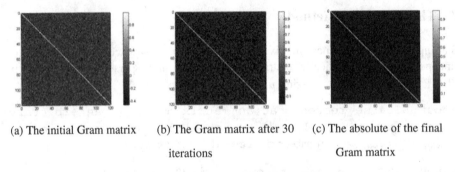

(a) The initial Gram matrix   (b) The Gram matrix after 30   (c) The absolute of the final

                              iterations   Gram matrix

Fig. 1. Compare the Gram matrix

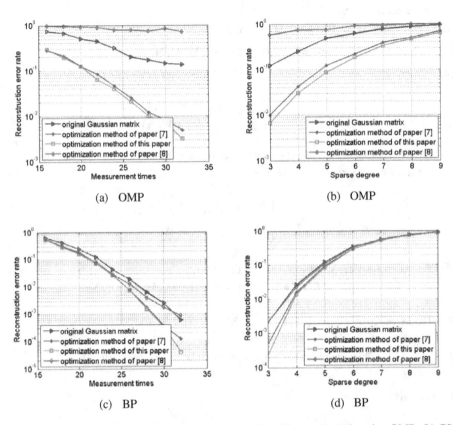

(a) OMP   (b) OMP

(c) BP   (d) BP

Fig. 2. (a) CS relative errors as a function of the number of measurements using OMP; (b) CS relative errors as a function of sparse degree using OMP; (c) CS relative errors as a function of the number of measurements using BP; (d) CS relative errors as a function of sparse degree using BP.

Subsequently we examine the performance of the proposed method and compare it with methods in paper [7, 8]. In the first experiment, we used a random dictionary of size 80*120. We generate 50000 sparse vectors of length 120 with 4 non-zeros in each. The nonzero locations were chosen at random and populated with i.i.d. zero-mean and unit variance Gaussian values. Varying values of measurement times in the range [16, 40]. The relative error rate was evaluated as a function of measurement times for both OMP and BP algorithms before and after projection optimization. When more than 200 errors were accumulated, the test was stopped and the average was used instead. As expected, as measurement times grow, the average performance error decline slowly, the proposed optimized projection lead to better performance compared to the original and other methods in paper [7, 8]. The second experiment fixed measurement times equal to 25 and varied sparse degree from 3 to 9. As the sparse degree grows, the performance error increases slowly. The proposed method outperforms the others slightly (Fig. 2).

5   Discussion and Conclusion

In this paper optimization of the measurement matrix in compressed sensing was addressed. Although random sampling has been used widely so far in the framework, it has been shown recently that smaller mutual coherence with respect to sparse transform matrix can improve the performance significantly. More importantly, the presented numerical results reveals that by using the optimized measurement matrices one can get the same performance as that obtained using the original random matrices, but with fewer number of measurements. On the other hand, the optimized measurement matrices can be applied to a wider range of signals than the original random matrices. Experiments verify the success of the optimized method.

References

1. Donoho, D.L., Elad, M., Temlyakov, V.N.: Stable recovery of sparse overcomplete representations in the presence of noise. IEEE Trans. Inf. Theor. **52**(1), 6–18 (2006)
2. Candes, E.J., Romberg, J.K., Tao, T.: Robust uncertainty principles: exact signal reconstruction from highly incomplete frequency information. IEEE Trans. Inf. Theor. **52**(2), 489–509 (2006)
3. Candes, E.J., Romberg, J.K., Tao, T.: Stable signal recovery from incomplete and inaccurate measurements. Commun. Pure Appl. Math. **59**(8), 1207–1223 (2006)
4. Candes, E.J.: The restricted isometry property and its implications for compressed sensing. ComptesRendusMatheMatique **346**(9), 589–592 (2008)
5. Baraniuk, R., Davenport, M., Devore, R., et al.: A simple proof of the restricted isometry property for random matrices. Constr. Approximation **28**(3), 253–263 (2008)
6. Xu, J., Pi, Y., Cao, Z.: Optimized projection matrix for compressive sensing. EURASIP J. Adv. Sig. Process. **2010**(1), 560349 (2010)
7. Elad, M.: Optimized projections for compressed sensing. IEEE Trans. Sig. Process. **55**(12), 5695–5702 (2007)

8. Rui-zhen, Z.H.A.O., Zhou, Q.I.N., Shao-hai, Hu: An optimization method for measurement matrix based on eigenvalue decomposition. Sig. Process. **28**(5), 653–658 (2012)
9. Duarte-Carvajalino, J.M., Sapiro, G.: Learning to sense sparse signals: simultaneous sensing matrix and sparsifying dictionary optimization. IEEE Trans. Image Process. **18**(7), 1395–1408 (2009)

Non-rigid Point Set Registration
Based on Iterative Linear Optimization

Hongbin Lin[(⊠)] and Daqing Zhang

Yanshan University, Qinhuangdao, China
honphin@ysu.edu.cn, 1401766632@qq.com

Abstract. This paper presents a novel point set registration algorithm based on iterative linear optimization, which can be used to register both rigid and non-rigid point set. Firstly, a new cost function was constructed to evaluate the summation of squared distance between the two point sets, in which rigid transformation, non-rigid elastic deformation and complex deformation were all included for consideration. Secondly, the proposed cost was linearized using to obtain a linear cost function of registration parameters. Thirdly, the registration parameters were solved by iterative optimization using Tikhonov regularization. Experimental results validated the performances of proposed method.

Keywords: Point set registration · Non-rigid point set · Cost function · Tikhonov regularization · Linear optimization

1 Introduction

With the rapid development of 3d scanning technology, 3d point set could be obtained more and more conveniently. As an important part, registration of rigid and non-rigid point set has become popular for the researchers who proposed many registration algorithms. For example, Fitsgibbon et al. [1] developed a robust iterative closest point algorithm, which optimize the registration energy function via LM algorithm, making registration error minimum. Although the algorithm greatly reduces the possibility of trapping in local minima, it is not consider noise perturbation in the matrix of coefficients, thus leading to poor stability. Hasler et al. [2] obtained the statistical modeling of interference noise before maximum likelihood estimation to register the point set. Bing et al. [3] proposed a novel point cloud registration method based on GMM, obtained sound registered results for rigid point set. In the field of non-rigid point set registration, the most famous algorithm was proposed by Chui et al. [4], in which thin plate splint was taken as the deformation template, and deterministic annealing technique was adopted. Although, this algorithm occluded abnormal shrinkage points, the speed is rather slow. Sofien et al. [5] presented a more efficient algorithm for non-rigid point set registration via the constraint of the energy change generated by the single template during registration process. But it will be accompanied by a large number of abnormal shrinkage points.

Main contents of this paper were organized as follow: Sect. 2 presented the basic principle and the pipeline of the algorithm. Section 3 constructed a new cost function for non-rigid point registration, followed by the linearization of the cost function in

© Springer Science+Business Media Singapore 2016
T. Tan et al. (Eds.): IGTA 2016, CCIS 634, pp. 167–175, 2016.
DOI: 10.1007/978-981-10-2260-9_19

Sect. 4. In Sect. 5, the register parameters were solved by iterative linear optimization. And Sect. 6 presented the experimental results. The main achievements of this paper were concluded in Sect. 7.

2 Pipeline of the Algorithm

Let S and M be two 3d point sets(S is the Scene point set, M is the Model point set). Due to the registration was performed in an iterative manner, the intermediate point sets M^t and S^t were defined as illustrated in Fig. 1. In order to evaluate the degree of transformation, translation, deformation and distance between the point sets, cost functions $Cost(M^t, M^{t+1})$, $Cost(S^t, S^{t+1})$ and $Cost(M^t, S^{t+1}; S^{t+1}, M^{t+1})$ were defined, and the total cost function of t th iteration was defined by weighted summation of the three cost functions. Based on the cost function, Tikhonov regularization was used to linearize the cost function. In addition, linear optimization was used to solve the registration parameters in each step. This process was iterated until preset tolerance was achieved. Pipeline of overall algorithm was illustrated in Fig. 2.

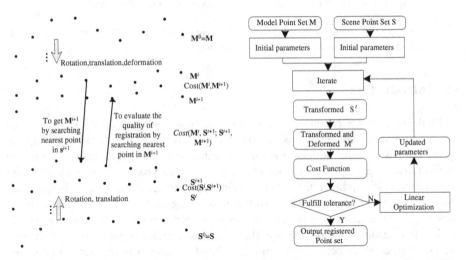

Fig. 1. Basic principle of proposed method   **Fig. 2.** Pipeline of the proposed algorithm

3 Cost Function for Non-rigid Point Set Registration

In rigid or non-rigid point set registration, a proper cost function is very important to avoid the iteration trapped in local minima, as well as speed up the convergence progress. In our construction, the cost function was divided into three parts, which were $Cost\left(M^i, M^{i+1}\right)$, $Cost\left(S^i, S^{i+1}\right)$ and $Cost\left(M^t, S^{t+1}; S^{t+1}, M^{t+1}\right)$, as illustrated in Fig. 1. And the total cost function $Cost(i, i+1)$ was defined by weighted summation of the three parts as

$$Cost(i, i+1) = w_1 Cost(\mathbf{M}^i, \mathbf{M}^{i+1}) + w_2 Cost(\mathbf{M}^i, \mathbf{S}^{i+1}; \mathbf{S}^{i+1}, \mathbf{M}^{i+1}) + w_3 Cost(\mathbf{S}^i, \mathbf{S}^{i+1})$$

$$(1)$$

where w_1, w_2 and w_3 are the weights, used to control the relative significance during registration.

For $Cost(\mathbf{M}^i, \mathbf{M}^{i+1})$, this cost function was defined to evaluate the averaged distance between point set $\mathbf{M}^i$ and $\mathbf{M}^{i+1}$. In which, rigid and non-rigid were both involved. Further more, for non-rigid transformation elastic deformation and complex deformation should be involved to perform complex deformation. Thus the cost function $Cost(\mathbf{M}^i, \mathbf{M}^{i+1})$ between $\mathbf{M}^i$ and $\mathbf{M}^{i+1}$, was defined by

$$Cost(\mathbf{M}^i, \mathbf{M}^{i+1}) = w_{11} Cost_{rigid}(\mathbf{M}^i, \mathbf{M}^{i+1}) + w_{12} Cost_{nonrigid}(\mathbf{M}^i, \mathbf{M}^{i+1}) \quad (2)$$

where w_{11} and w_{12} were the weights, fulfilling $w_{11} + w_{12} = 1$, $Cost_{rigid}(\mathbf{M}^i, \mathbf{M}^{i+1})$ was the cost function describing rigid transformation of the point set, $Cost_{nonrigid}(\mathbf{M}^i, \mathbf{M}^{i+1})$ was the cost function describing non-rigid transformation of the point set defined below

$$Cost_{nonrigid}(\mathbf{M}^i, \mathbf{M}^{i+1}) = w_{121} Cost_{elastic}(\mathbf{M}^i, \mathbf{M}^{i+1}) + w_{122} Cost_{complex}(\mathbf{M}^i, \mathbf{M}^{i+1})$$

$$(3)$$

where w_{121} and w_{122} were the weights. $Cost_{elastic}(\mathbf{M}^i, \mathbf{M}^{i+1})$ was the cost function describing elastic deformation of the point set, $Cost_{complex}(\mathbf{M}^i, \mathbf{M}^{i+1})$ was the cost function describing complex deformation of the point set. $Cost_{elastic}(\mathbf{M}^i, \mathbf{M}^{i+1})$ and $Cost_{complex}(\mathbf{M}^i, \mathbf{M}^{i+1})$ were defined in following subsections.

For $Cost(\mathbf{M}^i, \mathbf{S}^{i+1}; \mathbf{M}^{i+1}, \mathbf{S}^{i+1})$, the cost function was defined to evaluate the averaged distance between point set $\mathbf{M}^i$ and $\mathbf{S}^{i+1}$ and between point set $\mathbf{M}^{i+1}$ and $\mathbf{S}^{i+1}$, a symmetrical distance was defined based on projection to nearest plane in our work.

For $Cost(\mathbf{S}^i, \mathbf{S}^{i+1})$, the cost function was defined to evaluate the degree of rigid transformation between point set $\mathbf{S}^i$ and $\mathbf{S}^{i+1}$, because only rigid transformation was involved for scene point set. Thus,

$$Cost(\mathbf{S}^i, \mathbf{S}^{i+1}) = Cost_{rigid}(\mathbf{S}^i, \mathbf{S}^{i+1}) \quad (4)$$

3.1   Cost Function for Rigid Point Set Transformation

In order to evaluate the degree of rigid transformation, $Cost_{rigid}(\mathbf{X}^i, \mathbf{X}^{i+1})$ was defined in this subsection. Due to $\mathbf{X}^{i+1}$ is the transformed point set of $\mathbf{X}^i$, the cost function was defined by summation of squared distance between the points in $\mathbf{X}^i$ and their transformed points in $\mathbf{X}^{i+1}$. The $Cost_{rigid}(\mathbf{X}^i, \mathbf{X}^{i+1})$ was defined by

$$Cost_{rigid}\left(\mathbf{X}^i, \mathbf{X}^{i+1}\right) = \sum_{k=1}^{N} \left\| \mathbf{x}_k^{i+1} - \left(\mathbf{R}\mathbf{x}_k^i + \mathbf{t}\right) \right\|_2^2 \qquad (5)$$

where $\mathbf{x}_k^i$ and $\mathbf{x}_k^{i+1}$ are the kth point in $\mathbf{X}^i$ and $\mathbf{X}^{i+1}$, $\mathbf{R}$ is the rotation matrix, $\mathbf{t}$ is the translation vector.

Equation (5) could be used in the definition of $Cost\left(\mathbf{S}^i, \mathbf{S}^{i+1}\right)$ and rigid part of $Cost\left(\mathbf{M}^i, \mathbf{M}^{i+1}\right)$.

On the contrary, in the definition of $Cost\left(\mathbf{M}^i, \mathbf{S}^{i+1}; \mathbf{M}^{i+1}, \mathbf{S}^{i+1}\right)$, symmetrical distance was defined based on projection to nearest plane, the point projection was illustrated in Fig. 3.

Let $\mathbf{m}_j$ be a point in $\mathbf{M}^i$, $\mathbf{s}_k$, $\mathbf{s}_{k+1}$ and $\mathbf{s}_{k+2}$ were three nearest points in $\mathbf{S}^{i+1}$, Π is the nearest plane defined by point $\mathbf{s}_k$, $\mathbf{s}_{k+1}$ and $\mathbf{s}_{k+2}$, $p(\mathbf{m}_j)$ is the point on Π projected by $\mathbf{m}_j$, $d_{ms}(j) = \left\| \mathbf{m}_j - p\left(\mathbf{m}_j\right) \right\|_2^2$ is the squared distance between $\mathbf{m}_j$ and its projected point. In the same way, the squared distance between point $\mathbf{s}_j$ (a point in $\mathbf{S}^{i+1}$) and its projected point can also be computed by $d_{sm}(j) = \left\| \mathbf{s}_j - p\left(\mathbf{s}_j\right) \right\|_2^2$. Thus the cost function $Cost\left(\mathbf{M}^i, \mathbf{S}^{i+1}; \mathbf{S}^{i+1}, \mathbf{M}^{i+1}\right)$ was defined symmetrically, by

$$Cost\left(\mathbf{M}^i, \mathbf{S}^{i+1}; \mathbf{S}^{i+1}, \mathbf{M}^{i+1}\right) = \sum_{j=1}^{N} d_{ms}(j) + \sum_{j=1}^{M} d_{sm}(j) \qquad (6)$$

where N and M are the point numbers of $\mathbf{M}^i$ and $\mathbf{S}^{i+1}$.

3.2 Cost Function for Non-rigid Point Set Transformation

During registration, the model point set was deformed non-rigidly, thus the deformation model constraints the deformation performances, a simple model often causes inadequate deformation or abnormal deformation, and a complex model would reduce the efficiency of the algorithm. Thus, in our construction, elastic deformation and complex deformation model were used in our construction.

3.2.1 Cost Function for Elastic Deformation
Let $\mathbf{m}_1$, $\mathbf{m}_2$, $\mathbf{m}_3$ and $\mathbf{m}_4$ be four points in $\mathbf{M}^i$, $\mathbf{q}_1$, $\mathbf{q}_2$, $\mathbf{q}_3$ and $\mathbf{q}_4$ be the corresponding deformed points, as illustrated in Fig. 4.

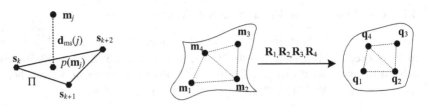

Fig. 3. Illustration of point projection   Fig. 4. Illustration of elastic deformation

In this paper, the elastic deformation cost $Cost_{elastic}(\mathbf{M}^i, \mathbf{M}^{i+1})$ was defined

$$Cost_{elastic}(\mathbf{M}^i, \mathbf{M}^{i+1}) = \sum_{j=1}^{N} \sum_{k \in \eta_j} \left\| (\mathbf{q}_j - \mathbf{q}_k) - \tilde{\mathbf{R}}_j(\mathbf{m}_j - \mathbf{m}_k) \right\|_2^2 \tag{7}$$

where N is the point number of $\mathbf{M}^i$, η_j is the neighboring index set of point $\mathbf{m}_j$, $\tilde{\mathbf{R}}_j$ is the rotation matrix. Equation (7) performed a block rotation to deformable template elastically or approximate elastically, but for every block, one block correspond to one rotation matrix, presenting approximate rigid transformation within the block, maintaining local structure.

3.2.2   Cost Function for Complex Deformation

In complex deformation, former elastic deformation model is not enough to describe the deformation form, thus, a data driven method was adopted to evaluate the complex deformation quantitatively.

Let $\mathbf{M}$ be a point set, represented by a $N \times d$ matrix, where N is the point number, d is the dimension, $\mathbf{P}^0$, $\mathbf{P}^1$, $\mathbf{P}^2$, ..., $\mathbf{P}^{N-1}$ be the circular shifted point sets of $\mathbf{M}$. Representing $\mathbf{M}$ and its ith circular shifted form $\mathbf{P}^i$ by

$$\mathbf{M} = \mathbf{P}^0 = \begin{bmatrix} x_{11} & x_{12} & \cdots & x_{1d} \\ x_{21} & x_{22} & \cdots & x_{2d} \\ \vdots & \vdots & \vdots & \vdots \\ x_{N1} & x_{N2} & \cdots & x_{Nd} \end{bmatrix} \tag{8}$$

$$\mathbf{P}^i = \begin{bmatrix} x_{(i+1)1} & x_{(i+1)2} & \cdots & x_{(i+1)d} \\ x_{(i+2)1} & x_{(i+2)2} & \cdots & x_{(i+2)d} \\ \vdots & \vdots & \vdots & \vdots \\ x_{N1} & x_{N2} & \cdots & x_{Nd} \\ x_{11} & x_{12} & \cdots & x_{1d} \\ \vdots & \vdots & \vdots & \vdots \\ x_{i1} & x_{i2} & \cdots & x_{id} \end{bmatrix}, \quad i = 1, 2, \cdots, N - 1 \tag{9}$$

Then, a complex deformed point set $\mathbf{M}'$ was defined by linear combination of $\mathbf{P}^0$, $\mathbf{P}^1$, $\mathbf{P}^2$ ... $\mathbf{P}^{N-1}$, represented by

$$\mathbf{M}' = \sum_{i=0}^{N-1} \lambda_i \mathbf{P}^i \tag{10}$$

where $\lambda_i, i = 0, 1, \cdots, N - 1$ are the coefficients and $\lambda_0 = 1$.

Defining the deformation cost performed by Eq. (10) according to the summation of squared distance between the two point sets, by

$$Cost_{complex}(\mathbf{M}, \mathbf{M}') = \sum_{k=1}^{N} \|\mathbf{m}_k - \mathbf{m}'_k\|_2^2 \qquad (11)$$

where $\mathbf{m}_k$ and $\mathbf{m}'_k$ are the kth point in point set $\mathbf{M}$ and $\mathbf{M}'$ respectively.

In above section, the cost function to register two point sets was defined (see Eq. (1)) rigidly or non-rigidly. The type of registration the algorithm performed depends on the weights w_{12} in Eq. (2), if $w_{12} = 0$, rigid registration would be performed, or non-rigid registration would be performed, a larger w_{12} often leads to a more flexible deformation during registration.

4   Linearization of the Cost Function

Based on constructed cost function in above section, optimal registration parameters could be solved by minimizing the cost function using linear or non-linear optimization. In this paper, the cost function was firstly linearized, then, the registration parameters were solved by Tikhonov regularization.

For non-rigid registration, the total cost for ith iteration can be written as

$$Cost(i, i+1) = w_1 \sum_{k=1}^{N} \|\mathbf{m}_k^{i+1} - (\mathbf{R}_1\mathbf{m}_k^i + \mathbf{t}_1)\|_2^2 + w_2 \sum_{j=1}^{N} \sum_{k \in \eta_j} \|(\mathbf{q}_j - \mathbf{q}_k) - \tilde{\mathbf{R}}_j(\mathbf{m}_j - \mathbf{m}_k)\|_2^2 +$$
$$w_3 \sum_{k=1}^{N} \|\mathbf{m}_k - \mathbf{m}'_k\|_2^2 + w_4 \sum_{j=1}^{N} \|\mathbf{m}_j - p(\mathbf{m}_j)\|_2^2 + w_5 \sum_{j=1}^{M} \|\mathbf{s}_j - p(\mathbf{s}_j)\|_2^2 +$$
$$w_6 \sum_{k=1}^{M} \|\mathbf{s}_k^{i+1} - (\mathbf{R}_2\mathbf{s}_k^i + \mathbf{t}_2)\|_2^2$$

$$(12)$$

Equation (12) is a non-linear function of registration parameters, especially on the aspects of the rotating angles in $\mathbf{R}_1$ and $\mathbf{R}_2$, in which, sine and cosine computation were involved. Because the point sets were transformed slightly, the rotating angles in $\mathbf{R}_1$ and $\mathbf{R}_2$ are all very small, thus $\mathbf{R}_1$ and $\mathbf{R}_2$ could be approximated by

$$\mathbf{R}_1 = \begin{bmatrix} 1 & -\gamma_1 & \beta_1 \\ \gamma_1 & 1 & -\alpha_1 \\ -\beta_1 & \alpha_1 & 1 \end{bmatrix}, \quad \mathbf{R}_2 = \begin{bmatrix} 1 & -\gamma_2 & \beta_2 \\ \gamma_2 & 1 & -\alpha_2 \\ -\beta_2 & \alpha_2 & 1 \end{bmatrix} \qquad (13)$$

Substitute Eq. (13) to Eq. (12), besides $p(\bullet)$ in Eq. (12) is a linear projection operator. Thus, Eq. (12) was transformed into a linear model, rewrite Eq. (12) in the following form

$$Cost(i, i+1) = w_1 \|\mathbf{A}_1\mathbf{x} - \mathbf{b}_1\|_2^2 + w_2\|\mathbf{A}_2\mathbf{x} - \mathbf{b}_2\|_2^2 + w_3\|\mathbf{A}_3\mathbf{x} - b_3\|_2^2 + w_4\|\mathbf{x} - b_4\|_2^2 +$$

$$w_5\|\mathbf{x} - b_5\|_2^2 + w_6\|\mathbf{A}_6\mathbf{x} - \mathbf{b}_6\|_2^2 \quad (14)$$

$$= \left\| D^{0.5}(\mathbf{A}\mathbf{x} - \mathbf{b}) \right\|_2^2 + \|\Gamma\mathbf{x}\|_2^2$$

where $\mathbf{x}$ is the state variable induced by rotation angles in $\mathbf{R}_1$, $\mathbf{R}_2$, the translating vector $\mathbf{t}_1$, $\mathbf{t}_2$ and the new point set $\mathbf{M}^{i+1}$, $\mathbf{S}^{i+1}$. D was a coefficient matrix who encoded w_1, w_2, w_3, w_4, w_5 and w_6. A was encoded $\mathbf{A}_1$, $\mathbf{A}_2$, $\mathbf{A}_3$ and $\mathbf{A}_4$, in which point sets $\mathbf{M}^i$ and $\mathbf{S}^i$ were used. $\mathbf{b}$ was the biased vector who encoded $\mathbf{b}_1, \mathbf{b}_2, \mathbf{b}_3$ and $\mathbf{b}_4$, in which point sets $\mathbf{M}^i$, $\mathbf{S}^i$ and the two linear projection operators were used. Γ was a coefficient matrix to involve the solution of rotation angles in $\mathbf{R}_1$, $\mathbf{R}_2$ and the translating vector $\mathbf{t}_1$, $\mathbf{t}_2$. Thus, non-rigid registration was transformed into the problem of linear minimization of Eq. (14).

5   Tikhonov Regularization

Up to now, non-rigid point set registration can be solved by minimizing linear optimization proved by Eq. (14). In this paper, Tikhonov regularization was used to minimize the two formulas. According to Tikhonov regularization method, the extreme of $\|\mathbf{A}\mathbf{x} - \mathbf{b}\|_2^2 + \|\Gamma\mathbf{x}\|_2^2$ expressed by

$$\underset{\mathbf{x}}{\arg\min} \|\mathbf{A}\mathbf{x} - \mathbf{b}\|^2 + \|\Gamma\mathbf{x}\|^2 \quad (15)$$

can be solved by

$$\mathbf{x}^* = \left(\mathbf{A}^T\mathbf{A} + \Gamma^T\Gamma\right)^{-1}\mathbf{A}^T\mathbf{b} \quad (16)$$

This optimization was performed step by step, until preset tolerances were reached.

6   Experimental Results

In order to validate the performances of proposed method, point sets were registered non-rigidly, using both proposed method and the method in [5]. Non-rigid registration results of 3D wolf point sets were shown in Fig. 5. It can be seen from the registered point sets, in our method, the model point set and the scene point set were registered accurately(corresponding points overlapped accurately), while [5] obtained slightly biased result, which means, our proposed method could reduce the residue error appeared in [5]. Numerical results were listed in Table 1. In Table 1, residue addition, our proposed method maintained more points after registration. It indicates our proposed method is more robust to point contraction than [5]. There will also offer relationship curves of non-rigid registration experiment to illustrate the change of residue error and maintained points with the registration in Figs. 6 and 7. In addition, our proposed method maintained more points after registration. It indicates our proposed

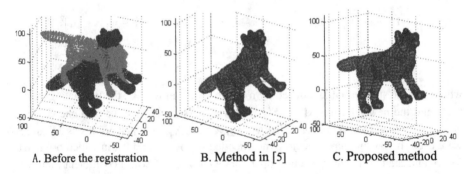

| A. Before the registration | B. Method in [5] | C. Proposed method |

Fig. 5. Non-rigid registration test of method in [5] and proposed method

Table 1. The residual and abnormal contraction points after registration

Non-rigid registration	Method in [5]	Proposed method
Original points	4344	4344
Residue error	1.7471×10^{-12}	1.9333×10^{-14}
Maintained points	2622	3894

method is more robust to point contraction than [5]. There will also offer relationship curves of non-rigid registration experiment to illustrate the change of residue error and maintained points with the registration in Figs. 6 and 7.

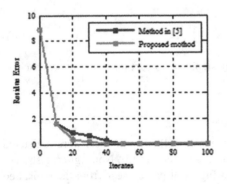
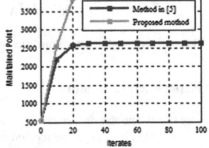

Fig. 6. Relationship curve between residue error and iteration number

Fig. 7. Relationship curve between maintained point and iteration number

7 Conclusions

This paper presented a novel point set registration method based on newly constructed cost function, linearization and Tikhonov regularization based optimization. The proposed method can be used in registration of both rigid and non-rigid point sets, achieving relative smaller residue error and larger maintained points. Experimental results indicate the proposed method is more accurate and robust than traditional method on the aspect of abnormal contraction.

Acknowledgments. This research was supported by National Natural Science Foundation of China (Grant No. 51305390, 61501394) and Natural Science Foundation of HeBei Province (Grant No. F2016203312).

References

1. Fitsgibbon, A.W.: Robust registration of 2D and 3D point set. Image Vis. Comput. **21**(13), 1145–1153 (2001)
2. Hasler, D., Sbaiz, L., SÜSstrunk, S.: Outlier modeling in image matching. IEEE Trans. Pattern Anal. Mach. Intell. **25**(3), 301–315 (2003)
3. Jian, B., Vemuri, B.: A robust algorithm for point set registration using mixture of Gaussians. In: IEEE International Conference on Computer Vision, vol. 2, pp. 1246–1251(2005)
4. Chui, H., Rangarajan, A.: A new point matching for non-rigid registration. Comput. Vis. Image Underst. **89**(2–3), 114–141 (2003)
5. Sofien, B., Andrea, T.: Dynamic 2D/3D registration. The Eurographics Association. http://lgg. epfl.ch/2d3dRegistration

An Independently Carrier Landing Method Using Point and Line Features for Fixed-Wing UAVs

Jia Ning[1,2(✉)], Lei Zhihui[1,2], and Yan Shengdong[1]

[1] College of Aerospace Science and Engineering,
National University of Defense Technology, Changsha 410073, Hunan, China
m15580074030@163.com
[2] Hunan Provincial Key Laboratory of Image Measurement
and Vision Navigation, National University of Defense Technology,
Changsha, China

Abstract. In this paper, we put forward a kind of visual landing algorithm which is straightforward and undemanding to realize for the special environment of deck. Firstly, the algorithm calculates roll angle according to sky-sea line and the vanish point according to edges of runway. According to the nature of vanish point, we can calculate the yaw angle and pitching angle; then on the basis of the landmark and track lines' collinear equation, utilizing least square solutions estimate the three position parameters. Thus all the pose parameters are obtained. The digital simulation experiment results show that the algorithm is effective and quickly, and the error of each parameters is within 10^{-10}. Even if there is a certain feature extraction error, it can get adequate results. Compared with other algorithms, the algorithm is more accurate. The algorithm is quick, accurate, easy to realize, and doesn't need iteration.

Keywords: Independently · Carrier landing · UAV · Mark point · Track line

1 Introduction

It is necessary to obtain pose parameters between ship and aircraft for landing successfully. The relative pose estimation can be estimated by detecting the existing marks on the ship, such as the track line and runway center line [1].

There are a lot of research about landing and carrier landing based on vision. Michael C. Nechyba used airborne visual sensor to obtain UAV's roll angle and pitch angle [2]. Sasa presented a method which used track line and horizon to estimate the UAV landing pose parameters [3]. Dusha extraced the horizon using the optical flow method, so as to solve the fixed-wing UAVs' attitude angles [4]. Zhou Langming proposed a visual navigation method using structured line features [5]. There are also some domestic research about the carrier landing. For example Tang Daquan discusses how to use the guidance of machine vision, during the last phase of auto-landing of UAV on deck, to make the UAV identifying and tracking the naval ship, and finally fly into the intercept net fixed on the rear deck of naval ship placidly and accurately [6].

© Springer Science+Business Media Singapore 2016
T. Tan et al. (Eds.): IGTA 2016, CCIS 634, pp. 176–183, 2016.
DOI: 10.1007/978-981-10-2260-9_20

Compared with landing, carrier landing is more complicated and difficult. The length of deck is very limited, the characteristic of dots and lines distribute clutter, the ship is in the rock all the time. These factors put forward higher requirements for the carrier landing. At present, landing method has developed from the initial optical landing system, such as Mirror Optical Landing System, Fresnel Lens Optical Landing System and Remote Optical Landing System, to All Weather Carrier Landing System, Joint Precision Approach and Landing System, and so on [7].

2 Problem Description

We assume the installation angles and displacement of camera are known. When the pose parameters of camera is estimated, we can get UAV's pose parameter through rigid transformation. In this paper camera pose is equivalent to the UAV pose. And the camera calibration has been done. So the coordinate of center point in the image and the focal length which appears in the following contents is known, and the lens distortion has been corrected.

The purpose of this paper is to estimate pose parameters of UAVs when we can accurately extract the sign points (e.g. Fresnel Lens) and the edges of runway in the late stage of carrier landing. As Fig. 1 showing the ship 3D model downloaded on the internet, the model set five sphere logo, four of all is above the track line, another is located at the edge of the deck, which represents the mark dot such as Fresnel Lens. The features used in the algorithm is one mark point and both sides of the track way edges, which are marked in Fig. 1.

As shown in Fig. 2, there are four coordinate system, deck coordinate system $O_W - X_W Y_W Z_W$, image pixel coordinate system $I - xy$, image center point coordinate system $o - uv$ and camera coordinate system $O_C - X_C Y_C Z_C$.

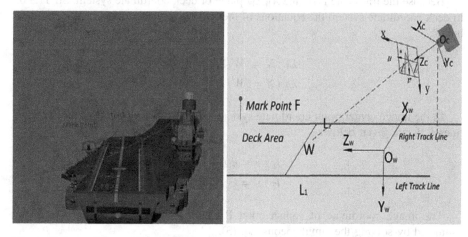

Fig. 1. Point and line in 3D model of the ship

Fig. 2. The coordinate system

According to the central perspective projection model, the coordinate system has transformation relations shown in formula (1) [8] :

$$u = f\frac{r_0(X_W - X_O) + r_1(Y_W - Y_O) + r_2(Z_W - Z_O)}{r_6(X_W - X_O) + r_7(Y_W - Y_O) + r_8(Z_W - Z_O)}$$
$$v = f\frac{r_3(X_W - X_O) + r_4(Y_W - Y_O) + r_5(Z_W - Z_O)}{r_6(X_W - X_O) + r_7(Y_W - Y_O) + r_8(Z_W - Z_O)}$$

(1)

3   Algorithm Principle

The solving process of the algorithm is mainly divided into the following two steps:

- Estimate the angle parameters: calculate roll angle using sky-sea line, and solve yaw and pitch angle according to the nature of vanish point which is the intersection of the two runway edges in the image;
- Estimate the position parameters: according to collinear equations of one point and two line, using the least squares method, calculate the three position parameters.

3.1   Estimate the Angle Parameters

The sky-sea line in the image is intersection of the image line and sea level. The roll angle can be obtained directly from the parameters of the sky-sea line, and the accuracy can be achieved at 10" [9]. There are many researches about how to estimate roll angle by extracting sky-sea line or the horizon. The related technology is mature, and its result is stable and reliable. This paper will focus on the solution of the other 5 parameters other than how to estimate roll angle in this way.

Because the track line is on the $X_W Z_W$ plane of deck coordinate system. So $Y \equiv 0$. In deck coordinate system the equations of the two runway edge lines L_1, L_2 are given below:

$$L_1 : X = W/2, Y = 0$$
$$L_2 : X = W/2, Y = 0$$

(2)

In the image center point coordinate system, the equations of the two runway edge lines l_1, l_2 are given below:

$$l_1 : v = k_1 u + j_1$$
$$l_2 : v = k_2 u + j_2$$

(3)

The image coordinate of vanish point P which is given as formula (4) can be estimated by solving the simultaneous Eq. (3):

$$u_p = \frac{j_2 - j_1}{k_1 - k_2}$$
$$v_p = k_1 u_p + j_1 \tag{4}$$

The deck coordinate of vanish point P has the nature that $Z_W \gg X_W, Y_W$, thus its collinear equation are given below [5]:

$$u_p = f\frac{r_2}{r_8} = -f\frac{\tan Ay}{\cos Ax}$$
$$v_p = f\frac{r_5}{r_8} = f\tan Ax \tag{5}$$

According to the coordinate of vanish point (u_p, v_p), we can estimate the yaw and pitch angle by further consolidation:

$$Ax = \tan^{-1}\frac{-v_p}{f} \tag{6}$$

$$Ay = \tan^{-1}(u_p\frac{\cos Ax}{f}) \tag{7}$$

As a result, we get complete attitude parameters.

3.2 Estimate the Position Parameters

The collinear equations of the right track line L_2 are given below:

$$\begin{cases} u = f\frac{r_0(B-X_O)+r_1(0-Y_O)+r_2(Z-Z_O)}{r_6(B-X_O)+r_7(0-Y_O)+r_8(Z-Z_O)} \\ v = f\frac{r_3(B-X_O)+r_4(0-Y_O)+r_5(Z-Z_O)}{r_6(B-X_O)+r_7(0-Y_O)+r_8(Z-Z_O)} \end{cases} \tag{8}$$

And its image coordinate is:

$$l_2 : v = a_2 u + b_2 \tag{9}$$

Combining formula (9) with formula (8), we can get formula (10):

$$a_1 X_O + b_1 Y_O + c_1 Z_O = d_1 \tag{10}$$

The algebras in Eq. (10) are given below:

$$a_1 = fr_3 - k_2 fr_0 - j_2 r_6$$
$$b_1 = fr_4 - k_2 fr_1 - j_2 r_7$$
$$c_1 = fr_5 - k_2 fr_2 - j_2 r_8 \tag{11}$$
$$d_1 = a_1 W/2$$

In the same way, the left track line can provide an equation like formula (10). The collinear equations of the mark point F are given below:

$$\begin{cases} u_f = f\frac{r_0(X_F-X_O)+r_1(Y_F-Y_O)+r_2(Z_F-Z_O)}{r_6(X_F-X_O)+r_7(Y_F-Y_O)+r_8(Z_F-Z_O)} \\ v_f = f\frac{r_3(X_F-X_O)+r_4(Y_F-Y_O)+r_5(Z_F-Z_O)}{r_6(X_F-X_O)+r_7(Y_F-Y_O)+r_8(Z_F-Z_O)} \end{cases} \tag{12}$$

The formula (12) can be sorted into the following form:

$$a_2X_O + b_2Y_O + c_2Z_O = d_2 \tag{13}$$

$$a_3X_O + b_3Y_O + c_3Z_O = d_3 \tag{14}$$

$$\begin{aligned} a_2 &= fr_0 - u_f r_6 \\ b_2 &= fr_1 - u_f r_7 \\ c_2 &= fr_2 - u_f r_8 \\ d_2 &= [a_2 \quad b_2 \quad c_2][X_F \quad Y_F \quad Z_F]^T \\ a_3 &= fr_3 - u_f r_6 \\ b_3 &= fr_4 - u_f r_7 \\ c_3 &= fr_5 - u_f r_8 \\ d_3 &= [a_3 \quad b_3 \quad c_3][X_F \quad Y_F \quad Z_F]^T \end{aligned} \tag{15}$$

A mark point provides two collinear equations as formulas (13) and (14), then we can get 4 equations combinating them with collinear equations of the two track lines. So full position parameters can be estimated through least square method.

4 Experiments

The idea of the simulation experiment is: 1. simulate the point and lines image coordinates according to the true value of the deck coordinates of point and lines which are set in advance; 2. estimate the pose parameters using this algorithm and those image coordinates. Then we get the error of the calculated value.

In the experiment, according to the real UAVs landing, we set the focal length $f = 1150$, the center point of the image $(x_o, y_o) = (640, 512)$, the width of runway $W = 26$ m, the mark point $F(0.292, 0, -55.251)$. And we set 1000 groups of pose data as the following Table 1 and Fig. 3. In Table 1 these parameters is set at the initial position. Figure 3 is each parameter of the 1000 groups.

We can calculate the error curve between the true value and calculated value in this method. These curves are shown in Fig. 4. We can refer literature [8] on how to estimate roll angle by sky-sea line. Here we only verify the other five parameters in addition to roll angle.

We can find the errors of each parameter is within 10^{-10} from Fig. 4 which proved the algorithm is effective. In Fig. 4(a, b), we can find the angle parameters' error become smaller as the ship closer, which is in line with expectation.

Table 1. The parameters of initial position

Parameters	Initial value
Roll angle	−0.401°
Pitch angle	−8.116°
Yaw angle	−0.566°
Height	61.10 m
Leteral offset	1.25 m
Runway direction distance	−998.96 m

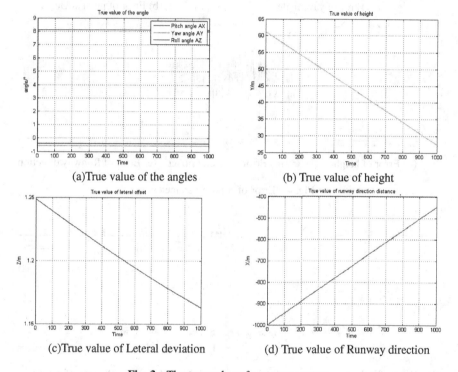

(a)True value of the angles

(b) True value of height

(c)True value of Leteral deviation

(d) True value of Runway direction

Fig. 3. The true value of pose parameters

Taking into account that the feature extraction process bring about extraction error, and the extraction of line is more accurate than point extraction usually. We give the mark point 1 pixel error to test the algorithm. Through the algorithm principle we can found the extraction error of the mark point only affects the location parameters. So we only analysis the error of three position parameters. The calculation results are the red lines shown in Fig. 5.

To prove this method is effective, we compare it with Zhou's method [5]. Zhou Langming proposed a visual navigation algorithm using the structural line features on the runway plane [5]. His algorithm is based on the both sides of runway edge lines and

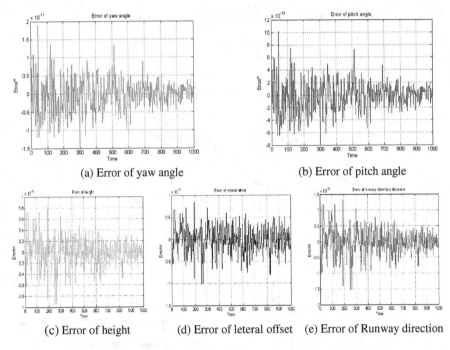

(a) Error of yaw angle   (b) Error of pitch angle

(c) Error of height   (d) Error of leteral offset   (e) Error of Runway direction

Fig. 4. Error of 5 pose parameters

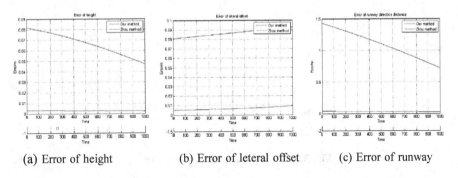

(a) Error of height   (b) Error of lateral offset   (c) Error of runway

Fig. 5. Comparison between the two methods

a lateral structural line. We realize Zhou's algorithm and add 1 pixel error to an endpoint of the structural line, then the errors of each parameters are shown in Fig. 5.

By Fig. 5 we can found when there is 1 pixel error, the three errors of height, the lateral offset and runway direction distance are less than 0.01 m, 0.004 m, 0.04 m respectively. The result is sufficiently accurate, conforms to the expected design. The three errors in Zhou's algorithm are less than 0.10 m, 0.09 m, 1.5 m. So under this circumstance our method is more accurate than Zhous'.

5 Conclusion

In this paper, a new algorithm based on point and line feature is proposed. Taking into account the imaging characteristics in the UAV landing stage, and the distribution of point and line on the deck, we estimate the roll angle with sky-sea line, solve the other 5 parameters using the track lines and feature points (such as Fresnel and other known landmarks).

The numerical simulation results show that the error of each parameter calculated by the algorithm is within 10^{-10} at the range of 1000 m–500 m from the origin of the deck. And the effectiveness of the algorithm is proved. Even if we give 1 pixel error to the mark point, the error of all the three position parameters is within 0.01 m. This paper also compared the Zhou Langming's algorithm, although his algorithm is to solve the UAV position for landing on the runway, it also has a certain reference for this paper. The comparison results show that our algorithm is more accurate.

The advantages of the method are: special features are not required, we can use the existing features of the deck directly. The estimation of angle and position parameters is independent, and the coordinate of the point only affect the position parameters. The method is quickly because it doesn't use iteration, it is also reliable and easy to project implementation.

The limitations of this method lies in the fact that in the process of landing, the roll angle is calculated by the sky-sea line, which is vulnerable to weather. And the roll angle is an absolute angle of the UAV in relation to the world coordinate system, rather than the angle relative to the deck, so when the ship shakes seriously, this method is limited.

References

1. Zhang, X.M.: Research of Key Technology and Methods of Vision-landing and Visual Guiding. National university of defense technology (2008). (in Chinese)
2. Ettinger, S.M., Nechyba, M.C., Ifju, P.G., et al.: Vision-guided flight stability and control for micro air vehicles. J. Adv. Rob. 3(7), 2134–2140 (2002)
3. Sasa, S., Gomi, H., Ninomiya, T., et al: Position and attitude estimation using image processing of runway. In: Aerospace Sciences Meeting and Exhibit (2000)
4. Dusha, D., Boles, W.W., Walker, R.: Fixed-wing attitude estimation using computer vision based horizon detection. J. Comput. Vis. 34(5), 599–621 (2007)
5. Zhou, L., Zhong, Q., Zhang, Y., et al.: A vision-based landing method using structured line features of runway surface for Fixed-Wing UAVs. (in Chinese)
6. Daquan, T., Yang, Y., Xin, D.: Study of the guidance methods of machine vision during the last phase of auto-landing of UAV on deck. J. Aviat. Metrol. Measur. Technol. 4(24), 4–9 (2004). (in Chinese)
7. Daquan, T., Bo, B., Xushang, W., et al.: Summary on technology of automatic landing/carrier landing. J. Chin. Inert. Technol. 18(5), 550–555 (2010). (in Chinese)
8. Yu, Q., Yang, S.: Video Metrics Principles and Researches, pp. 95–196. Science Press, Beijing (2009). (in Chinese)
9. Zhang, Y., Liu, H., Su, A., et al.: Real-time estimation of ship's horizontal attitude based on horizon tracking. Optik-Int. J. Light Electron. Opt. 126(23), 4475–4483 (2015)

Pose Estimation of Space Objects Based on Hybrid Feature Matching of Contour Points

Xin Zhang$^{(\boxtimes)}$, Haopeng Zhang, Quanmao Wei, and Zhiguo Jiang

Image Processing Center, School of Astronautics,
Beihang University, Beijing Key Laboratory of Digital Media, Beijing, China
{zhangxxag,zhanghaopeng,weiqm,jiangzg}@buaa.edu.cn

Abstract. This paper presents an improved pose estimation algorithm for vision-based space objects. The major weakness of most existing methods is limited convergence radius. In most cases they ignore the influence of translation, only focusing on rotation parameters. To breakthrough these limits, we utilizes hybrid local image features to explicitly establish 2D-3D correspondences between the input image and 3D model of space objects, and then estimate rotation and translation parameters based on the correspondences. Experiments with simulated models are carried out, and the results show that our algorithm can successfully estimate the pose of space objects with large convergence radius and high accuracy.

Keywords: Pose estimation · Space object · Hybrid local image features · 2D-3D correspondences

1 Introduction

Determining the pose parameters of a space object is one of the fundamental issues in space missions. In recent years, optical imaging system has been widely used in aerospace for many applications such as automatic rendezvous and docking, on-orbit self-serving,etc [1]. There is an urgent demand for vision-based pose estimation algorithms which can be applied to space objects. On the other hand, with the rapid development of high quality imaging sensors, images which contain more details can serve as the input of the pose estimation process, which is critical for improving accuracy of pose parameters estimated by vision-based methods.

2D-3D pose estimation is a fundamental task for computer vision applications and many feasible approaches have been proposed to solve this problem [2–8]. The main difficulty of vision-based pose estimation lies in the establishment of certain correspondences between the image and 3D model. Focusing on this point, the existing methods can be generally divided into three categories: (1) The first kind of methods separate the pose estimation process into two parts directly, i.e. first determining the correspondences through local feature extraction such as SIFT [9], stable region extraction [10], etc., and then estimating

© Springer Science+Business Media Singapore 2016
T. Tan et al. (Eds.): IGTA 2016, CCIS 634, pp. 184–191, 2016.
DOI: 10.1007/978-981-10-2260-9_21

pose parameters base on these features. However, the performance of these methods largely depends on the capacity of certain feature, and the results are not always satisfying. (2) The second kind of methods aims at bypassing the problem of determining 2D-3D correspondences by the technique of image matching. A number of silhouette images of space object's 3D model are projected beforehand with different view angle and translation, and then the object's pose is regarded as the pose parameters of the most similar silhouette image measured by calculating the similarity between the input image and each of the silhouette images. This kind of methods can roughly determine the pose parameter, but the number of silhouette images grows exponentially when a more accurate estimation result is required. (3) The third category employs iterative mechanism to determine correspondence and estimates pose parameters simultaneously. Compared with methods of the first two categories, the advantages of these methods are that no silhouette image is needed to generate beforehand and are stabler than methods using certain feature extraction. However, they suffer from the limits of convergence speed and convergence radius.

Images of space objects often have relative small size and low resolution, and thus lack of texture information. These characteristics make it difficult to accurately estimate pose parameters for space objects using vision-based methods. In this paper, we propose a contour-based approach which does not need texture information and broadly belongs to the third category. This method is motivated by the work in [5] which employs distance map to establish tentative 2D-3D point correspondences, then estimates pose parameters and updates correspondences simultaneously and iteratively. Our improvements mainly lie in two aspects: (1) Instead of using distance map for point-matching, we exploit hybrid local feature of contour points to establish tentative 2D-3D correspondences, which is more accurate and robust to translation. (2) In order to avoid interpolation, we use the original points given in 3D model to establish 2D-3D correspondences, making our method computationally much more efficient.

The rest of the paper is arranged as follows. In Sect. 2 we detail our method by describing the establishment of 2D-3D correspondences and the orthogonal iteration algorithm. Section 3 presents the simulation experiments and the results. Finally the conclusion is given in Sect. 4.

2   Iterative Pose Estimation Based on Contour Points' Hybrid Feature

This section presents the details of our algorithm and analysis them theoretically. Given the 3D model of a space object which contains vertex and normal information, our goal is to find the 3D (Euclidean) transformation making the model coincide with the object in the referential coordinate attached to a calibrated camera.

2.1 Notation

Camera model and coordinate systems configuration are presented in Fig. 1. Subscripts u, p and v respectively indicate camera coordinate system, image plane coordinate system and object self-centered coordinate system.

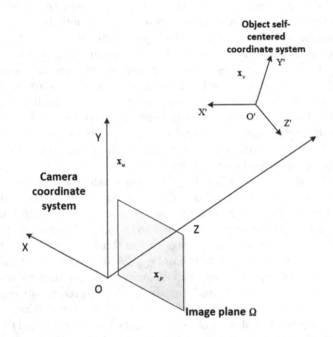

Fig. 1. Camera model and coordinate frames configuration

Let $\mathbf{x}_u = [X, Y, Z]^T$ denotes the coordinates of a point in R^3 measured with respect to a referential coordinate attached to the imaging camera. We denote by $\Omega \subset R^2$ the image plane, and assume that the camera is modeled as an ideal perspective projection: $\pi : R^3 \rightarrow \Omega$; $\mathbf{x}_u \rightarrow \mathbf{x}_p$, where $\mathbf{x}_p = [x, y]^T = [X/Z, Y/Z]^T$ denotes coordinates in Ω. Object self-centered coordinate system and camera coordinate system are related by the rigid transformation as

$$\mathbf{x}_u = \mathbf{R}\mathbf{x}_v + \mathbf{t} \tag{1}$$

where $\mathbf{R}$ is the rotation matrix and $\mathbf{t}$ is the translation vector. The image plane coordinate system and object self-centered coordinate system are related by the equation

$$\begin{pmatrix} \mathbf{x}_p \\ 1 \end{pmatrix} \sim \mathbf{K}(\mathbf{R}|\mathbf{t}) \begin{pmatrix} \mathbf{x}_v \\ 1 \end{pmatrix} \tag{2}$$

where symbol '$\sim$' means equal in homogeneous manner, and $\mathbf{K}$ is the inner camera parameter matrix which is known as a priori.

2.2 Establishing 2D-3D Point Correspondence

We firstly establish the 2D-2D correspondence between contour of the input image and contour of the projection image which is generated by projecting object's 3D model onto the image plane. Border following algorithm proposed in [11] is utilized to produce binary and single-pixel wide contours.

The contour point's hybrid feature extracted in our method consists of pixel's position and curvature in the image. We construct a vector which represents local feature by the following equation

$$\mathbf{f} = (f_1, f_2, f_3)^T = (x, y, \omega k)^T \tag{3}$$

where $(x, y)^T$ represents the position of the pixel, and k is the curvature of the contour at this point. For discrete contour image it is difficult to calculate curvature, so we calculate USAN [12] value as an alternative. USAN describes the target to the background ratio in a circle template, it is robust to noise and has scale invariant property. ω is a weighting coefficient, and we can rectify the relative effects between feature components to reflect the structure of the feature space accurately by adjusting the coefficient. The choice of ω has to guarantee that when the difference between the input image and the projection image is relative small, the curvature feature will not overwhelm the effect of x and y; meanwhile when the difference between the input image and the projection image is conspicuous, the curvature feature has to play a major role. In our current implementation, the value of ω is set to 6, and tests show that the correspondence result is relative good. The curve of correspondence error between contour of input image and contour of projection image is presented in Fig. 2.

Let $\mathbf{C}_i$ denotes the set of feature vector of the input image contour points and $\mathbf{C}_p$ denotes the set of feature vector of the projection image contour points. Given a point F_p in projection image contour with feature vector $\mathbf{f_p} = (f_{p1}, f_{p2}, f_{p3})^T$,

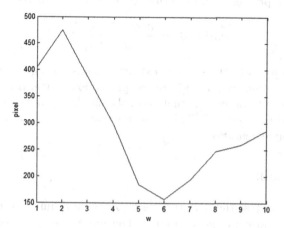

Fig. 2. Curve of correspondence error

the feature vector $\mathbf{f_i}$ of its correspondence point F_i in input image contour can be described as follow

$$\mathbf{f_i} = (f_{i1}, f_{i2}, f_{i3})^T = \min_{\mathbf{g}} \parallel \mathbf{f_p} - \mathbf{g} \parallel, \forall \mathbf{g} \in \mathbf{C}_i \qquad (4)$$

where symbol '$\parallel \cdot \parallel$' means calculate two-norm of the vector.

When we create a projection image, we dye each vertex of the 3D model with different color. Then by using color attribute as index, we can efficiently retrieve the required 3D coordinate of the vertex from object's 3D model, and carry the established 2D-2D point correspondence relationship forward to the final 2D-3D point correspondences.

The algorithm in [5] establishes 2D-2D correspondences for each point in projection image, then back-projects them to 3D model by interpolation to get 2D-3D correspondences. Such approach is not only a waste of computation, but may also bring in error in the process of interpolation. As an improvement, we choose the points in projection image that exactly correspond to vertices in 3D model to establish 2D-3D correspondences. In our implementation, the number of points in projection image contour is about 600, and after our filtration, the number of 2D-3D correspondences can be reduced to about 50. The decrease of calculation is remarkable.

2.3 Estimating Pose Parameters Based on 2D-3D Correspondence

After the establishment of 2D-3D point correspondences between the input image and object's 3D model, the next step is the process of point-based pose estimation. As in [5], we adopt the orthogonal iteration (OI) algorithm proposed in [2] which is fast and numerically precise.

We define a similarity function by employ the XNOR operation '$\odot$' to the binary input image contour and the binary projection image contour, to measure the fitness of the pose estimation result returned by our method.

$$Similarity = \frac{area(\mathbf{C}_{in} \odot \mathbf{C}_{pr})}{area(\mathbf{C}_{pr})} \qquad (5)$$

in which $\mathbf{C}_{in}$ represents the contour extracted from the input image, and $\mathbf{C}_{pr}$ represents the contour extracted from the projection image. If the pose estimation result is close to object's actual pose, the similarity value after the XNOR operation would be close to 1. This measurement is utilized as termination criterion in our implementation.

3   Experiment

In this section, we test the performance of our pose estimation method in convergence speed and convergence radius. The method in [5] is the baseline for comparison. All the codes involved in our algorithm are implemented in C++ and run on a PC with 2.6 GHz CPU and 8 GB RAM.

Figure 3 presents twelve frames from two pose estimation runs to give a clear inspection about the convergence process of our method. We initiate the iteration with a conspicuous deviation for rotation and translation. The six frames in (a) and (b) are extracted from a total of 100 iterations in a pose estimation run.

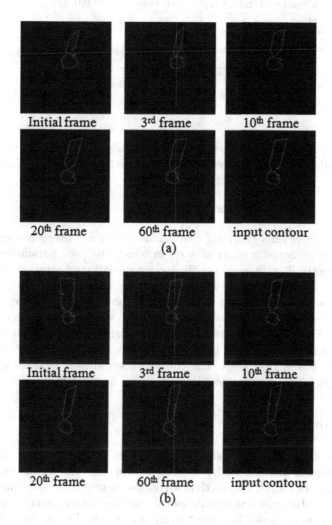

Fig. 3. Convergence illustration of our method

Table 1 summarizes the convergence speed and convergence radius of our methods and the method in [5]. The threshold of similarity is set to 0.96. For pose sample density, we set the intervals to 20° for all the three Euler angles (yaw angle ψ, pitch angle θ and roll angle ϕ). The initial pose solution required by the iterative methods is obtained randomly within the range

$$\Delta\psi \times \Delta\theta \times \Delta\phi = [-45°, 45°] \times [-45°, 45°] \times [-45°, 45°] \tag{6}$$

Table 1. Convergence speed and convergence radius

	Method of [5]	Our method
Average iteration number	25.8	22.7
Time per iteration (s)	0.1840	0.07357
Min radius (°)	19.7	18.5
Max radius (°)	41.2	41.7
Mean radius (°)	30.6	31.2
Error of rotation (°)	1.542	1.243
Error of translation (pixel)	3.1	2.8

For each pose we run 100 tests to explore its neighborhoods. We use the same formula as [5] to calculate convergence radius for the convenience of comparison.

$$R_{convergence} = \sqrt{\frac{N_{sucess}}{N_{total}}} \cdot R_{total} \tag{7}$$

where N_{total} represents the total number of tests for convergence radius, and $N_{success}$ represents the number of tests in which the pose parameters are calculated correctly. R_{total} represents the largest deviation of rotation angle in the tests. In our implementation, we have $N_{total} = 100$, $R_{total} = 45°$. The error of rotation and translation are the average of the deviation between estimated pose parameters and the true value in 100 tests in which the algorithm converges successfully. From the statistics in Table 1 we can see that for our method, it usually takes tens of iterations before successfully converging, and the time cost per iteration is less than 0.1 s. The convergence radius is close to that of the method in [5] which is wide enough for practical application.

4   Conclusion

In this article, we focus on vision-based pose estimation of space objects. An improved contour-based iterative method is proposed which runs fast and has wide convergence radius. Our method solves the feature correspondence problem and pose estimation problem simultaneously and iteratively, and no priori feature correspondences is needed between the input monocular image and object's 3D model. Experimental results show that our method can successfully achieve space object pose estimation and meet the requirement of practical application.

Acknowledgments. This work was supported in part by the National Natural Science Foundation of China (Grant Nos. 61501009, 61371134 and 61071137), and the Fundamental Research Funds for the Central Universities.

References

1. Aghili, F., Kuryllo, M., Okouneva, G., English, C.: Robust vision-based pose estimation of moving objects for automated rendezvous and docking. In: International Conference on Mechatronics and Automation, pp. 305–311 (2010)
2. Lu, C.P., Hager, G.D., Mjolsness, E.: Fast and globally convergent pose estimation from video images. IEEE Trans. Pattern Anal. Mach. Intell. **22**(6), 610–622 (2000)
3. Dambrevile, S., Sandhu, R., Yezzi, A., Tannenbaum, A.: A geometric approach to joint 2D region-based segmentation and 3D pose estimation using a 3D shape prior. SIAM J. Imaging Sci. **3**(1), 110–132 (2010)
4. Iwashita, Y., Kurazume, R., Konishi, K., Nakamoto, M., Hashizume, M., Hasegawa, T.: Fast alignment of 3D geometrical models and 2D grayscale images using 2D distance maps. Syst. Comput. Jpn. **38**(14), 1889–1899 (2007)
5. Leng, D.W., Sun, W.D.: Contour-based iterative pose estimation of 3D rigid object. IET Comput. Vis. **5**(5), 291–300 (2011)
6. Ansar, A., Daniilidis, K.: Linear pose estimation from points or lines. IEEE Trans. Pattern Anal. Mach. Intell. **25**(5), 578–589 (2003)
7. Rosenhahn, B., Perwass, C., Sommer, G.: Pose estimation of free-form contours. Int. J. Comput. Vis. **62**, 267–289 (2005)
8. Dambreville, S., Sandhu, R., Yezzi, A., Tannenbaum, A.: Robust 3D pose estimation and efficient 2D region-based segmentation from a 3D shape prior. In: Proceedings of European Conference on Computer Vision, pp. 169–182 (2008)
9. Lowe, D.G.: Distinctive image features from scale-invariant keypoints. Int. J. Comput. Vis. **60**(2), 91–110 (2004)
10. Donoser, M., Bischof, H.: Efficient maximally stable extremal region (MSER) tracking. Comput. Vis. Pattern Recogn. **1**, 553–560 (2006)
11. Suzuki, S., Abe, K.: Topological structural analysis of digitized binary images by border following. Comput. Vis. Graph. Image Process. **30**(1), 32–46 (1985)
12. Smith, S.M., Brady, J.M.: Susan-a new approach to low level image processing. Int. J. Comput. Vis. **23**(1), 45–78 (1997)

A Software Watermarking Algorithm Based on the Full Array of Expression Coefficients

Cheng Cheng[✉], Niande Jiang, Huiyuan Li, and Rong Zeng

Department of Information Engineering,
East China University of Technology, Nanchang, Jiangxi, China
592711713@qq.com

Abstract. In order to solve the problem of low message hidden rate and against attacks, this paper proposed an algorithm based on a full array of expressions coefficient. Algorithm through coefficient expressions of permutations and binary number and sequence number of one-to-one correspondence to construct a mapping dictionary. Then the mapping dictionary is used to embedding and extracting watermark. At last, the program which embedded watermark is encrypted by AES module. This algorithm is used to concrete some real examples on the SandMark platform, and then it is compared with the Monden algorithm, Mohammad algorithm and inverse number algorithm in performance. Theoretical analysis and experimental results proves that the algorithm is significantly improved anti attack and data rate.

Keywords: Software watermarking · Expression coefficient · Mapping dictionary · Ordinal arrangement

1 Introduction

With the rapid development of computer network and software industry, the piracy of digital products has become increasingly easy, so the protection of digital property right is concerned by more and more people. Nowadays there are many software protection technologies. The software can be protected by encryption, serial number, key files, dongles (hardware key), etc. Whether the author of the software, or software developers need to spend a lot of financial and material resources in the software protection. Software watermarking technique is proposed by the researchers at this time. Its purpose is to protect the intellectual property rights of software authors, and it can identify illegal copying and theft of software products.

In 2000, Akito et al. proposed a watermarking algorithm [2], which to add a mute function in the source code (Monden Algorithm). Some mute functions are added to the conditional statements. The if condition is false all the time, the mute function will never run, and the watermark is hidden in the mute function. While adding code to the source code is easy to implement, but it reduces the running speed of the program, and this method can be easily found by the attacker. Shirali-Shahreza et al. proposed to hide the watermark by expression operand reorder and the difference of binary tree around the subtree. This method does not need to add extra code, but its hidden data rate is relatively low [2] (Mohammad Algorithm). In 2009, Hua et al. proposed a software

© Springer Science+Business Media Singapore 2016
T. Tan et al. (Eds.): IGTA 2016, CCIS 634, pp. 192–199, 2016.
DOI: 10.1007/978-981-10-2260-9_22

watermarking algorithm based on inverse number of expression [4] (Reverse Number Algorithm). Through the arrangement of reverse the number and structure of binary code mapping dictionary to implement the watermark embedding and extraction. The algorithm running speed and hide information has improved so much, but it is less secure, attacks are more likely to figure out its hidden watermark in accordance with their arrangement.

Based on the above research, a software watermarking scheme is proposed based on the full permutation of the expression coefficients. Let the software copyright and author information hiding in the binary number, and then according to arrange permutations and ordinal expression coefficients corresponding relation with the binary structure mapping dictionary. Put the expression of the corresponding coefficient into the source code. Finally, the program is encrypted by AES encryption method, and the software watermarking algorithm is realized by SandMark platform.

2 Software Watermarking Based on Full Array of Expression Factor

2.1 The Main Idea of the Algorithm

The main idea of this algorithm is that the whole arrangement of coefficient expression. The watermark information is hidden in the expression coefficient by using the watermark information and the expression coefficient of one to one. At the same time, the function of the expression remains unchanged.

This algorithm has the following main steps: construct watermark→construct mapping dictionary→embedding watermark→extracting watermark.

2.2 Constructing Watermark

The author's information and copyright information and other information to be saved in accordance with certain rules (Rules can be defined by the software owner) into binary code. Many of these programs have many different versions because of various of different needs. Different versions of the watermark information can be constructed. And this method is also an important means of a software copyright protection.

2.3 Construct Mapping Dictionary

There are a lot of expressions in each program. It have such expressions: The operating coefficients of the expression are exchangeable, and such an exchange does not affect the function of the program. Expressions such as a combination of additions and multiplication

$$a_1X_1 + a_2X_2 + a_3X_3 + \ldots + a_nX_n \tag{1}$$

To find such expressions in the program. The coefficients are extracted and the coefficients are arranged. Record the total arrangement number M. Specifies the digit for each random permutation (Digital range is 1–M, and shall not repeat the specified). We define the number of such figures as the order number. Specify a binary code for each permutation, watermark is a binary code hidden among them. When the expression coefficient is 5, the map dictionary is constructed as shown in Table 1:

Table 1. Mapping dictionary

Binary code	Expression coefficient permutation	Permutation number
1100101100011	a_1, a_2, a_3, a_4, a_5	98
110000110000101	a_1, a_3, a_2, a_4, a_5	76
0001101100011	a_4, a_2, a_1, a_5, a_3	118
....	....	....
11110100011011	a_2, a_4, a_1, a_3, a_5	35

2.4 Embedding Watermark

To find expressions in the program such as (2):

$$(a_1X_1 + a_2X_2 + a_3X_3 + \ldots + a_nX_n) + (b_1Y_1 * b_2Y_2 * b_3Y_3 * \ldots * b_mY_m) \tag{2}$$

$$(a_1, a_2, a_3, \ldots a_n) \& (b_1, b_2, b_3, \ldots b_m) \tag{3}$$

$$(X_1 \ldots X_n) \& (Y_1 \ldots Y_m) \tag{4}$$

Data (3) is called coefficients. Data (4) is called operand.

To hide the watermark in (2), steps are as follows:

a. There are two groups of interchangeable coefficients in (3), two sets of data were ordered, and then according to the above method to construct maps dictionary. Hide the converted watermark information in the construction of the dictionary.

b. According to the arrangement and the arrangement ordinal number mapping dictionary watermark information and expression coefficients one to one relationship, and then according to the arrangement of the watermark information corresponding expression coefficients obtained two expressions watermarked.

c. Finally, the embedded watermark is embedding into the source program.

2.5 Extracting Watermark

The extraction of the watermark is the inverse process of watermark embedding. If now extract the watermark from the S sets of coefficients exchangeable expressions. The steps are as follows:

a. Firstly, the coefficients of the S group are arranged according to their relative positions in the expression: $K_1, K_2, K_3, \ldots K_S$.
b. According to the arrangement of the coefficient of expression in the mapping dictionary to find out its corresponding arrangement number, and then according to the arrangement number to find the corresponding binary number.
c. Finally, the watermarking data is compared with the watermark information. If the same, the copyright is proved, if not, the watermark is destroyed or subject to attack.

3   AES Code Encryption

In order to further strengthen the protection of the program, after embedding the watermark, the AES encryption module is used to encrypt the program, and the program code can be converted into an encrypted cipher code. First, mark the code segment of the embedded watermark (Also including non-watermarked sensitive code segment).

$$(CEB_1, CEB_2, CEB_3, \ldots CEB_n) \tag{5}$$

Then calculate the abstract of the unlabeled code segment, and then call the AES encryption function. At last, encrypt the code.

$$CEB_i, CEB_i' = AES(CEB_i, key_i). \tag{6}$$

When the program is executed, if you encounter a cipher block CEB_i', first call the decryption function to decrypt, and then execute the code block. In the process of encryption, the use of the unlabeled code segment of the message digest $SHA1$ as a parameter, that it could effectively prevent the entire program is being tampered with. After the program is finish-end, the encryption module is called to protect the embedded watermark code section and the sensitive code segment.

4   The Simulation Experiment and Performance Analysis

This article choose to implement software watermarking algorithm proposed on open source software watermarking test platform SandMark. The testing platform integrates many software watermarking algorithms, which can be used to study and verify various algorithms. The system is based on the. Jar type file as the research object. SandMark software testing platform mainly consists of two parts: embedded device and identifier. The embedded file and watermark information as input to generate a new embedded watermark file. Recognition will generate a new file as inputs and outputs the watermark information. Experiments will be conducted to evaluate the algorithm from 3 aspects: data rate, concealment and anti attack. The experimental flow chart is shown in Fig. 1:

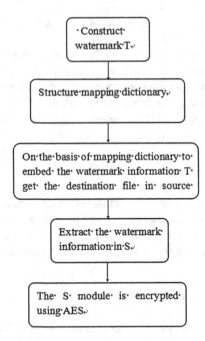

Fig. 1. Algorithm flow chart of the simulation experiments

4.1 Data Rate

Data rate is the maximum amount of watermark information embedded in a program, which is an important indicator of the software watermarking system. In this paper, the algorithms is realized on the SandMark platform, with this algorithm in different amount of code in the program are compared. The results are shown in Table 2:

Table 2. Four algorithms to hide the watermark data rate

Algorithm	Lines of code		
	1000	3000	5000
Monden	17	13	31
Mohammad	15	19	28
Reverse number	20	44	76
The algorithm of this paper	23	48	86

As can be seen from the table when fewer lines of code, the algorithm advantage is not obvious. But with the increase of the amount of code, the algorithm of data rate rises to be higher than the previous 3 kinds of algorithms. Four algorithms comparison data rate line chart shown in Fig. 2.

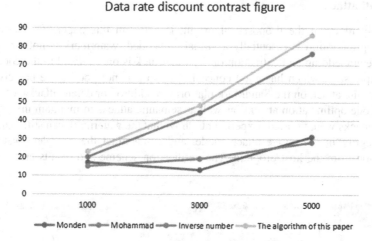

Fig. 2. Data rate discount contrast figure

4.2 Concealment

Concealment is used to measure the watermark information embedded in the program is found and the location of the attacker and the ease of positioning [5]. On this basis, the paper [4] proposes a feature value of the watermark information and its surrounding code and the non-embedded watermark to represent the concealment of the watermark. Characteristic value calculation formula:

$$d = \sum_{i=0}^{k} \sqrt{(n_i - m_i)^2} \tag{7}$$

$\{n_i\}$ is the process of the embedded watermark after the percentage of each byte code instruction, $\{m_i\}$ is the percentage of the general program of various byte code instructions. The smaller the characteristic value, the better the concealment of the watermark. Four kinds of algorithms is characterized by calculated values as shown in Table 3:

As can be seen from the table. This algorithm has some advantages in terms of concealment. In this paper, we use the mapping dictionary, but because the algorithm does not use additional encryption method, it still has good performance in the concealment.

Table 3. Four kinds of watermarking algorithm characteristic value

Algorithm	Characteristic value
Monden	0.0993
Mohammad	0.1011
Inverse number	0.1034
The algorithm of this paper	0.0988

4.3   Anti-attack

The transparency of the proposed algorithm is better in this paper. The watermark embedding algorithm is essentially a virtual embedded, watermark is not written the code. The embedding and extraction of the watermark is only related to the coefficient of the expression, which has good concealment, so it is not good to be perceived. In this paper, the attack on the SandMark platform in addition or delete attacks, distortion attacks, code optimization attacks, as well as semantic attacks to maintain the attack of the four attacks were verified. Experiments show that the watermark can still maintain a good integrity in the above attack mode, and can extract the complete watermark information from the host program. The verification scheme and results are shown in Fig. 3:

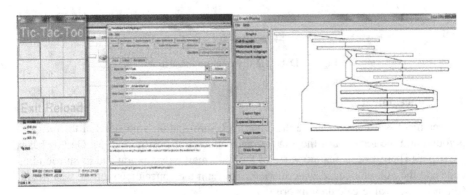

Fig. 3. Experimental methods and results

This algorithm's resistance to aggressive from four aspects below are analyzed.

(1) Add or remove attacking

An attacker on software for data add or remove. Since this method does not add additional information in the program, the watermark embedding and extraction are associated with the coefficient of expression. An attacker to add the code will only make the program becomes cumbersome, and will not affect the extraction of the watermark. If you remove the code will destroy the watermark and so does not work properly, so this method of watermarking is invalid.

(2) Distortion attacking

Assume that the attacker already knows the watermark is hidden in the expression, and the data in the expression change to achieve the purpose of destroying the watermark. Since the coefficient with the author and the user's information expression is one to one, after such transformation extracted watermark is not find information or to find the information is wrong.

(3) Code optimization attacking

Attackers find watermark embedding location, on watermarked code for code optimization, aimed at undermining the watermark. For the algorithm in this paper, the expression of the embedded watermark is the optimal form, so the code optimization is doesn't work on it. Developers can still extract the watermark.

(4) Semantic holding attacking
This algorithm is the use of the code confusion technology transformation program, do not change under the premise of the program features and functions disrupted its original structure. For this algorithm, if the coefficient of the expression is changed, the expression is not written in the standard form, then the watermark is destroyed or attacked.

5 Conclusion

In this paper, a software watermarking scheme is proposed, which is based on the full permutation of the expression coefficients, Operand coefficients extracted and its full array, specify the arrangement ordinal number for each arrangement, the arrangement and the number of one to one mapping of binary relations dictionary by constructing ordinal number and arrangement of each expression coefficient to achieve embedding and extraction. Simulation results on SandMark platform show that the proposed algorithm is improved in data rate, concealment and anti attack.

References

1. Zhang, L., Yang, Y., Niu, X.: Overview of software watermarking. Softw. J. **14**(2), 268–277 (2003)
2. Akito, M., Hajimu, I., Ken-ichi M., et al.: A practical method for watermarking Java programs. In: Proceedings of the 24th Computer Software and Applications Conference (2000)
3. Patel, S.J., Pattewar, T.M.: Software birthmark based theft detection of Java Script programs using agglomerative clustering and frequent subgraph mining. In: 2014 International Conference on Embedded Systems (ICES) (2014)
4. Hua, J., Sha, Z., Xuan, A.: Software watermarking algorithm based on inverse number of expression. Comput. Appl. **09**(06), 3189–3190 (2009)
5. Zhou, L.: Evaluation of Software Watermarking Algorithm. Jilin Universiy, Ji Lin (2010)
6. Cui, X.: Software Encryption and Decryption, pp. 378–488. People's Posts and Telecommunications Press, Beijing (2012)
7. Chan, P.P.F., Hui, L.C.K., Yiu, S.M.: Heap graph based software theft detection. In: IEEE Transactions on Information Forensics and Security (2013)
8. Tang, Z.Y., Fang, D.Y., Shu, L.: A tamper resistant software watermarking scheme based on code encryption. J. Univ. Sci. Technol. China **41**(7), 599–606 (2011)
9. Ying, G., Lu, L., Wang, L.: The research and practice of computer graphics teaching reform based on algorithm demonstration and algorithm training. J. East China Inst. Technol. (Soc. Sci.) **32**(1), 78–80 (2013)

A Framework Analysis of Measuring the Index Node Considering Local and Global Networks

Xinyi Fan, Shan Liu[✉], and Jianping Chai

School of Information Engineering, Communication University of China,
Beijing 100024, China
liushan@cuc.edu.cn

Abstract. This paper proposes a solution using multi-index method to evaluate node importance locally and globally with adjusted parameters in the network by considering several evaluation indexes. Especially, it adheres to the principles that the node importance of the network is relevant to the value of the node itself together with the centrality of neighbor nodes from a local point of view. Moreover, this paper considers both spreading information and speed of node in dynamic network. The chief influence on adjusted parameters in different network has been estimated. We can rank the influence of users and analyze their tags of interest from the result. In addition, we can make valuable classification of users and improve the service for more personalized services, which is very important for data mining.

Keywords: Social network · Date mining · Network construction · Visualization analysis

1 Introduction

In the late 20th century, two concepts of specific networks were proposed. Watts and Strogatz put forward small-world networks [1], and Barabasi and Albert proposed a standard scale-free networks [2], claim that there are common, unified and non-trivial features in a wide variety of network architectures. A large number of complex network systems in nature can be described through relative network. And they are all based on "six degrees of separation theory "of the network. Each person's social network social property and interests determine their social relationships and dating range. In the social network used to describe the complex system [3, 4], people are acted as the nodes in social network, simultaneously the links of certain relationships between people are considered as the connecting sides.

By analyzing the network, we can clearly understand the connection and the mutual influence between users. The dissemination of information in the network can be manageable and controllable by monitoring the propagation path and dissemination source of the information. We can also make personalized recommendation by monitoring users' relationships in the network and their attention.

Dissemination of information in the social network is carried out by the strength of the relationships between people. It is essential to make analysis of the node importance to study the network. We can quantify the index of the node importance in order

© Springer Science+Business Media Singapore 2016
T. Tan et al. (Eds.): IGTA 2016, CCIS 634, pp. 200–208, 2016.
DOI: 10.1007/978-981-10-2260-9_23

to strengthen the protection of the users, which are in the important key nodes. In this way, we can improve the robustness of the network, control the speed of information dissemination and public opinion and cut the dissemination of harmful information. On the other hand, it plays a supporting role for the "word of mouth" and "viral marketing" [5]. We only need to make product promotion to a small number of influential customers and get their approval so that the members of this group will recommend the product to their friends. Obviously, it can help us save our time, effort and cost compared to widely recommendation without direction. How to exactly find the users with important influence? We are required to rank the importance of nodes in the network to accurately identify valuable users.

Current researches on the influence of the individual nodes are mostly focused on communication content, interacted node relationship, information-processing of influence, etc. Analyzing social network, centrality is used to mark the most influential node. Pastor-Satorras R. and some scholars use degree centrality to measure the most influential node. Opsahl T. use closeness centrality to describe the degree of difficulty from one node to another. Kitsak M. determine the most influential monophyletic node through K-shell factorization [6]. However, measuring the influence of nodes only in one aspect is one-sided.

This paper illustrated that node importance in the network is relevant to the value of the node itself and the centrality of neighbor nodes from a local point of view. A multi-index method of evaluating node importance locally and globally with adjusted parameters in the network is put forward in this paper considering several evaluation indexes.

2 Measuring the Index Node Considering Local and Global Networks

There are several common evaluation indexes, such as degree centrality, betweenness centrality, closeness centrality, eigenvector centrality, etc. We can establish a system to analysis the node importance by choosing different indicators. The detail framework is shown in Fig. 1 is.

2.1 The Analysis of the Node Importance Index

The importance of node depends on its direct influence, position in the structure and the indirect impact of the neighboring nodes in the network [8–10]. In the actual social network, we generally consider the influence of the nodes in the following sections:

(1) Direct influence of users in the node [11]. Users who own a large number of friends in the actual social network can unite greater influence. That corresponds to the degree of the nodes in the network structure.
(2) The control of nodes in the network. The control of nodes can be seen by calculating the betweenness of node.

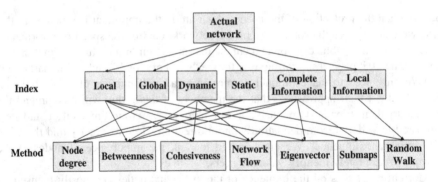

Fig. 1. Framework Overview [7]. The results are evaluated using the same network using different analysis methods. Thereby, we can combine different sub-system to find out a more universal and accurate way.

(3) The indirect influence of nodes in the network, which is the influence contribution of neighboring. Users indirectly enhance their influence by connecting influential neighboring nodes. In the actual performance of social network, people who are in the social circle of important users also have a high impact, corresponding to the influence contribution of the neighboring nodes in the network. As shown in Fig. 2 is an example for social network:

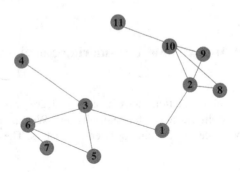

Fig. 2. Simple Social Network. The importance of Node 1 in the graph is related to the number of directly connected neighbor nodes and the influence of the neighbor nodes in the network. Meanwhile, Node 5, 6, 9 and 10 must be indirectly connected through Node 1, acting as a bridge.

We should combine three factors, including the value of degree centrality and betweenness centrality and the contribution of the neighbor nodes, to sort for the node importance (Fig. 3).

As it can be seen from Table 1, according to the degree centrality, the importance of Node 2 and 3 is consistent ranking the first while the importance of Node 1, 4, 5, 6 and 7 is consistent ranking lowest. In the view of the closeness centrality, the importance of Node 5 ranks the first; The importance of Node 2 and 3 is the number two; The importance of Node 4,5,6 and 7 is the last. And removing Node 5 will break

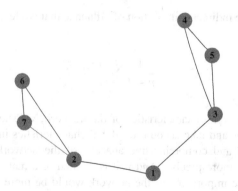

Fig. 3. Topological Diagram of the Network. The contribution of the neighbor nodes depends on network locations of nodes and the relevance between the neighbor nodes and other nodes in the network [12], both of them are indispensable.

the entire network, which make the network incomplete to the greatest extent. Therefore, the importance of Node 5 ranks the first. The calculation result of closeness centrality agrees with the actual situation whose accuracy is higher than the degree centrality index. More structural features can be described node in the network globally.

Table 1. Value of degree centrality and closeness centrality

Node sequence	1	2	3	4	5	6	7
Degree centrality	0.333	0.500	0.500	0.333	0.333	0.333	0.333
Closeness centrality	0.600	0.545	0.545	0.4	0.4	0.4	0.4

We use the value of closeness centrality as one factor when calculating the contribution of neighbor nodes. The contribution of the Node V_j's neighbor node is expressed by the contribution weighted sum. For a n-node network, the indirect contribution of influence that Node V_i contact with Node V_j is expressed as:

$$C_h(i) = \sum_{j=1}^{n} \frac{B(j)}{C(j)}, i \neq j \qquad (1)$$

Wherein B (j) representing the betweenness of Node V_j, C (j) representing by the closeness value of Node V_j, the closeness value of Node V_j which is defined as 1/C (j) contributes to its neighboring nodes. The node whose closeness value is higher makes little contribution to the contribution of its neighboring nodes under the certain circumstance that the distance of adjacent nodes are 1 and the betweenness of nodes is constant. The value of contribution is considered zero regardless of nonadjacent nodes. When the neighbor node of Node V_i is at the edge of the network or the value of the betweenness centrality is zero, the influence contribution to Node V_i is zero.

The formula needs to be standardized to compare the influence of different scale of the network. In a network with n nodes, the neighbor node number of one node can be n − 1 at large. So, the indirect contribution of influence that Node V_i contact with Node V_j is expressed as:

$$C_o(i) = \frac{1}{n-1} \sum_{j=1}^{n} \frac{B(j)}{C(j)}, \ i \neq j \tag{2}$$

Considering the overall characteristics of the network, we should highlight direct influence of the nodes and take account of global characteristics in which way we can make more effective and comprehensive analysis of the network nodes so that the sorting result will be more precise. And if it is applied to a real network, our sorting result of the influence importance of the network would be more universal (Fig. 4).

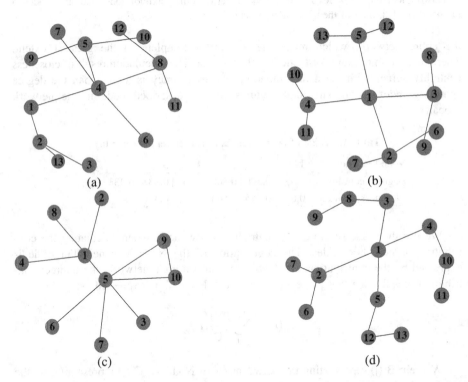

Fig. 4. Comparison between the Importance Index of the Network. The betweenness and the indirect influence of Node 1 is constant while the degree of nodes changes in the Fig. (b) compared to Fig. (a). And there is an obvious reduction of the importance of the network; The degree of Node 1 and the contribution of indirect influence that the neighbor nodes act on Node 1 is constant in the Fig. (c) compared to Fig. (a). The betweenness of the node has changed. It can be seen that its influence in the network significantly reduced; In the Figure (d) compared to Fig. (a), the degree of Node 1 and the betweenness is unchanged. The contribution of indirect influence that the neighbor nodes act on Node 1 has changed, its influence in the network reducing significantly. Those three indicators are independent, indispensable with emphasis on different meaning in practical networks.

2.2   Evaluation Importance Formula

The formula is proposed by measuring the index node considering local and global adjusts of the network together with considering the degree, the betweenness and the contribution of neighbor nodes. In this paper, the influence that represents the importance of nodes is defined as:

$$H(i) = \alpha D(i) + \beta B(i) + \lambda C_O(i) \tag{3}$$

In which α, λ, β are adjustable parameters, D (i) representing degree centrality value of node V_i, B(i) representing betweenness centrality value of node V_i and C_o (i), representing the indirect contribution of influence that of node V_i. In order to balance the indicators, it is set that $\alpha > \lambda > \beta$ and $\alpha + \beta + \lambda = 1$. The value of α can be appropriately increased because we focus more on the users' directly influence in social networks. And the size of parameters in this method can be adjusted for the actual network. Let's take an example that we need to find out the network node carrying a large amount of information in transportation networks. So, we increase the value of β and decrease the value of α and λ. Another example is that we need to focus on infected users in infectious disease network to control the epidemic in which the indirect influence of neighboring nodes should be mainly taken into consideration. So, we increase the value of λ and decrease the value of α and β.

In order to make comparison between different networks easily, the parameter indicators need to be normalized to eliminate the consequences resulted from different size of networks. The normalized formula is as follows:

$$H'(i) = \frac{H(i)}{\sum_{i \in n} H(i)} \tag{4}$$

In which $\sum_{i \in n} H(i) = 1$, the importance index of nodes being limited in [0,1] in order to make comparison of different networks efficiently (Fig. 5).

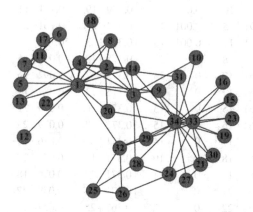

Fig. 5. Topology of Relationship between the United States Karate Clubs. In order to make full and clear comparison between the method we put forward and several other sorting methods and verify the accuracy and applicability of the method, we select the most classic American karate social network for verification.

3 Verification of Experimental Results

Under the analysis of social network, our main focus is the direct influence of users. Therefore, when $\alpha > \lambda > \beta$ and $\alpha + \beta + \lambda = 1$, we set that $\alpha = 0.5$, $\beta = 0.1$, $\lambda = 0.4$ for the sequence of importance. We selected sorting method using degree centrality, betweenness centrality, closeness centrality and eigenvector centrality for comparison.

Table 2. Sorting table of importance indicators in karate network

Degree centrality		Betweenness centrality		Closeness centrality		Eigenvector centrality		Our method	
Node	Value	Node	Value	Node	Value	Node	Value	Node	Value
34	0.515	1	0.438	1	0.569	34	0.373	34	0.0999
1	0.485	34	0.304	3	0.559	1	0.355	1	0.0992
33	0.364	33	0.145	34	0.550	3	0.317	33	0.0724
3	0.303	3	0.144	32	0.541	33	0.309	3	0.0609
2	0.273	32	0.138	9	0.516	2	0.266	2	0.0515
4	0.182	9	0.056	14	0.516	9	0.227	32	0.0434
32	0.182	2	0.054	33	0.516	14	0.226	9	0.0358
9	0.152	14	0.046	20	0.5	4	0.211	14	0.0353
14	0.152	20	0.032	2	0.485	32	0.191	4	0.0353
24	0.152	6	0.030	4	0.465	31	0.175	24	0.0317
6	0.121	7	0.030	28	0.458	8	0.171	31	0.0270
7	0.121	28	0.022	31	0.458	24	0.150	28	0.0261
8	0.121	24	0.018	29	0.452	20	0.148	30	0.0260
28	0.121	31	0.014	8	0.440	30	0.135	8	0.0245
30	0.121	4	0.012	10	0.434	28	0.133	6	0.0242
31	0.121	26	0.004	24	0.393	29	0.131	7	0.0242
5	0.091	30	0.003	6	0.384	10	0.103	20	0.0236
11	0.091	25	0.002	7	0.384	15	0.101	29	0.0217
20	0.091	29	0.002	30	0.384	16	0.101	5	0.0183
25	0.091	10	0.001	5	0.379	19	0.101	11	0.0183
26	0.091	5	0.001	11	0.379	21	0.101	26	0.0183
29	0.091	11	0.001	18	0.375	23	0.101	25	0.0168
10	0.061	8	0	22	0.375	18	0.092	15	0.0158
13	0.061	12	0	25	0.375	22	0.092	16	0.0158
15	0.061	13	0	26	0.375	13	0.084	19	0.0158
16	0.061	15	0	13	0.371	6	0.079	21	0.0158
17	0.061	16	0	15	0.371	7	0.079	23	0.0158
18	0.061	17	0	16	0.371	5	0.076	10	0.0153
19	0.061	18	0	19	0.371	11	0.076	27	0.0143
21	0.061	19	0	21	0.371	27	0.076	18	0.0134
22	0.061	21	0	23	0.371	26	0.059	22	0.0134
23	0.061	22	0	12	0.367	25	0.057	13	0.0132
27	0.061	23	0	27	0.363	12	0.053	17	0.0105
12	0.030	27	0	17	0.284	17	0.024	12	0.0079

The experimental results are shown in Table 2: Node 34, 33 and 1 are fairly important nodes. They are all at the center of the network and have big influence. And we can see that the results are too rough using degree centrality when it comes to distinguish the characteristics of nodes in the network because there are many nodes with the same degree. Compared with degree centrality, using betweenness centrality to sort out the results is rather good. However, we cannot distinguish the nuances with Node 22 and Node 17 whose degrees are uniform. Let's take Node 25 and Node 29 for an example. Their quantized values of degree centrality are the same, but, as the topological diagram shows, Node 29 is in a more central position than Node 25 in the network. Therefore, the sort method using betweenness centrality index is not accurate. As for closeness centrality, Node 1, 3 and 34 are important ones and the importance of Node 9, 14 and 33 is uniform. As the topological diagram shows, Node 33 is at the center of the community network. And its destructive effect is more crucial than the other two nodes if deleted while Node 33 is not distinguished from others as an important node. We are more concerned about the influence of neighbor nodes when using eigenvector centrality to analyze nodes. The importance of Node 4 increased because it is connected with Node 1 which is at the center. Node 32 is a bridge connecting two community in the network whose destructive effect is more crucial than Node 4 after removal. So, it is inaccurate to judge the importance for some relatively important nodes.

4 Conclusion

This paper introduces a method of evaluating node importance combined with three factors that affect the node importance to synthetically estimate the node importance. Especially, the work is highlighted by the node influence for more details: (1) The differences between the nodes are highlighted in the network structure, the actual significance and a global perspective is objectively; (2) Forum websites is used according to sociology, graph theory and communication; (3) The method makes up for the deficiency of the existing calculation methods on the accuracy and completeness to some extent. The result of this work is valuable because it has a broader applicability. We can use this method to compute the importance of the nodes of network in various big data application areas, such as communication network and infectious disease network. From ranking the influence of users and analyzing their tags of interest, we can make value classification of users for more personalized services. Our future work will bring the framework to different areas and develop different models to evaluate the user behavior in the data mining.

References

1. Watts, D.J., Strogatz, S.H.: Collective dynamics of 'small-world' networks. Nature **393**, 440–442 (1998)
2. Barabasi, A.-L., Albert, R.: Emergence of scaling in random networks. Science **286**(5439), 509–512 (1999)

3. Wasserman, S., Faust, K.: Social Network Analysis: Methods and Applications, pp. 28–35. Cambridge University Press, Cambridge (1994)

4. Scott, J.: Social Network Analysis: a Handbook, pp. 113–152. Sage Publications, London (2000)

5. Tao, X., Chen, Y., Zhang, W., Lu, Y.: Survey of influence in social networks. J. Comput. Appl. **34**(4), 980–985 (2014)

6. Jian, X.: Application and development of office automation technology in COSCO Shipyard. Softw. Guide (3) (2014)

7. Li, R., Guo, T., Wang, J.: Complex central network nodes. Shanghai Univ. Technol. **30**(3), 227–230 (2008). doi:10.3969/j.issn.1671-7597.2011.15.005

8. Si, W.: Based communication network node network performance gradient on the importance of evaluation method. Tsinghua Univ.: Nat. Sci. Ed. **15**, 541–544 (2011). doi:10.3969/j.issn.1671-7597.2011.15.005

9. Wu, J., Tan, Y.J.: Finding the most vital node by node contraction in communication networks. In: IEEE Proceeding of International Conference on Communications, Circuits and Systems, pp. 1282–1286. IEEE Press, Changsha (2005)

10. Chen, Y., Hu, A., Hu, X.: Evaluation of the importance of communication network nodes. Communications **25**(8), 129–134 (2004). doi:10.3321/j.issn:1000-436X.2004.08.018

11. Freeman, L.C.: Centrality in social networks conceptual clarification. Soc. Netw. **1**(3), 215–239 (1978)

12. Zhao, X., Wang, X.: A formula for calculating the importance of communication network node. Northeastern Univ.: Nat. Sci. Ed. **35**(5), 663–666 (2014)

Image Content Authentication and Self-recovery Using Rehashing and Matrix Combined Method

Xue-Jing Li, Wan-Li Lyu[✉], and Jie Xie

Key Laboratory of Intelligent Computing and Signal Processing of Ministry of Education,
School of Computer Science and Technology, Anhui University, Hefei 230039, China
xjalcatraz@outlook.com, wanly_lv@163.com, csis_ahu@qq.com

Abstract. Numerous image content authentication schemes have been proposed to solve potential security problems in transmitting digital images via the Internet. Aiming at achieving high detection successful rates in image tamper areas localization, a novel image content authentication and self-recovery algorithm using rehashing model and reference matrix M is proposed in this study. A series of hash functions compose a rehashing model for the sake of avoiding numerous collisions of the random authentication numbers in the procedure of image tamper detection. This scheme utilize the rehashing authentication information as the digital watermark to be embedded into the original image by means of the reference matrix M, in order to authenticate the integrity of the received image. The experiment results demonstrate that the proposed method can detect tamper areas more accurately and recover image tamper content nearly up to 50 % with an acceptable visual quality.

Keywords: Content authentication · Image self-recovery · Rehashing model · Digital watermarking

1 Introduction

Generally, the image content authentication and self-recovery technology of digital images has been more popular in recent years. When receivers get images from the Internet, the primary issue they ought to take into consideration is the integrity of the received images. Supposing that the transmitted image has been tampered, the recovery procedure of the tampered image is necessary even though the visual quality of the regained self-recovery image will diminish. In the past decades, several effective digital watermarking techniques are used for the image integrity authentication, such as [1–6]. The principal idea of these schemes is embedding the extracted feature information into the original image, i.e., what they pay attention to is how to extract the representative feature of the image and how to embed the information into the image with an acceptable visual quality, hence it is a main focus where researchers seek more effective methods. Some digital watermarking authentication schemes divide the original image into several non-overlapping blocks; therefore, the block-based watermarking technique utilizes few bits, on behalf of the feature of this image block, as a watermarking unit to be embedded into another image block. Nonetheless, even though the ideal feature

© Springer Science+Business Media Singapore 2016
T. Tan et al. (Eds.): IGTA 2016, CCIS 634, pp. 209–219, 2016.
DOI: 10.1007/978-981-10-2260-9_24

information of the image block, such as Integer Wavelet Transform coefficients or the average intensity of a block, is extracted, it still doesn't ensure the accurate tamper areas localization. Since the tamper attack will influence the subsequent work of image authentication. In a nutshell, presume that the representative feature of block i is embedded into block j, if block i is tampered, the feature information extracted from block j will not equal the feature of tampered block i, which impacts the localization of the tampered areas.

Subsequently, Lin et al. [3] brought up the concept of the watermark payload, which is composed of the authentication information embedded into this image block and the recovery information embedded into another image block. Hence, a series of block-based watermarking authentication algorithms [4–6] utilize a chaotic and random number as authentication information to represent an image block. Only the image blocks without tamper attack have the correct number values, so the tampered areas can be located more accurately. On account of the limited payload of watermark and the design of random numbers, a series of hash-based authentication algorithms have been proposed [7–9] which map the block features to short hash authentication numbers via the hash function. Nevertheless, if more than two distinct keys in the key space are hashed to the same address, and then collisions occur, which will influence the accurate localization of tampered regions. The perfect hash function, which is proposed by Sprugnoli [10], denotes that the keys in key space can be mapped to the address space one-to-one. Later, Du et al. brought up a new perfect scheme [11] named the rehashing model with the help of the HIT (the hash indicator table), which will be expounded on in Sect. 2 at great length. Therefore, the design of the hash function is to evade the numerous collisions of random authentication numbers.

In this paper, a novel image content authentication and self-recovery method, which has the desired visual quality and greater security, is discussed in detail. This algorithm is based on the rehashing model and two-dimensional reference matrix M; namely, the feature recovery information which is extracted from the original image block and the HIT authentication information which is generated by the rehashing model, as a watermarking unit to be embedded into the original image by means of the reference matrix M. Compared with simply embedding watermarks into the LSBs (the least significant bits) of the original image pixels, this algorithm has the higher PNSR (peak signal-to-noise ratio) and enhances the security.

The rest of this paper is organized as follows. Section 2 briefly introduces the related schemes including EMD, Sudoku and EMD-2, and Sect. 3 is the proposed method described in detail. The experiment results and conclusion will be stated in Sects. 4 and 5, respectively.

2 Preliminaries

2.1 Du et al.' Rehashing Model

Presume that a single random hash function h_i is selected from a set of the map $h_{n \times m}$ from the n distinct entries key space to the m entries address space, which will lead to numerous collisions in the address space. Concretely, $P_j(n, m)$ evaluates the probability of the $j(0 \leq j \leq min(n, m))$ address entries hash function with mere one key mapped to them, which is descried by Eq. (1), where $e_j(n, m)$ can be calculated by following Eq. (2). To summarize, $j's$ expected values for $P_j(n, m)$ are 3.874, 7.547, and 11.224. Furthermore, while $j \geq 0.8 \times n$ and $n = m = 10, 20, 30$, the corresponding expected values of $P_j(n, m)$ are 1.670 %, 0.021 %, and 0.0003 %, respectively. The expected value of j for $P_j(n, m)$ nearly approaches n/e, which is exceedingly large, while $n = m$.

$$P_j(n, m) = \frac{e_j(n, m)}{m^n} \tag{1}$$

$$e_j(n, m) = n! \binom{m}{j} \sum_{r=0}^{n-j} (-1)^r \binom{m-j}{r} \frac{(m-r-j)^{n-r-j}}{(n-r-j)!} \tag{2}$$

The numerous collision problems can be evaded, if a hash function satisfies mapping the key space to the address space is one-to-one, which is called perfect hash function by Sprugnoli [10]. A novel perfect hash method named rehashing model, put forward by Du et al. [11], maps the key space to the address space without numerous collisions by using a series of hash functions $\{h_1, h_2, \cdots, h_k\}$ (i.e., the rehashing model). In a nutshell, for each key in the n entries key space, the n entries HIT stores the corresponding sequence numbers of the selected hash functions and the n entries HAT (the hash address table) stores the corresponding hashed address. Additionally, $P_j^k(n, m)$ estimates the probability of the j entries address space with mere one key in the key space hashed to them, which can be computed by following Eqs. (4) and (5). Summarily, the expected values of j for $P_j^7(n, m)$ are 8.800, 17.464, and 26.070. Moreover, the corresponding $P_j^7(n, m)'s$ values are 96.41 %, 97.17 %, and 97.84 % while $j \geq 0.8 \times n$ and $n = m = 10, 20, 30$, respectively.

$$P_j^k(n, m) = \sum_{r=0}^{j} P_r^{k-1}(n, m) \times Q_{j-r}(n, m, r), where P_j^1(n, m) = P_j(n, m) \tag{4}$$

$$Q_j(n, m, s) = \left(\frac{s}{m}\right)^{n-s} \sum_{r=0}^{n-s} \binom{n-s}{r} \frac{e_i(r, m-s)}{s^r} \tag{5}$$

In a nutshell, the proposed algorithm uses the rehashing model composed of seven functions to evade numerous collisions compared with a single random hash function, which can authenticate the intensity of a received image commendably.

2.2 Digital Watermarking's Embedding Reference Matrix

As there are simple modifications of LSBs (the least significant bits) of the original image pixels to embed the digital watermark, the security and visual quality of the authentication image is not satisfied. Here, an effective digital watermarking's embedding reference matrix $\mathbf{M}$ and the corresponding theoretical principle is expounded on at great length. The proposed method takes two pixels (p_i, p_j) as an image block. Aiming at embedding two base-8 digits, which are authentication and recovery information, into the original pixel pair with a desired visual quality, we make full use of the proposed matrix M, whose abscissa and ordinate values range from 0 to 255, via modifying original pixel pair twice. The entire matrix M consists of several 3×3 sub-grids with regular combination, which contain all of base-8 digits; ultimately, the formative 256×256 reference matrix M is indicated in Fig. 1. More momentously, all of the 3×3 sub-grids' middle elements, as the overstriking character shown in Fig. 1, compose a two-dimensional 85×85 key matrix B once again presented in Fig. 2. In the sub-matrix B, each element can constitute a 3×3 box with circumambient elements similarly.

	0	1	2	3	4	5	6	7	8	9	10	11	12	13	14	15	16	17	18	19	20	21	22	23	24	25	⋯	254	255
0	2	7	5	3	0	6	4	1	7	5	2	0	6	3	1	7	4	2	0	5	3	1	6	4	2	7	⋯	1	7
1	3	0	6	4	1	7	5	2	0	6	3	1	7	4	2	0	5	3	1	6	4	2	7	5	3	0	⋯	2	0
2	4	1	7	5	2	0	6	3	1	7	4	2	0	5	3	1	6	4	2	7	5	3	0	6	4	1	⋯	3	1
3	4	1	7	5	2	0	6	3	1	7	4	2	0	5	3	1	6	4	2	7	5	3	0	6	4	1	⋯	3	1
4	5	2	0	6	3	1	7	4	2	0	5	3	1	6	4	2	7	5	3	0	6	4	1	7	5	2	⋯	4	2
5	6	3	1	7	4	2	0	5	3	1	6	4	2	7	5	3	0	6	4	1	7	5	2	0	6	3	⋯	5	3
6	7	4	2	0	5	3	1	6	4	2	7	5	3	0	6	4	1	7	5	2	0	6	3	1	7	4	⋯	6	4
7	0	5	3	1	6	4	2	7	5	3	0	6	4	1	7	5	2	0	6	3	1	7	4	2	0	5	⋯	7	5
8	1	6	4	2	7	5	3	0	6	4	1	7	5	2	0	6	3	1	7	4	2	0	5	3	1	6	⋯	0	6
9	1	6	4	2	7	5	3	0	6	4	1	7	5	2	0	6	3	1	7	4	2	0	5	3	1	6	⋯	0	6
10	2	7	5	3	0	6	4	1	7	5	2	0	6	3	1	7	4	2	0	5	3	1	6	4	2	7	⋯	1	7
⋯	⋯	⋯	⋯	⋯	⋯	⋯	⋯	⋯	⋯	⋯	⋯	⋯	⋯	⋯	⋯	⋯	⋯	⋯	⋯	⋯	⋯	⋯	⋯	⋯	⋯	⋯	⋯	⋯	⋯
254	6	3	1	7	4	2	0	5	3	1	6	4	2	7	5	3	0	6	4	1	7	5	2	0	6	3	⋯	6	4
255	6	3	1	7	4	2	0	5	3	1	6	4	2	7	5	3	0	6	4	1	7	5	2	0	6	3	⋯	6	4

Fig. 1. The 256×256 reference matrix M

	0	1	2	3	4	5	6	7	8	9	10	11	⋯	83	84
0	0	1	2	3	4	5	6	7	0	1	2	3	⋯	3	4
1	2	3	4	5	6	7	0	1	2	3	4	5	⋯	5	6
2	5	6	7	0	1	2	3	4	5	6	7	0	⋯	0	1
3	7	0	1	2	3	4	5	6	7	0	1	2	⋯	2	3
4	2	3	4	5	6	7	0	1	2	3	4	5	⋯	5	6
5	4	5	6	7	0	1	2	3	4	5	6	7	⋯	7	0
6	7	0	1	2	3	4	5	6	7	0	1	2	⋯	2	3
7	1	2	3	4	5	6	7	0	1	2	3	4	⋯	4	5
8	4	5	6	7	0	1	2	3	4	5	6	7	⋯	7	0
⋯	⋯	⋯	⋯	⋯	⋯	⋯	⋯	⋯	⋯	⋯	⋯	⋯	⋯	⋯	⋯
83	7	0	1	2	3	4	5	6	7	0	1	2	⋯	2	3
84	2	3	4	5	6	7	0	1	2	3	4	5	⋯	5	6

Fig. 2. The 85×85 sub-matrix B

The $M(p_i, p_j)$ denotes the concrete location of an original pixel pair (p_i, p_j) in the reference matrix M, while the box $B_M(b_i, b_j)$ contains nine $M(p_i, p_j)$ elements, where $p_i \in \{3b_i, 3b_i + 1, 3b_i + 2\}$ and $p_j \in \{3b_j, 3b_j + 1, 3b_j + 2\}$. Additionally, the middle number of each 3×3 box can present its value, i.e., $B_M(b_i, b_j) = M(3b_i + 1, 3b_j + 1)$. In the sub-matrix B, which is composed by all center digits of 3×3 boxes in reference matrix M, the circumambient nine boxes for each $B_M(b_i, b_j)$ generates a novel 3×3 cell $C_B(b_i, b_j)$ defined as Eq. (6), where $\lfloor b_i = p_i/3 \rfloor$ and $\lfloor b_j = p_j/3 \rfloor$. For each box $B_M(b_i, b_j)$ and cell $C_B(b_i, b_j)$, the corresponding elements $M(p_i, p_j)$ and the elements $B_M(b_i, b_j)$ are all 8-ary notational system digits from 0 to 7.

$$C_B(b_i, b_j) = \begin{matrix} B_M(b_i - 1, b_j - 1) & B_M(b_i - 1, b_j) & B_M(b_i - 1, b_j + 1) \\ B_M(b_i, b_j - 1) & B_M(b_i, b_j) & B_M(b_i, b_j + 1) \\ B_M(b_i + 1, b_j - 1) & B_M(b_i + 1, b_j) & B_M(b_i + 1, b_j + 1) \end{matrix} \qquad (6)$$

3 Proposed Scheme

The proposed method take two pixels as an image block, and this block needs to embed the HIT data of itself and the recovery data of another image block by means of the reference matrix M. Presume that the size of the original image is $M \times N$, hence the total sum of divided image blocks is $M \times N/2$. Concretely, this novel image content authentication and self-recovery algorithm is divided into four procedures, i.e., the construction of HIT, the embedding phase, the extraction phase, the image tamper detection and self-recovery procedure.

3.1 The Construction of HIT

The location of each pixel pair in the original image is unique; therefore, it can be taken as the key of Du et al.' rehashing model. The construction procedure of seven random hash functions $\{h_1, h_2, \cdots, h_7\}$ and HIT (the hash indicator table) is descried later.

Initially, select a random digit seed R to obtain seven random digits $\{R_1, R_2, \cdots, R_7\}$, which are used to generate seven random hash functions $\{h_1, h_2, \cdots, h_7\}$ by means of the random number generators. The range of $h_i(j)$ is from 1 to $M \times N/2$, while i which denotes the sequence number of hash function, and j which denotes the serial number of image block make the $1 \leq i \leq 7$ and $1 \leq j \leq M \times N/2$ hold. Subsequently, construct HIT. Initialize $HIT[1:M \times N/2] = 0, i = 1$ and $j = 1$, if $i \leq 7$ and the $h_i(j)$ hashed address is not visited, and then $HIT(j) = i$; or else, set $i = i + 1$ until find the $h_i(j)$ hashed address without visit then $HIT(j) = i$. Set $j = j + 1$ and repeat above phase while $j \leq M \times N/2$. Ultimately, we will obtain the correct HIT that all keys correspond to. The HIT stores the sequence number of hash function, i.e., by using from 1 to i hash functions can gain the only address that the key hashed to.

3.2   The Embedding Phase

The proposed algorithm embeds the average intensity of a block, which is taken as the feature information with the aim of the subsequent self-recovery work, and the HIT, which is taken as the authentication information with the aim of the tamper detection work, into the original image to generate the authentication image. With the help of the reference matrix M, the embedding phase is indicated as follows.

Initialize $i = 1$ and then locate the concrete location $M(p_i, p_{i+1})$ in the reference matrix M for each pixel pair (p_i, p_{i+1}) of the original image block. Additionally, the located element $M(p_i, p_{i+1})$ belongs to the box $B_M(b_x, b_y)$, where $\lfloor b_x = p_i/3 \rfloor$ and $\lfloor b_y = p_{i+1}/3 \rfloor$. Read the digital watermark $(s_i, s_{i+1})_8$, where s_i denotes the $HIT((i+1)/2)$ and s_{i+1} represents the average intensity of a block, i.e., MSBs (the most significant bits) of the $(i+1)/2 - th$ image block. If $s_i = B_M(b_x, b_y)$, no modification of directions is needed; otherwise, find a box $B_M(b'_x, b'_y)$ which satisfies $s_i = B_M(b'_x, b'_y)$. Then, judge the value of s_{i+1}, if it equals $B_M(b'_x, b'_y)$, maintain the current location; otherwise, select an element $M(p'_i, p'_{i+1})$ in the 3×3 box $B_M(b'_x, b'_y)$ which satisfies $s_{i+1} = M(p'_i, p'_{i+1})$. Ultimately, $(s_i, s_{i+1})_8$ is embedded into the cover pixel pair (p_i, p_{i+1}) meanwhile, which makes $s_i = B_M(b'_x, b'_y)$ and $s_{i+1} = M(p'_i, p'_{i+1})$ hold. Set $i = i + 2$ and repeat the above procedure, until all of original image blocks have been embedded the corresponding watermarks. Therefore, the authentication image I', which is used for image tamper detection, has been constructed.

3.3   The Extraction Phase

Similarly, the watermarking messages S, which contains the authentication and recovery information, can be exactly retrieved from the authentication image I' by means of the following extraction phase.

Obtain pixel pair (p'_i, p'_{i+1}) from grayscale authentication image I' and compute current location $M(p'_i, p'_{i+1})$ to represent s_{i+1}, which is used for the self-recovery work, and then calculate the box $B_M(b'_x, b'_y)$ that $M(p'_i, p'_{i+1})$ belongs to, where $b'_x = p'_i/3$ and $b'_y = p'_{i+1}/3$, so $s_i = B_M(b'_x, b'_y) = HIT((i+1)/2)$, i.e., the authentication information of the $(i+1)/2 - th$ image block has been extracted. If all the watermarks have been traversed, the extraction phase is finished.

3.4   The Image Tamper Detection and Recovery Procedure

To verify the integrity of the received image I', which has been embedded authentication data anteriorly, and to recover tampered areas, the TLM (tamper location map) and RM

(Recovery Map), whose size are both equal to the sum of the received image's blocks (i.e., $M \times N/2$), are used in the subsequent image tamper detection and recovery procedure.

Input: The received image blocks $\left\{ B'_1, B'_2, \cdots, B'_{M \times N/2} \right\}$

Output: The element set of TLM $\{TLM(1), \cdots, TLM(M \times N/2)\}$ and RM $\{RM(1), \cdots, RM(M \times N/2)\}$, the tamper detection image I_{tamper} and self-recovery image $I_{recovery}$

Step 1. According to the above extraction phase, obtain the corresponding watermark messages S, and initialize $TLM[1:M \times N/2] = 0$, $RM[1:M \times N/2] = 0$ and $i = 1$, then proceed to Step 2.

Step 2. Judge the value of $s_{2 \times i-1}$, if $HIT(i) = s_{2 \times i-1}$, and then $TLM(i) = 1$ indicates the block B'_i hasn't been tempered. Otherwise, $TLM(i) = 0$ represents the block B'_i has been tampered.

Step 3. Set $RM(i) = s_{2 \times i}$ while $TLM(i) = 0$, otherwise maintain the status quo.

Step 4. If all the received image blocks have been traversed, and then move to Step 5; or else, set $i = i + 1$ and repeats Steps 2 to 3.

Step 5. Convert the TLM and RM into the tamper detection image I_{tamper} and self-recovery image $I_{recovery}$, respectively. The specific converted norms are shown as Eqs. (7) and (8), where $x = (i - 1)/(N/2) + 1, (1 \leq x \leq M)$ and $y = 2 \times ((i - 1)mod(N/2) + 1) - 1, (1 \leq y \leq N)$.

$$\begin{cases} I_{tamper}(x, y) = TLM(i) \\ I_{tamper}(x, y + 1) = TLM(i) \end{cases} \tag{7}$$

$$\begin{cases} I_{recovery}(x, y) = I'(x, y) \text{ and } I_{recovery}(x, y + 1) = I'(x, y + 1), \text{ if } TLM(i) = 1 \\ I_{recovery}(x, y) = RM(i) \text{ and } I_{recovery}(x, y + 1) = RM(i), \text{ if } TLM(i) = 0\} \end{cases} \tag{8}$$

4   Experimental Results

The novel image content authentication scheme proposed in this study not only obtains higher detection successful rate in the tampered areas, but also maintains the relatively desired image visual quality. To certify the great performance of the proposed algorithm, four grayscale original test images of the common size 512×512, shown as Fig. 3's Group a., are used for the subsequent experiment, and the corresponding authentication images are presented as Fig. 3's Group b. All experiments were performed using MATLAB R2014a software.

In this experiment, the peak signal-to-noise ratio (PSNR) and the average detection probability (ADP) are two criteria used to evaluate the final test results, which represent the visual quality of authentication image and the detection successful rate of tampered image, respectively. The PSNR of a $M \times N$ grayscale image is calculated by Eq. (9), where x_{ij} denotes the original image pixel's value and $\bar{x}_{ij}$ indicates the value of the authentication image pixel.

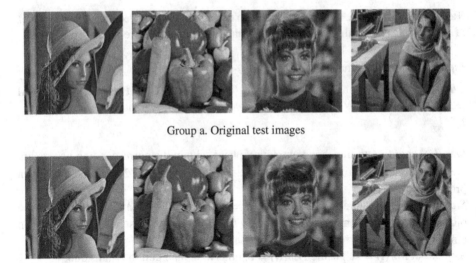

Group a. Original test images

Group b. Corresponding authentication images

Fig. 3. Original and authentication grayscale images with the proposed algorithm using Lena, Pepper, Zelda and Barbara

$$PSNR = 10 \times \log_{10} \frac{255^2}{\frac{1}{M \times N} \times \sum_{i=1}^{M} \sum_{j=1}^{N} \left(x_{ij} - \bar{x}_{ij}\right)^2} \tag{9}$$

Additionally, the ADP of an $M \times N$ tampered image is described as following Eq. (10) in detail. In Eq. (10), P_a and P_d can be computed as Eq. (11), where N_a and N_d denote the total sum of intact pixels which are detected invalid and the total sum of tampered pixels which are detected valid, respectively.

$$ADP = \left(1 - \frac{P_a + P_d}{2}\right) \times 100\% \tag{10}$$

$$P_a = \left(\frac{N_a}{M \times N}\right) \times 100\%, P_d = \left(\frac{N_d}{M \times N}\right) \times 100\% \tag{11}$$

The following Table 1 shows the tampered images with different type of attack, images of tamper detection localization, self-recovery images and the corresponding ADP. While Table 2 indicates the comparisons of PSNR and ADP with 50 % content tampered among the related methods and the proposed method.

Table 1. Tampered images, tamper detection images, recovery images and the corresponding ADP

Type of Attack	Tampered Image	Tamper Detection	Recovery Image	ADP (%)
(a) no tamper				100.00
(b) 10% tampered				99.98
(c) 30% tampered				99.70
(d) 50% tampered				99.34

Table 2. Comparisons of PSNR and ADP with 50 % content tampered of the related methods and the proposed method

Images	PSNR (db)		ADP (%) with 50 % content tampered		
	LSB	Proposed	Kim et al. [12]	He et al. [13]	Proposed
Lena	38.6062	39.4753	95.03	99.29	99.34
Pepper	38.5435	39.7633	95.03	99.29	99.34
Zelda	38.7526	39.4475	95.03	99.29	99.34
Barbara	38.4465	39.4913	95.03	99.29	99.34

The above experiment results demonstrate that the average detection successful rate of this proposed scheme is much higher than other published schemes. Meanwhile, it still offers a desired image visual quality, i.e., the average PSNR of the authentication image approaches 39.54 *db* on average. On account of the rehashing model and the reference matrix M, the novel method stands out in obtaining a much greater image visual quality of the authentication image, higher security against uncomplicated analysis attack and detection successful rate when compared to other works previously mentioned.

5 Conclusions

A novel image tamper detection and self-recovery algorithm based on the rehashing model and embedding reference matrix M is reviewed in this paper. The utilization of the rehashing model is to evade numerous collisions of the random authentication numbers, and the reference matrix M is to enhance the digital watermarking's security compared with simply replacing the least significant bits of the original image. The above experiment results certify that the proposed method has a desired image visual quality and great performance in the tamper detection successful rate; more specifically, the PNSR of the authentication image and corresponding ADP with the 50 % content tampered are 39.54 *db* and 99.34 % on average, respectively.

Acknowledgements. This research work is supported by Provincial Training Projects of Innovation and Entrepreneurship for Undergraduates of Anhui University under Grant No.J1018515315.

References

1. Lin, C.Y., Chang, S.F.: SARI: Self-authentication-and-recovery image watermarking system. In: Proceedings of the Ninth ACM International Conference on Multimedia, pp. 628–629. ACM (2001)
2. Chamlawi, R., Khan, A., Usman, I.: Authentication and recovery of images using multiple watermarks. Comput. Electr. Eng. **36**(3), 578–584 (2010)
3. Lin, P.L., Hsieh, C.K., Huang, P.W.: A hierarchical digital watermarking method for image tamper detection and recovery. Pattern Recogn. **38**(12), 2519–2529 (2005)
4. Chang, C.C., Fan, Y.H., Tai, W.-L.: Four-scanning attack on hierarchical digital watermarking method for image tamper detection and recovery. Pattern Recogn. **41**(2), 654–661 (2008)
5. Tong, X., Liu, Y., Zhang, M., Chen, Y.: A novel chaos-based fragile watermarking for image tampering detection and self-recovery. Sig. Process. Image Commun. **28**(3), 301–308 (2012)
6. Lee, C.W., Tsai, W.H.: A data hiding method based on information sharing via PNG images for applications of color image authentication and metadata embedding. Sig. Process. **93**(7), 2010–2025 (2013)
7. Tagliasacchi, M., Valenzise, G., Tubaro, S.: Hash-based identification of sparse image tampering. IEEE Trans. Image Process. **18**(11), 2491–2504 (2009)
8. Ahmed, F., Siyal, M.Y., Uddin Abbas, V.: A secure and robust hash-based scheme for image authentication. Sig. Process. **90**(5), 1456–1470 (2010)
9. Lei, Y., Wang, Y., Huang, J.: Robust image hash in radon transform domain for authentication. Sig. Process. Image Commun. **26**(6), 280–288 (2011)

10. Sprugnoli, R.: Perfect hashing functions: a single probe retrieving method for static sets. Commun. ACM **20**(11), 841–850 (1977)
11. Du, M.W., Hsieh, T.M., Jea, K.F.: The study of a new perfect hash scheme. IEEE Trans. Softw. Eng. **SE-9**(3), 305–313 (1983)
12. Kim, K.S., Lee, M.J., Lee, J.W., Oh, T.W., Lee, H.Y.: Region-based tampering detection and recovery using homogeneity analysis in quality-sensitive imaging. Comput. Vis. Image Underst. **115**(9), 1308–1323 (2011)
13. He, H., Chen, F., Tai, H.M., Kalker, T., Zhang, J.: Performance analysis of a block-neighborhood-based self-recovery fragile watermarking scheme. IEEE Trans. Inf. Forensics Secur. **7**(1), 185–196 (2012)

A Perfect Hash Model Used for Image Content Tamper Detection

Jing Sun[1] and Wan-Li Lyu[2(✉)]

[1] NARI Technology Development Co., Ltd.,
Anhui NARI Zenith Electricity & Electronic Co., Ltd., Hefei 230088, China
sunjing3@sgepri.sgcc.com.cn
[2] Key Laboratory of Intelligent Computing and Signal Processing of Ministry
of Education, School of Computer Science and Technology,
Anhui University, Hefei 230039, China
wanly_lv@163.com

Abstract. An effective image content temper detection scheme that uses perfect hash model is proposed in this paper. Aiming at low detection failing rates and high detection successful rates in image tamper localization, the proposed scheme uses perfect hash model to overcome easy collisions of the random numbers to enhance the effectiveness in authentication procedure. This scheme embeds perfect hash information in the LSBs of the original image to protect image content. The experimental results demonstrate that the proposed scheme has a good performance and can be used for image authentication applications.

Keywords: Data hiding · Image authentication · Rehashing · Perfect hash

1 Introduction

When users get images from the Internet, they want to confirm the integrity of the received images. Currently, two main techniques are used for the image content authentication. One is based on image hash methods [1–6] and the other is based on the digital watermark methods [7–9]. Certify images only using image hash methods requires adding labels to original images. In other words, the features are extracted from the original images first, and then the authentication messages are saved as labels and transmit them with original images together. Although it is difficult to penetrate these labels, these labels still can be separated from the related images. Once these labels have been removed, the corresponding images cannot be verified anymore. To overcome above weakness, the use of digital watermark method adds a watermark into an image, the added watermark becoming an integral part of the image. Watermark information can be author's signatures or the features of the original image. However, the use of digital watermark method may affect the quality of the original image. Some watermarking schemes divide the original image into blocks [9, 10]. Block-based watermarking authentication methods use few bits to represent the features of each block as watermark bits and then embed these generated watermark bits into the other block later, e.g., and average intensity of a block, important quantized DCT coefficients or Integer Wavelet Transform coefficients. The hidden watermark bits can be used to verify

© Springer Science+Business Media Singapore 2016
T. Tan et al. (Eds.): IGTA 2016, CCIS 634, pp. 220–229, 2016.
DOI: 10.1007/978-981-10-2260-9_25

whether tampering has occurred and where it is located in a potential modified image. Some proposed approaches use chaotic or random number [11–13] to generate authentication data. Some block-based watermarking authentication schemes concatenate a watermark unit with a random number [14], which also is sent to the receiver, aiming at locating tamper regions more accurately. With Lee et al.'s [14] scheme, only the unmodified blocks have the correct random values, so that the tampered blocks are located. Because the embedding capacity of watermarking algorithms is limited, the length of random numbers is very short. A lot of blocks have a same random number, making it impossible to locate many of the tamper units. In fact, the design of the random number is important to avoid unsuccessful authentication results.

Hashing is a key-to-address transformation technique in which the key space can be mapped into the address space. It is considered to be an effective means of organizing and retrieving data in practical applications, such as database management, compiler construction, and many other applications [15]. When over two different keys have a same hashing value, collisions are occurred. If a hash function has the feature that maps the set of keys in the key space to the address space is one-to-one, it will make the hash function much easier to be used because the key collision problem can be avoided. Sprugnoli [15] called the one-to-one hash function the 'perfect hashing function.' Du et al. [16] proposed a rehashing model to design a perfect hash function with an indicator table called the hash indicator table (HIT). With the help of HIT, several random hash functions can be organized to construct the desired perfect hash function. The rehashing model uses a number of hash functions $\{h_1, h_2, \cdots, h_s\}$ to reduce collisions.

The proposed scheme aims at locating tamper regions more accurately; therefore, perfect hash method is utilized for image authentication innovatively to overcome easy collisions of the random numbers and enhance the ability to resist various attacks. To verify the use of perfect hash model can improve the performance in tamper localization, the proposed scheme simply uses the least significant bits (LSBs) plane of an image for watermark embedding.

The rest of this paper is organized as follows. Section 2 briefly introduces and discusses Du et al' rehashing technology [16]. In Sect. 3, our image authentication scheme based on perfect hash model is described in detail. Experimental results are reported in Sect. 4 to prove the performance of the proposed scheme. Finally, a short of conclusion is given in Sect. 5.

2 Du et al.' Perfect Hashing Method

Hashing is an effective method to map the key space into the address space for organizing and retrieving data. If a hash function is one-to-one map from the key space to the address space, the hash function will become much easier to use because the key collision problem can be evaded. Sprugnoli [15] called such one-to-one hash function as perfect hashing function.

Assume that there are n distinct keys $\{K_1, K_2, \cdots, K_n\}$ in the key space, and m entries in the address space $\{A_1, A_2, \cdots, A_m\}$, we denote the set of key mapping from the key space to the address space as $F_{n \times m}$. If there is a single random hash function

$h \in F_{n \times m}$ is employed, the collisions are occurred in the address space. Let $P_i(m,n)$ denote the probability that the hash function has $i(0 \leq i \leq \min(m,n))$ entries in the address space with only one key hashed to them. The $P_i(m,n)$ can be computed as shown in Eq. (1):

$$P_i(m,n) = \frac{e_i(m,n)}{m^n}, \tag{1}$$

where $e_i(m,n) = n! \binom{m}{i} \sum_{r=0}^{n-i} (-1)^r \binom{m-i}{r} \frac{(m-r-i)^{n-r-i}}{(n-r-i)!}$.

However, the rehashing model which employed a number of hash functions $\{h_1, h_2, \cdots, h_s\}$ can reduce lots of collisions. The keys will find their right positions in the address space if there are only one key hashed in entries by h_1. Then, the remainder keys perform the same method using h_2 to find their right positions in the remainder entries in the address space. The similar procedure will be repeatedly performed with different hash function until all keys have their unique positions.

Let $P_i^s(m,n)$ denote the probability of the rehashing model has $i(0 \leq i \leq \min(m,n))$ entries in the address space with only one key hashed to them. The $P_i^s(m,n)$ can be computed with Eq. (2):

$$P_i^s(m,n) = \sum_{r=0}^{i} P_r^{s-1}(m,n) \cdot Q_{i-r}(m,n,r), \tag{2}$$

where $Q_i(m,n,j) = \left(\frac{j}{m}\right)^{n-j} \sum_{r=0}^{n-j} \binom{n-j}{r} \frac{e_i(r,m-j)}{j^r}$, and $P_i^1(m,n) = P_i(m,n)$.

Furthermore, the q segments address space rehashing model which divided the address space into q segments can reduce more of collisions. The address space which divides into q segments is denoted as $\{A_1, A_2, \cdots, A_q\}$ with size of $\{m_1, m_2, \cdots, m_q\}$. The keys will use the rehashing model method to find their right positions in the first segment A_1. Then the remainder keys perform the same method to find their right positions in the second segment A_2. All procedures are repeatedly performed until A_q has been searched.

Let $R_i^s(m,n)$ denote the probability has entries in the address space with only one key hashed to them. The $R_i^s(m,n)$ can be computed with Eq. (3):

$$R_i^s(n,\overline{qm},q) = \sum_{i_q=0}^{i} R_{i-i_q}^s(n,\overline{(q-1)m},q-1) \cdot P_{i_q}^s(n-(i-i_q),m_q), \tag{3}$$

where $R_i^s(n,\overline{1m},1) = P_i^s(n,m_1)$.

The expected values of i for $P_i^7(m,n)$ are 8.8000, 17.4644, and 26.0698, and the probabilities are 96.41 %, 97.17 % and 97.84 % when and $m = n = 10, 20, 30$, respectively. Compared with using a single hashing function, using q segments address space rehashing model, numerous collisions are decreased. In other words, it is suitable for calculating the address and can be used for processing the authentication messages.

The proposed scheme uses 7 hash functions with 4 segments address space rehashing model to implement image authentication and utilizes LSB to embed HIT information.

3 Proposed Scheme

The proposed image authentication scheme consists of three phases: seven random hash functions with 4 segments design and HIT construction phases, hiding HIT secret bits into original image phases and HIT secret bits extracting and tamper detection phases.

3.1 The Construction of Seven Random Hash Functions with 4 Segments

For an image, many different pixels may have a same pixel value. Having same pixel values leads to having same hashing values. Since these pixels cannot be distinguished from each other, they are not suitable for serving as hash keys. However, the locations of all of the pixels in an image are distinctive, so the proposed scheme uses the locations of pixels as keys of hash functions.

The 7 random hash functions with 4 segments designing and HIT construction procedure are shown in Fig. 1.

Fig. 1. Illustration of 7 random hash functions with 4 segments designing and HIT procedure construction

Supposes the size of image I is $M \times N$ in Fig. 1. After interlaced sampling is performed on the image I, the image I can be divided into 4 sub-images I_1, I_2, I_3, I_4 and each one has the size of $\lfloor \frac{M}{2} \rfloor \times \lfloor \frac{N}{2} \rfloor$. Use S as the seed for a random number generator to generate four random numbers S^1, S^2, S^3, S^4, and then use each random number as sub-seed to derive seven random numbers. Finally, 28 random numbers $S_1^1, S_2^1, \cdots, S_7^1, S_1^2, S_2^2, \cdots, S_7^2, \cdots, S_1^4, S_2^4, \cdots, S_7^4$ are generated as random number generators to construct hash functions $h_1^1, h_2^1, \cdots, h_7^1, h_1^2, h_2^2, \cdots, h_7^2, \cdots, h_1^4, h_2^4, \cdots, h_7^4$, each of which has the size of $\frac{M}{2} \times \frac{N}{2}$, and the range of the values of the hash functions is $1 \leq h_\alpha^\beta(x, y) \leq \frac{M}{2} \times \frac{N}{2}$, where $1 \leq \alpha \leq 7$, $1 \leq \beta \leq 4$, $1 \leq x \leq \frac{M}{2}$ and $1 \leq y \leq \frac{N}{2}$. The coordinate of a pixel in the i-th sub image I_i donates as (x, y). The procedure of constructing the HIT table of i-th sub image I_i is described in Algorithm 1. In Algorithm 1, a hash address table (HAT) and a flag table (FT) are used to help constructing the HIT table (Fig. 2).

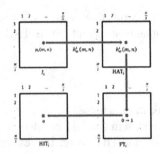

Fig. 2. Illustration of using Algorithm 1 to compute $HIT_i(m,n)$, $HAT_i(m,n)$ and $FT_i(m,n)$ of a pixel $p_i(m,n)$ in sub image I_i

Algorithm 1: Construct HIT_i and HAT_i of i-th sub image I_i

Input: Sub-image I_i, which has the size of $\frac{M}{2} \times \frac{N}{2}$, and a random number seed S^i

Output: HIT_i and HAT_i of Sub–image I_i

Step 1. Use S^i as the seed for a random number generator to get seven random numbers $S_1^i, S_2^i, \cdots, S_7^i$; then use $S_1^i, S_2^i, \cdots, S_7^i$ as the random number generators to construct seven random hash functions $h_1^i, h_2^i, \cdots, h_7^i$, each of which has the size of $\frac{M}{2} \times \frac{N}{2}$.

Step 2. Initialize HIT_i, HAT_i, and a flag table (FT_i) for each sub-image, which has the size of $\frac{M}{2} \times \frac{N}{2}$ and zero contents.

Step 3. Set five variables $\alpha = 1$, $x = 1, y = 1$, $m = 1$ and $n = 1$.

Step 4. If $\alpha \leq 7$, goto Step 5; otherwise, set $\alpha = 1$, $m = m+1$ and goto Step 5.

Step 5. If $m \leq \frac{M}{2}$, goto Step 6; otherwise, set $x = 1$, $y = 1$, $m = 1$, $n = 1$ and goto Step 8.

Step 6. If $n \leq \frac{N}{2}$, goto Step 7; otherwise, set $m = m+1$ and goto Step 5.

Step 7. If $FT_i(m,n) = 0$, set $FT_i(h_\alpha^i(m,n)) = 1$, $HIT_i(m,n) = i$, $HAT_i(m,n) = h_\alpha^i(m,n)$, $n = n+1$, and goto Step 6; otherwise, set $\alpha = \alpha+1$, $m = 1$, $n = 1$, and goto Step 4.

Step 8. Scan the HIT_i and FT_i tables, if $HIT_i(m,n) = 0$ and $FT_i(m,n) = 0$, set $HAT_i(x,y) = (m,n)$ and $FT_i(m,n) = 1$, until $x = \frac{M}{2}, y = \frac{N}{2}, m = \frac{M}{2}$, and $n = \frac{N}{2}$.

Algorithm 1 uses a flag table (FT) to indicate whether the address space is occupied which can speed up the execution time. $HAT_i(m,n)$ records the hash value $h_\alpha^i(m,n)$ and $HIT_i(m,n)$ records the α-th hash function.

3.2   The Embedding Phase

In this paper, we focus on the efficiency of perfect hashing method used for temper detection, so, the proposed scheme uses the least three significant bits (LSBs) to embed watermark and this is the simplest method to embed data into original image.

For a pixel $p_i(m,n)$ in i-th sub image I_i, $1 \leq m \leq \frac{M}{2}$ and $1 \leq n \leq \frac{N}{2}$, the authentication message $HIT_i(m,n)$ will be embedded into the pixel whose location is $HAT_i(m,n)$, Eq. (4) shows the proposed embedding strategy.

$$p_i(HAT_i(m,n)) = p_i(HAT_i(m,n)) - p_i(HAT_i(m,n)) \bmod 8 + HIT_i(m,n) \quad (4)$$

When all sub images contains HIT message, reconstruct the sub images to watermarked image I'.

3.3 The Image Tamper Detection Phase

Once receiver received the image I', he may want to verify whether tampers have occurred in the received image content. First, the receiver performs Interlaced sampling on the image I' to get HIT'_i and HAT'_i of sub-image I'_i, $1 \leq i \leq 4$.

Later, receiver uses Algorithm 2 to verify the reality of sub-image I'_i.

Algorithm 2: Verify the reality of sub-image I'_i

Input: Sub image I'_i, which has the size of $\frac{M}{2} \times \frac{N}{2}$, and a random number seed S^i, which was used in Algorithm 1

Output: Verifying results T'_i of sub image I'_i

Step 1. Initialize a tamper location map T'_i, which has the size of $\frac{M}{2} \times \frac{N}{2}$ and element values are set as 1.

Step 2. Set variables $\alpha = 1$, $x = 1, y = 1$, $m = 1$ and $n = 1$ and goto Step 3.

Step 3. If $m \leq \frac{M}{2}$, goto Step 4; otherwise, goto Step 7.

Step 4. If $n \leq \frac{N}{2}$, goto Step 5; otherwise, goto Step 6.

Step 5. For a pixel $p'_i(m,n)$ in sub image I'_i, use Eq. (5) to get tamper position location $T'_i(m,n)$ and set $n = n+1$, goto Step 4.

$$T'_i(m,n) = \begin{cases} 1, \text{if } HIT_i(m,n) = p'_i(HAT_i(m,n)) \bmod 8 \\ 0, \text{if } HIT_i(m,n) \neq p'_i(HAT_i(m,n)) \bmod 8 \end{cases} . \quad (5)$$

Step 6. set $m = m+1$, goto Step 3.

Step 7. Output verify results T'_i.

When all verifying results T'_i of sub image I'_i are gained, construct the authentication result T_i.

4 Experimental Results

The purpose of our scheme is to locate tamper regions more accurately. To accomplish this purpose, the proposed scheme uses the perfect hash method to authenticate the integrity of an image's content. To prove the performance of the proposed scheme, eight 512×512 gray images shown in Fig. 3, were used as original images for comparisons of tamper detection. All experiments were performed using MATLAB R2014a software.

Table 1 shows the tamper images and the authentication results.

The parameter N_t denotes the number of actually tampered pixels, the number of tampered pixels which are detected valid is denoted by N_{fd} and the number of intact pixels which are detected invalid is denoted by N_{fa}. The total number of tampered

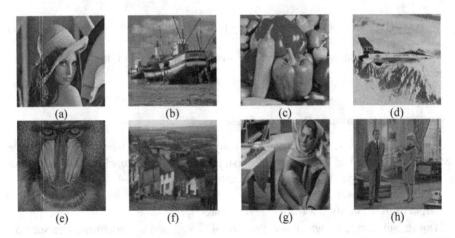

Fig. 3. Original test images (a) Lena, (b) Boat, (c) Baboon, (d) Jet, (e) Baboon, (f) Goldhill, (g) Barbara and (h) Couple

Table 1. The tamper images and their corresponding tamper detection locating image

Attack	Tamper Image	Tamper Detection	Attack	Tamper Image	Tamper Detection
(a) no tamper			(e) 40% modify		
(b) 5% modify			(f) 50% modify		
(c) 10% modify			(g) irregular modify		
(d) 30% modify			(h) irregular modify		

pixels which are falsely detected is $N_{fd} + N_{fa}$. Then, the tamper detection probability (TDP), the false detection probability (FDP), false alarm probability (FAP) and average detection probability (ADP) are defined as Eqs. (8), (9), (10) and (11).

$$\text{TDP} : R_{td} = \left(\frac{N_t - N_{fd}}{N_t} \right) \times 100\%, \tag{8}$$

$$\text{FDP} : R_{fd} = \left(\frac{N_{fd}}{M \times N} \right) \times 100\%, \tag{9}$$

$$\text{FAP} : R_{fa} = \left(\frac{N_{fa}}{M \times N} \right) \times 100\%, \tag{10}$$

$$\text{ADP} : R_{ad} = \left(1 - \frac{R_{fd} + R_{fa}}{2} \right) \times 100\%, \tag{11}$$

The FDP and FAP are detection failing rates, and the ideal cases would be nearly to 0 %. The TDR and ADP are detection successful rates and the ideal cases would be nearly to 100 %. Table 2 uses statistic results to show tamper detection accuracy.

Table 2. Statistics of experimental results

Tamper rate (Image size 512 × 512)	No. of tampered pixels	No. of correct detected pixels (R_{td})	N_{fd}	N_{fa}	FDP (%)	FAP (%)	ADP (%)
Table 1(a)	0	0	0	0	0	0	100
Table 1(b)	13287	13176 (99.16 %)	111	0	0.0423	0	99.98
Table 1(c)	26471	26352 (99.55 %)	119	0	0.0454	0	99.98
Table 1(d)	82497	80906 (98.07 %)	1591	0	0.6069	0	99.70
Table 1(e)	105370	102524 (97.30 %)	2846	0	1.0857	0	99.46
Table 1(f)	131610	128156 (97.38 %)	3454	0	1.3176	0	99.34
Table 1(g)	35389	35109 (99.21 %)	280	0	1.0681	0	99.95
Table 1(h)	14418	14212 (98.57)	206	0	0.0786	0	99.96

Table 3 shows that Lee and Tsai's method [14] ordinarily adds a random number, which led to frequently occurred collisions after processing, and the average false acceptance ratio was 12.5 %. Tang et al.'s method [17] only uses local color features to generate image hash for image content authentication, and the average false acceptance ratio was 12.5 %. Using the perfect hash method, our proposed scheme had the lowest false acceptance ratio of 0.4672 %, which is a significant advantage.

Table 3. Comparisons of existing color image authentication method and our proposed scheme

	Average FDP (%)	Average FAP (%)
Method of [14]	12.5	0
Method of [17]	11.15	0
Method of [18]	50	0
Proposed scheme	0.4672	0

5 Conclusions

An effective image tamper localization scheme that uses perfect hash technology is proposed in this paper. The proposed scheme utilizes a perfect hash model to overcome easy collisions of the numerous metadata in key space, thereby innovatively enhancing its effectiveness against attacks. The proposed scheme embeds image feature values in the LSBs of the original image to protect image content. The proposed scheme is realized with gray to test the scheme's quality. The experimental results demonstrate that the proposed scheme has a good performance in tamper location. Also, the experimental results verified that the proposed perfect hash method can be used for image authentication applications.

References

1. Venkatesan, R., Koon, S.M., Jakubowski, M.H., Moulin, P.: Robust image hashing. In: Proceedings of IEEE International Conference on Image Processing, vol. 3, pp. 664–666 (2000)
2. Fridrich, J., Goljan, M.: Robust hash functions for digital watermarking. In: Proceedings of IEEE International Conference on Information Technology: Coding and Computing, pp. 178–183 (2000)
3. Tagliasacchi, M., Valenzise, G., Tubaro, S.: Hash-based identification of sparse image tampering. IEEE Trans. Image Process. **18**(11), 2491–2504 (2009)
4. Ahmed, F., Siyal, M.Y., Uddin Abbas, V.: A secure and robust hash-based scheme for image authentication. Sig. Process. **90**(5), 1456–1470 (2010)
5. Lei, Y., Wang, Y., Huang, J.: Robust image hash in Radon transform domain for authentication. Sig. Process. Image Commun. **26**(6), 280–288 (2011)
6. Zhao, Y., Wang, S., Zhang, X., Yao, H.: Robust hashing for image authentication using Zernike moments and local features. IEEE Trans. Inf. Forensics Secur. **8**(1), 55–63 (2013)
7. Wu, M., Liu, B.: Watermarking for image authentication. In: Proceedings of IEEE International Conference on Image Processing, ICIP 1998, vol. 2, pp. 437–441 (1998)
8. Kundur, D., Hatzinakos, D.: Digital watermarking for telltale tamper proofing and authentication. Proc. IEEE **87**(7), 1167–1180 (1999)
9. Yang, L., Ni, R., Zhao, Y.: Segmentation-based image authentication and recovery scheme using reference sharing mechanism. In: 2012 International Conference on Industrial Control and Electronics Engineering, ICICEE 2012, pp. 863–866 (2012)
10. Preda, R.O.: Semi-fragile watermarking for image authentication with sensitive tamper localization in the wavelet domain. Measurement **46**(1), 367–373 (2013)

11. Chang, C.C., Fan, Y.H., Tai, W.L.: Four-scanning attack on hierarchical digital watermarking method for image tamper detection and recovery. Pattern Recognit. **41**(2), 654–661 (2008)
12. Rawat, S., Raman, B.: A chaotic system based fragile watermarking scheme for image tamper detection. AEU-Int. J. Electron. Commun. **65**(10), 840–847 (2011)
13. Tong, X., Liu, Y., Zhang, M., Chen, Y.: A novel chaos-based fragile watermarking for image tampering detection and self-recovery. Signal Process.: Image Commun. **28**(3), 301–308 (2012)
14. Lee, C.W., Tsai, W.H.: A data hiding method based on information sharing via PNG images for applications of color image authentication and metadata embedding. Signal Process. **93** (7), 2010–2025 (2013)
15. Sprugnoli, R.: Perfect hashing functions: a single probe retrieving method for static sets. Commun. ACM **20**(11), 841–850 (1977)
16. Du, M.W., Hsieh, T.M., Jea, K.F., Shieh, D.W.: The study of a new perfect hash scheme. IEEE Trans. Softw. Eng. **SE-9**(3), 305–313 (1983)
17. Tang, Z., Zhang, X., Dai, X., Yang, J., Wu, T.: Robust image hash function using local color features. AEU-Int. J. Electron. Commun. **67**(8), 717–722 (2013)
18. Byun, S.C., Lee, I.L., Shin, T.H., Ahn, B.H.: A public-key based watermarking for color image authentication. In: IEEE International Conference on Multimedia and Expo, vol. 1, pp. 593–596 (2002)

Vertebrae Detection Algorithm in CT Scout Images

Guodong Zhang[1,2], Ying Shao[1], Yoohwan Kim[2], and Wei Guo[1(✉)]

[1] School of Computer, Shenyang Aerospace University, Shenyang 110136, Liaoning, China
zhanggd@sau.edu.cn, shaoying613@163.com, 155381296@qq.com
[2] Department of Computer Science, University of Nevada Las Vegas,
Las Vegas, NV 89154, USA
Yoohwan.Kim@unlv.edu

Abstract. In order to solve the tedious and time-consuming works for CT scan planning manually, we proposed an automatic detection method of vertebrae in CT scout images. In this method, firstly, HOG features of the training samples were computed, which were imported into the random forest classifier for training. Then we rotated the CT scout images seven times for detecting multi-angle vertebrae. The trained classifier was employed to detect the vertebrae in test images. Finally, we merged the detection results with overlapping regions. For 76 images, experimental results show that the sensitivity of vertebrae detection by our method reached 95.18 % with 0.96 false positive per image.

Keywords: HOG · CT scout image · Random forest · Vertebrae detection

1 Introduction

In today's society, many people are deeply afflicted by spine diseases including bone hyperplasia, osteoporosis, fractures etc. CT examination can better distinguish lumbar vertebral body, pedicle and joint prominent bony tissue lesions. Image quality of CT image depends largely on scan planning. The existing study has already demonstrated that CT scout images not only have the role of developing the CT scan planning, also have the clinical diagnostic value [1]. However, due to different locations and orientations of different vertebrae, in order to obtain better CT vertebrae images, so we need radiological technologists to mark the scanning position and angle by reference line, according to the location and orientation of each vertebrae in the CT scout images. This way, the development of plans to scan manually, increases the workload of the technicians. Therefore, it's urgent to put forward a method for automatic detection of vertebrae in the CT scout images.

At present, the images used in medical image diagnosis of spine have X-ray, CT and MRI images. Because CT scout images are actually the approximate digital X-ray image, so the vertebrae detection algorithm in X-ray images can also be applied to CT scout images. Benjelloun et al. [2] proposed a method of cervical vertebrae detection based on active shape model (ASM), but this approach was more influenced by the initialization of mean shape model. Larhmam et al. [3] utilized a vertebrae mean shape model to detect the center of potential vertebrae by the method of template matching, which was

© Springer Science+Business Media Singapore 2016
T. Tan et al. (Eds.): IGTA 2016, CCIS 634, pp. 230–237, 2016.
DOI: 10.1007/978-981-10-2260-9_26

based on Generalized Hough Transform (GHT). In [4], the method of [3] was improved by combining template matching with K-means clustering to recognize cervical vertebrae. Masudur et al. [5] put forward a method to detect the cervical vertebral corners utilizing Haar-like features and modified Hough forest. In CT scan images, Stern et al. [6] estimated the location of the vertebrae center line through the edge points, and then determined centers of vertebral bodies and intervertebral discs, according to the gradient and intensity maps. Glocker et al. [7] localized vertebrae centers using regression forest and probabilistic graphical model, refined the results by a hidden Markov model. In MRI images, Pekar et al. [8] presented a method to determine the location of scan lines in the lumbar and cervical spine. This method can automatically detect and mark the vertebrae structure in the MRI scout images. Huang et al. [9, 10] applied an improved AdaBoost algorithm to locate the original vertebrae position, refine the detection results via robust curve fitting, and segment the vertebrae regions by an iterative normalized cut algorithm.

In summary, most of the above methods were based on the vertebrae model. The detection results were sensitive to the initialization of the model. Faced with the characteristics of vertebrae, the unknown number, various orientations, blurred edges, we proposed a novel detection algorithm of vertebrae in CT scout images.

2 The Method of Vertebrae Detection

In this paper, we rotated the CT scout images to make the vertebrae in a horizontal position in at least one of the rotated images according to the tilt angles of vertebrae. Then, we extracted HOG features, and used the constructed random forest classifier to detect the vertebrae in the rotated images. Finally, the detection results with overlapping regions were merged as the final detection results.

2.1 Rotating the Vertebrae

Because the different vertebrae has different tilt angles in the CT scout images, HOG features couldn't accurately describe the angle of the vertebrae. Therefore, it is necessary to rotate the detected image to make the vertebrae in a horizontal position in at least one of the rotated images. Therefore, multi-angle detection can detect more vertebrae than single angle detection, and multi-angle detection can detect the roughly angles of vertebrae. The angles of rotation were $-23°$, $-15°$, $-7°$, $-2°$, $0°$, $3°$ and $9°$, all these angles have covered the tilt angle range of vertebrae approximately.

2.2 Extracting the HOG Features

HOG (histogram of oriented gradient) [11] is a feature descriptor in computer vision and image processing for object detection. It describes the features of local object by calculating the gradient direction histogram of local region of the image. The HOG feature extraction process was described as follows:

(1) The input image was normalized by the Gamma correction method.
    Gamma compression formula is:

$$I(x, y) = I(x, y)^{gamma}, gamma = 1/2 \tag{1}$$

(2) Calculated the size and direction of the gradient of each pixel.

$$G_x(x, y) = H(x + 1, y) - H(x - 1, y) \tag{2}$$

$$G_y(x, y) = H(x, y + 1) - H(x, y - 1) \tag{3}$$

$$G(x, y) = \sqrt{G_x(x, y)^2 + G_y(x, y)^2} \tag{4}$$

$$\alpha(x, y) = tan^{-1}\left(\frac{G_y(x, y)}{G_x(x, y)}\right) \tag{5}$$

Where $H(x, y)$ is the value of the pixel (x, y) of the input image, $G_x(x, y)$ is the value of horizontal gradient of the pixel (x, y), $G_y(x, y)$ is the value of vertical gradient of the pixel (x, y). $G(x, y)$, $\alpha(x, y)$ are the size and direction of the gradient of the pixel (x, y) respectively.

(3) The image was divided into small spatial regions ("cells"), the size of each cell is 6 × 6 pixels. Then, the gradient direction of cell was divided into 6 directions ("bins"). The gradient of the pixels were mapped to different bin intervals according to their directions, and the gradient magnitude of each pixel was weighted by the weight of the projection to obtain the HOG of this cell.

(4) Each cell unit was combined into a larger spatial region ("blocks"). A block consists of 2 × 2 cells. In this way, the HOG feature of a block was obtained by connecting all the cell feature vectors of a block.

(5) The final feature vectors for classification were all HOG features of block, which were connected in series.

2.3   Vertebrae Detection Using Random Forest

Random Forest. After extracted the HOG features, we applied the constructed classifier to detect the vertebrae in the rotated CT scout images. As traditional classifier was prone to the problems of low accuracy and over-fitting, many scholars gathered more classifiers to improve the precision of prediction, which was called ensemble, or classifier combination. Random forest [12, 13] is an ensemble learning method for classification or regression, which is trained and predicted by a number of decision trees. Random forest constructed different training sets to increase the difference between the classification models, so as to improve the extrapolated predictive ability of the combination classification model. A classification model sequence, $\{h_i(x), i = 1, 2 \ldots, k\}$, was obtained by k rounds training. Finally, using them to form a mul-classification model system, the system determined its final classification results by a simple majority vote. The final classification decision is:

$$H(x) = argmax \sum_{i=1}^{k} I(h_i(x) = Y) \tag{6}$$

Where $H(x)$ indicates a combination classification model, $h_i(x)$ is a single classification model, Y represents the output variable (or target variable), $I(.)$ is a indicator function. The formula illustrates the final classification is determined by the approach of using the majority voting decision.

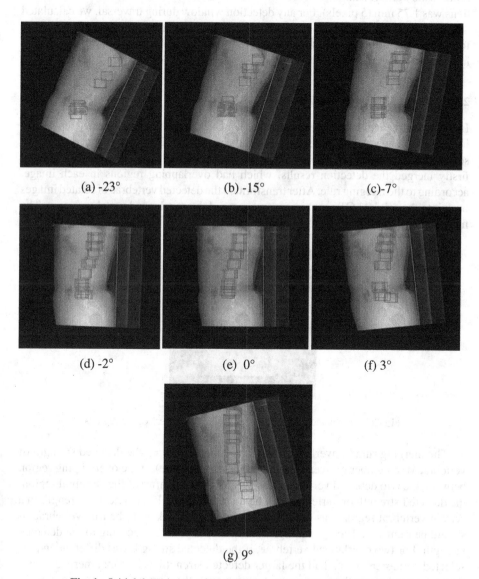

(a) -23°   (b) -15°   (c) -7°

(d) -2°   (e) 0°   (f) 3°

(g) 9°

Fig. 1. Initial detection results of vertebrae in the seven rotated images

Vertebrae Detection. In this experiment, the training set consists of 456 positive samples (vertebrae), 1311 negative samples (non-vertebrae). The positive sample was an inclined rectangular region, taking the center of vertebrae as the center, the average slope of the upper- edge and lower-edge as the slope. The size of the sample is 40 × 30 pixels. The negative sample was also a rectangular region with same size of the positive sample, randomly selected from the region of non-vertebrae in 76 CT scout images.

In the test progress, we moved detection window in accordance with the step length to traverse the whole image. The size of the detection window was 40 × 30 pixels, as same as the training samples. The length of moving step in horizontal and vertical directions was 1.75 mm (5 pixels). For any detection window during traversal, we calculated the HOG features, and then the detection window was classified according to the random forest classifier. Finally, we obtained the results of vertebrae detection in the rotated images, as shown in Fig. 1.

2.4 Merging the Detection Results

Due to the influence of the traversal step, the same vertebrae might be detected repeatedly in the same image. At the same time, due to the rotation of CT scout image, resulting in seven images, the same vertebrae might be detected in multiple images. Therefore, we firstly merged the detection results, which had overlapping regions in each image, according to the merging rule. After transformed the detected vertebrae of rotated images back into the original CT scout image, we merged the overlapped vertebrae again. The final detection results were shown as Fig. 2.

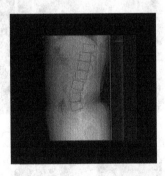

Fig. 2. Final detection results after merged the overlapping regions

The merging rule in overlapping regions is dependent on the detected strength of vertebrae (the number of overlapping with other vertebrae). If the overlapping region between the two detected vertebrae was greater than a quarter of the vertebral region, the detected strength of vertebrae will be increased by 1. If the detected strength in a certain vertebral region was only 1 or 2, so it was less likely to be true vertebrae, it should be removed. Then, we merged the detection results according to the detected strength. For two overlapped vertebrae, if the detected strength was different and we selected vertebrae, which had the larger detected strength as the final merged result; if the detected strengths were same, then we took the new vertebrae as the merged result. The new vertebrae were connected by the midpoints of the connections of the corresponding vertices of two vertebrae.

3   Results

3.1   Detection Results with Different Numbers of Trees

Random forest showed different classification performances with different numbers of trees. The detection results with different numbers of trees were given in Table 1. When the number of trees was set as 1200, random forest exhibited the optimal detection results, it could detect 434 vertebrae from 76 CT scout images, of which there are 456 vertebrae. The sensitivity reached 95.18 %, with 0.96 false positive per image. Generally speaking, random forest could show robust detection performance.

Table 1. Performance with different numbers of trees.

The number of trees	The number of detection	Sensitivity (%)	The number of false positive	FPs/image
400	426	93.42	94	1.24
600	431	94.52	90	1.18
800	426	93.42	89	1.17
1000	432	94.74	82	1.08
1200	434	95.18	73	0.96
1400	428	93.86	80	1.05
1600	432	94.74	85	1.12

3.2   Detection Results with Different Parameters of HOG

In this paper, we used HOG features to describe the vertebrae; the parameters used in computing features would influence the detection results. We conducted several experiments of vertebrae detection with changing the size of cell and the number of bin, while the random consisting of 1200 trees. The detection results with different parameters of HOG were given in Tables 2 and 3. When the cell size was 6*6 pixels, bin was 6, we could obtain the highest sensitivity, and the number of false positives was less.

Table 2. Performance with a bin of 9 and different sizes of cell

Cell (pixels)	The number of detection	Sensitivity (%)	The number of false positive	FPs/image
4*4	400	87.72	126	1.66
5*5	397	87.06	111	1.46
6*6	410	89.91	110	1.44
7*7	404	88.60	150	1.97
8*8	409	89.69	178	2.34
9*9	396	86.84	187	2.46

Table 3. Performance with a bin of 6 and different sizes of cell

Cell (pixels)	The number of detection	Sensitivity (%)	The number of false positive	FPs/image
4*4	397	87.06	102	1.34
5*5	419	91.89	71	0.93
6*6	434	95.18	73	0.96
7*7	405	88.82	148	1.95
8*8	400	87.72	181	2.38
9*9	394	86.40	205	2.70

4 Conclusion

This essay presented a novel vertebrae detection algorithm based on HOG features and random forest. This algorithm could automatically detect the vertebrae with various orientations by rotating CT scout images, also could detect the roughly angles of vertebrae. By experimental verification, the sensitivity of vertebrae detection by our method reached 95.18 % with 0.96 false positive per image. The radiological technologists could utilize the location and orientation of the detected vertebrae to make a scan planning. Therefore, this method could effectively reduce the workload of radiology technicians.

Acknowledgements. This work was supported in part by National Natural Science Foundation of China (No. 61373088 and 61402298), National Aerospace Science Foundation (No. 2013ZE54025), Shenyang Science and Technology Foundation (No. F13-316-1-35), the PhD Start-up Fund of SAU (No. 13YB16), and the CSC Visiting Scholarship.

References

1. Sener, R.N., Ripeckyj, G.T., Otto, P.M., Rauch, R.A., Jinkins, J.R.: Recognition of abnormalities on computed scout images in CT examinations of the head and spine. Neuroradiology **35**(35), 229–231 (1993)
2. Benjelloun, M., Mahmoudi, S., Lecron, F.: A framework of vertebra segmentation using the active shape model-based approach. Int. J. Biomed. Imaging (2011)
3. Larhmam, M.A., Mahmoudi, S., Benjelloun, M.: Semi-automatic detection of cervical vertebrae in X-ray images using generalized Hough transform. In: The 3rd International Conference on Image Processing Theory, Tools and Applications (IPTA), pp. 396–401, Istanbul-Turkey (2012)
4. Larhmam, M.A., Benjelloun, M., Mahmoudi, S.: Vertebra identification using template matching modelmp and K-means clustering. Int. J. Comput. Assist. Radiol. Surg. **9**(2), 177–187 (2013)
5. Masudur, R.A.A.S., Asad, M., Knapp, K., Gundry, M.: Cervical vertebral corner detection using haar-like features and modified Hough forest. In: Image Processing Theory, Tools and Applications (IPTA), pp. 417–422 (2015)

6. Stern, D., Likar, B., Pernus, F., Vrtovec, T.: Automated detection of spinal centrelines, vertebral bodies and intervertebral discs in CT and MR images of lumbar spine. Phys. Med. Biol. **55**(1), 247–264 (2010)
7. Glocker, B., Feulner, J., Criminisi, A., Haynor, D.R., Konukoglu, E.: Automatic localization and identification of vertebrae in arbitrary field-of-view CT scans. In: Ayache, N., Delingette, H., Golland, P., Mori, K. (eds.) MICCAI 2012, Part III. LNCS, vol. 7512, pp. 590–598. Springer, Heidelberg (2012)
8. Pekar, V., et al.: Automated planning of scan geometries in spine MRI scans. In: Ayache, N., Ourselin, S., Maeder, A. (eds.) MICCAI 2007, Part I. LNCS, vol. 4791, pp. 601–608. Springer, Heidelberg (2007)
9. Huang, S.H., Lai, S.H., Novak, C.L.: A statistical learning approach to vertebra detection and segmentation from spinal MRI. In: IEEE International Symposium on Biomedical Imaging: From Nano to Macro, pp. 125–128 (2008)
10. Huang, S.H., Chu, Y.H., Lai, S.H., Novak, C.L.: Learning-based vertebra detection and iterative normalized-cut segmentation for spinal MRI. IEEE Trans. Med. Imaging **28**(10), 1595–1605 (2009)
11. Dalal, N., Triggs, B.: Histograms of oriented gradients for human detection. IEEE Conf. Comput. Vis. Pattern Recogn. **1**, 886–893 (2005)
12. Breiman, L.: Random forests. Mach. Learn. **45**(1), 5–32 (2001)
13. Criminisi, A., Shotton, J.: Decision forests for computer vision and medical image analysis. In: Advances in Computer Vision and Pattern Recognition, pp. 273–293 (2013)

Retracted Chapter: Image Colorization Using Convolutional Neural Network

Yili Zhao[1,2(✉)], Dan Xu[1], and Yan Zhang[2]

[1] Yunnan University, Kunming 650091, Yunnan, China
ylzhao@vip.sina.com, danxu@ynu.edu.cn
[2] Southwest Forestry University, Kunming 650224, Yunnan, China
zydyr@163.com

Abstract. This paper presents an automatic grayscale image colorization method using convolutional neural network. Besides the gray target image, the user doesn't need to provide a reference color image nor manual guidance. First we train the convolutional neural network using residual connection based on the VGG-16 model. For colorization, a grayscale image is forwarded through the network and using the highest layer infers some color information, then it up-scales the color guess and adds in information from the next highest layer. Experimental results and user study on a large set of images demonstrate that our colorization method is competitive with previous state-of-the-art methods.

Keywords: Image colorization · Convolutional neural network · Color transfer

1 Introduction

Automatic image colorization is the task of adding colors to a new grayscale image without any user intervention. This problem is ill-posed in the sense that there is no unique colorization of a grayscale image without any prior knowledge. Indeed, many objects can have different colors. This is not only true artificial objects, such as plastic objects which can have random colors, but also for natural objects such as tree leaves which can have various nuances of green and brown in different seasons, without significant change of shape. In this paper, we present an automatic colorization method using the deep neural networks, which doesn't need any reference image nor user guidance. We evaluate our method on a broad range of images compromising random scene images and images with obvious foreground and background. Then we compare our results with existing methods and demonstrate our method can yield visually meaningful and appealing images.

© Springer Science+Business Media Singapore 2016
T. Tan et al. (Eds.): IGTA 2016, CCIS 634, pp. 238–244, 2016.
DOI: 10.1007/978-981-10-2260-9_27

2   Related Work

Colorization methods can be roughly divided into those based on user drawn scribbles and those that utilize example images. Scribble based methods propagate the colors from an initial set of user drawn strokes to the whole image. For example, Levin et al. [1] derived an optimization framework for this propagation to ensure that similar neighboring pixels are assigned a similar color. They formalize the color transfer using a quadratic cost function and obtain an optimization problem that can be solved efficiently using standard techniques. Yatziv et al. [2] combined the colors of multiple scribbles to colorize a pixel, where the combination weights depend on a distance measure between the pixel and the scribble. Qing et al. [3] present an interactive system to colorize the natural images of complex scenes by separating the colorization procedure into color labeling and color mapping.

Instead of relying on user scribbles for color information, example based methods transfer colors automatically from a color reference image of a similar scene. Reinhard et al. [4] propose color transfer which uses statistical analysis to impose one image's color characteristics on another. Welsh et al. [5] introduce a general technique for "colorizing" greyscale images by transferring color between a source color image and a destination, greyscale image. Irony et al. [6] present a new method for colorizing grayscale images by transferring color from a segmented example image. Rather than relying on a series of independent pixel-level decisions, they develop a new strategy that attempts to account for the higher-level context of each pixel. Charpiat et al. [7] perform color transfer by minimizing an energy function using the graph cut algorithm. Chia et al. [8] develop a method which obtains reference images from internet using a novel image filtering framework. Gupta et al. [9] introduce a method which adopts a fast cascade feature matching scheme to find the correspondences between target and reference images and develops an image space voting framework to enforce the spatial coherence.

Deep learning techniques have achieved amazing success in modeling large-scale data recently. It has shown powerful learning ability that even outperforms human to some extent [10] and deep learning techniques have been demonstrated to be very effective on various computer vision and image processing applications including image classification [11], pedestrian detection [12], and image super-resolution [13]. Cheng et al. [14] use an extremely large-scale reference database to solve the colorization problem. To ensure artifact free quality, a joint bilateral filtering based post-processing step is utilized.

3   Automatic Colorization

The models trained for large scale visual recognition challenge (ILSVRC) not only can be used for classification task, but also it can be used for feature extraction for computer vision tasks. Zeiler and Fergus [15] showed how to visualize what intermediate layers of a convolutional neural network (CNN) could represent, and it turns out that objects like car wheels and people already start becoming identifiable by layer three. Intermediate layers in classification models can provide useful color information. For this reason, we choose the pre-trained VGG-16 model [16] to extract features for

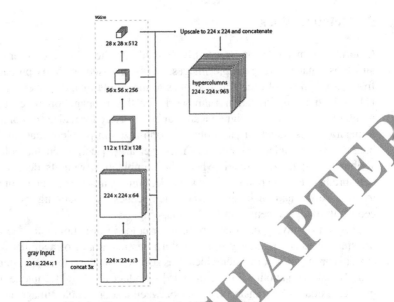

Fig. 1. Hypercolumns architecture.

colorization in this paper, and concatenate the extracted feature from CNN into hypercolumn [17]. A hypercolumn for a pixel in the input image is a vector of all the activations above that pixel. The input image is feed-forwarded through the VGG-16 network and the tensors before each of the first 4 max-pooling operations are extracted. Then we upscaling them to the original image size, and concatenating them all together as Fig. 1 illustrated.

The resulting hypercolumn tensor has the necessary information about what's in that image. This information can be used to color the image. Rather than reconstructing the entire color RGB image, we trained the models to produce two color channels that are concatenated with the grayscale input channel to produce a YUV image. The Y channel is intensity. This ensures that the intensity of the output will always be the same as the input.

3.1 Loss Function

The loss function is a Euclidean distance function between the network RGB output image and the true color RGB image. This works to some extent but we found models converged faster when a more complex loss function is used. Blurring the network output and the true color image and doing Euclidean distance can give the gradient decent help. More specifically, it averages the normal RGB distance and two blur distances with 3 and 5 pixel Gaussian kernels, and it only calculates the distance in the UV space. For network training, we quantify the closeness of the generated image to the actual image as the sum of the ℓ_2 norms of the difference of the generated image pixels and actual image pixels in the U and V channels:

$$L_{obj} = \left\| U_p - U_a \right\|^2 + \left\| V_p - V_a \right\|^2 \tag{1}$$

3.2 Network Architecture

We use rectified linear unit (ReLU) as activation functions throughout except at the last output to UV channels, there we use a sigmoid to squash values between 0 and 1. Batch norm (BN) instead of bias terms is used behind every convolution. A learning rate of 0.1 was used with standard SGD, and no weight decay. The model is trained on the ILSVRC 2012 classification training dataset. The same training set used for the pre-trained VGG-16 model. It's 147 GB and over 1.2 million images. Unlike in classification models there is no max pooling, and the output to be at full resolution as the input image.

Inspired by Microsoft Research's winning classification entry for ILSVRC 2015 in which they add residual connections skipping over every two layers [18]. We use residual connections to add in information as it works its way down the VGG-16 model. We name the model "residual encoder" as Fig. 2 illustrated, because it's almost an auto encoder but from black and white to color, with residual connections. The model forwards a grayscale image through the VGG-16 model and then using the

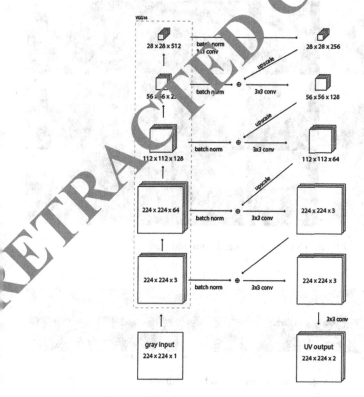

Fig. 2. Residual encoder architecture.

highest layer infers some color information. Then it up-scales the color guess and adds in information from the next highest layer, and so on working down to the bottom of the VGG-16 model until there is 224 × 224 × 3 tensor.

4   Experimental Results

The proposed method is tested on a number of images to illustrate its capabilities in Fig. 3. The first row presents the input grayscale images from different categories, namely beach, building, city, forest, field and road. Colorization results obtained from the proposed method are presented in the second row. The last row presents the corresponding ground-truth color images. We also compared the proposed method with other state-of-art colorization methods in Fig. 4. Note that (c)–(f) need to use a reference image and (g) adopts a large reference image dataset. Initially, we experimented with the HSV color space to address the under-saturation problem. In HSV color space, saturation is explicitly modeled as the individual S channel. Unfortunately, the results were not satisfying. Since saturation is directly estimated by the model, any prediction error became extremely noticeable, making the images noisy.

Fig. 3. Comparison with the ground truth.

(a) input   (b) proposed   (c) Gupta et al.   (d) Irony et al.   (e) Welsh et al.   (f) Charpiat et al.   (g) Cheng et al.

Fig. 4. Comparison with other methods.

5 Conclusion

This paper presents an automatic colorization method using deep neural networks to minimize user effort and the dependence on the example color images. Informative yet discriminative features are extracted and concatenated as hypercolumn and serve as the input to the neural network. Through experiments, we have demonstrated the efficacy and potential of using deep convolutional neural networks to colorize gray scale image. Future research includes modern model study and video colorization.

References

1. Levin, A., Lischinski, D., Weiss, Y.: Colorization using optimization. ACM Trans. Graphics (TOG) **23**(3), 689–694 (2004)
2. Yatziv, L., Sapiro, G.: Fast image and video colorization using chrominance blending. IEEE Trans. Image Process. **15**(5), 1120–1129 (2006)
3. Qing, L., Fang, W., Cohen-Or, D., Lin, L., Xu, Y.Q., Shum, H.Y.: Natural image colorization. In: Proceedings of the 18th Eurographics Conference on Rendering Techniques (EGSR 2007), Switzerland (2007)
4. Reinhard, E., Ashikhmin, M., Gooch, B., Shirley, P.: Color transfer between images. IIEEE Comput. Graphics Appl. **21**(5), 34–41 (2001)
5. Welsh, T., Ashikhmin, M., Mueller, K.: Transferring color to greyscale images. ACM Trans. Graphics (TOG) **21**(3), 277–280 (2002)
6. Irony, R., Cohen-Or, D., Lischinski, D.: Colorization by example. In: Proceedings of the 16th Eurographics Conference on Rendering Techniques (EGSR 2005), Switzerland (2005)
7. Charpiat, G., Hofmann, M., Schölkopf, B.: Automatic image colorization via multimodal predictions. In: Forsyth, D., Torr, P., Zisserman, A. (eds.) ECCV 2008, Part III. LNCS, vol. 5304, pp. 126–139. Springer, Heidelberg (2008)
8. Chia, A., Zhuo, S., Gupta, R., et al.: Semantic colorization with internet images. ACM Trans. Graphics (TOG) **30**(6) (2011). Article No. 156
9. Gupta, R., Chia, Y., Rajan, D., et al.: Image colorization using similar images. In: Proceedings of the 20th ACM International Conference on Multimedia, New York (2012)
10. He, K., Zhang, X., Ren, S., Sun, J.: Delving deep into rectifiers: surpassing human-level performance on ImageNet classification. In: IEEE International Conference on Computer Vision (ICCV), Santiago (2015)
11. Krizhevsky, A., Sutskever, I., Hinton, G.E.: Imagenet classification with deep convolutional neural networks. In: Advances in Neural Information Processing Systems (NIPS), pp. 1097–1105 (2012)
12. Ouyang, W., Wang, X.: Joint deep learning for pedestrian detection. In: Proceedings of the 2013 IEEE International Conference on Computer Vision (ICCV), pp. 2056–2063 (2013)
13. Dong, C., Chen, C.L., He, K., Tang, X.: Image super-resolution using deep convolutional networks. IEEE Trans. Pattern Anal. Mach. Intell. (PAMI) **38**(2), 184–199 (2014)
14. Cheng, Z., Yang, Q., Sheng, B.: Deep colorization. In: Proceedings of IEEE International Conference on Computer Vision (ICCV), pp. 415–423 (2015)

15. Zeiler, M.D., Fergus, R.: Visualizing and understanding convolutional networks. In: Fleet, D., Pajdla, T., Schiele, B., Tuytelaars, T. (eds.) ECCV 2014, Part I. LNCS, vol. 8689, pp. 818–833. Springer, Heidelberg (2014)
16. Simonyan, K., Zisserman, A.: Very deep convolutional networks for large-scale image recognition. In: Proceedings of International Conference on Learning Representations (ICLR), San Diego (2015)
17. Bharath, H., Pablo, A., Ross, G., Jitendra, M.: Hypercolumns for object segmentation and fine-grained localization. In: Proceedings of IEEE Conference on Computer Vision and Pattern Recognition (CVPR), Boston (2015)
18. He, K., Zhang, X., Ren, S., Sun, J.: Deep residual learning for image recognition. In: IEEE Conference on Computer Vision and Pattern Recognition (CVPR), Las Vegas (2016)

Retraction Note to: Image Colorization Using Convolutional Neural Network

Yili Zhao[1,2]($\boxtimes$), Dan Xu[1], and Yan Zhang[2]

[1] Yunnan University, Kunming 650091, Yunnan, China
ylzhao@vip.sina.com, danxu@ynu.edu.cn
[2] Southwest Forestry University, Kunming 650224, Yunnan, China
zydyr@163.com

Erratum to:
Chapter 27 in: T. Tan et al. (Eds.)
Advances in Image and Graphics Technologies
DOI: 10.1007/978-981-10-2260-9_27

This paper has been retracted because parts of the work were copied from the following publication: "Automatic Colorization" in http://tinyclouds.org/colorize/.

The updated original online version for this chapter can be found at
DOI: 10.1007/978-981-10-2260-9_27

Author Index

Printed in the United States
By Bookmasters